THE

Kabbalah Reader

THE

Kabbalah Reader

A Sourcebook of Visionary Judaism

Edited by Edward Hoffman

Foreword by Arthur Kurzweil

TRUMPETER ✦ *Boston & London* ✦ 2010

For Jeremy and Ortal

Trumpeter Books
An imprint of Shambhala Publications, Inc.
Horticultural Hall
300 Massachusetts Avenue
Boston, Massachusetts 02115
www.shambhala.com

9 8 7 6 5 4 3 2 1

First Edition
Printed in Canada

⊗This edition is printed on acid-free paper that meets the
American National Standards Institute z39.48 Standard.
♻This book was printed on 100% postconsumer recycled paper.
For more information please visit www.shambhala.com.
Distributed in the United States by Random House, Inc.,
and in Canada by Random House of Canada Ltd

Designed by James D. Skatges

The kabbalah reader: a sourcebook of visionary
Judaism/[compiled by] Edward Hoffman; foreword by
Arthur Kurzweil—1st ed.
p.   cm.
Includes bibliographical references.
ISBN 978-1-59030-656-7 (pbk.: alk. paper)
1. Cabala.   2. Mysticism—Judaism.   I. Hoffman, Edward, 1951–
BM525.A2K325 2010
296.1'6—dc22
2009034559

CONTENTS

PART THREE

Early Modern Thinkers,
ca. Sixteenth to Eighteenth Century

PART FOUR

Industrial Age Thinkers,
ca. Eighteenth and Nineteenth Century

PART FIVE

Twentieth-Century Thinkers

PART SIX

Contemporary Thinkers

FOREWORD

WE LIVE AT A TIME when the term *Kabbalah* is desperate for an accurate definition. As my teacher Rabbi Adin Steinsaltz of Jerusalem has said, the connection between "pop-culture Kabbalah" and the real thing is "the relationship between pornography and love."

Kabbalah is not a new age phenomenon, nor a Hollywood fad, nor superstition and good luck charms. Nor can Kabbalah be understood separate from the Torah of the Jewish people.

Kabbalah is the hidden, spiritual dimension of the revealed aspects of Torah.

Kabbalah is the theology of the Jewish people. It is the soul of the Torah.

Nearly thirty years ago, long before "Kabbalah" earned its own subject area in major bookstores, Dr. Edward Hoffman offered the world an extraordinary volume, *The Way of Splendor: Jewish Mysticism and Modern Psychology* (1981). Not only was it, at that time, one of the few books in English to explore basic notions of Kabbalah; it was also superb. And its publication introduced us to a teacher and writer who would go on to give us other important volumes in his clear, warm, friendly voice, filled with wisdom, understanding, knowledge, insight, and great depth.

In Jewish life, perhaps the highest compliment a person can receive is to be called a *talmid chacham,* which means "a student of the wise." How remarkable a tradition is that of the Jewish people, who elevate the student to the greatest of heights!

Dr. Edward Hoffman is a true *talmid chacham*. He has taken this holy posture for many years, and with the exceptional volume before you, *The Kabbalah Reader: A Sourcebook of Visionary Judaism,* Dr. Hoffman has generously arranged things so that we too can be students of the wise and sit before the great teachers of Kabbalah in order to drink from their nourishing words.

ARTHUR KURZWEIL

PREFACE

THE KABBALAH TODAY is undergoing a true renaissance of interest. Though inspiring Jews and non-Jews alike for more than a millennium, this vast tradition fell into disrepute with the rise of science and the industrial age. By the late nineteenth century, Kabbalistic notions about human existence—and our relation to the divine—had lapsed into obscurity in the West, and were scarcely known outside of Judaic scholars and insular Hasidic communities. To most educated persons, it was a tradition linked only to fanciful ideas and outmoded practices.

This situation began to change in the 1960s, slowly at first, then decisively. The televised popularization of Hasidic folktales like *The Dybbuk* was an important influence, as was the impassioned philosophical work of Martin Buber at the Hebrew University in the newly established State of Israel. Though he and colleague Gershom Scholem differed on many points regarding Jewish history, both viewed its mystical tradition as worthy of lifelong attention—and spurred scholarly investigation throughout the world. More broadly, the rediscovery of the relevance of many long-standing spiritual traditions from Sufism to Native American shamanism awakened long-dormant interest in the Kabbalah. From Southeast Asia to South America, explorations into this tradition are now occurring at a quickening pace. Not only has the subject of Jewish mysticism gained unprecedented respectability in academia, but it has also attracted a much wider audience of men and women of many backgrounds interested in spiritual wisdom for greater fulfillment in daily life.

Reflecting both types of audiences have been the publication of several anthologies devoted to Kabbalistic writings. Undoubtedly the first specifically meant for "spiritual seekers" was *Fragments of a Future Scroll,* produced by Rabbi Zalman M. Schachter-Shalomi. A small, evocative volume issued in the heyday of the American counterculture, *Fragments* helped catalyze my initial interest in the Kabbalah—and served as a valued reference when I authored *The Way of Splendor,* my first book on this topic, issued in 1981. I sent Reb Zalman (as he preferred to be known) a copy in gratitude for his inspiration, and he soon became my mentor, coauthor, and friend.

Since *Fragments,* a variety of Kabbalah anthologies have appeared. Though often erudite, they have conveyed all too little of the poetic allure and wisdom of this tradition. Indeed, most have been exceedingly dry in tone. In a way, this situation has appeared paradoxical to me, for historically, Jewish mystics have been accused of many things including heresy and self-messianism but never of being *boring.* Indeed, as writer Isaac Singer—the son of a Hasidic rabbi and another of my mentors—remarked ironically one blazing Miami afternoon as we discussed new books about Jewish mysticism, "Their authors have the unique gift of making dull even something as dazzling as the Kabbalah." I gazed into his twinkling blue eyes and nodded in agreement.

As the years passed, I gained an international reputation for my subsequent Judaica books. These included *Sparks of Light: Counseling in the Hasidic Tradition* (written with Rabbi Zalman M. Schachter-Shalomi), *The Heavenly Ladder, Opening the Inner Gates, Despite All Odds: The Story of Lubavitch, The Hebrew Alphabet: A Mystical Journey,* and *The Wisdom of Maimonides.* I also gave numerous lectures, courses, and workshops on the Kabbalah from my vantage point as a practicing psychologist. And repeatedly, I felt frustrated by the absence of a lively, informative anthology to recommend—especially for newcomers to this fascinating field. And so I managed professorially by distributing to my audiences excerpts of evocative works like the thirteenth-century *Zohar* (Book of Splendor) and *The Way of God* by Moses Chaim Luzzatto, written nearly a half-millennium later.

By the 1990s, the Kabbalah had, amazingly, become a household word in American popular culture, and I was increasingly invited by publishers to produce my own anthology. The editors shared my conviction that an appealing volume was needed, and their offers were usually enticing. Yet, I hesitated. Why? Chiefly, I think in retrospect, because I kept imagining that such an obviously worthwhile book would manifest while my project was still mired in laborious research—and thereby render my effort a needless duplication. Surprisingly, though, no such volume appeared, and I finally accepted the invitation of my Judaica editor, Beth Frankl, at Trumpeter Books. Under her guidance, the task has been a most enjoyable one.

My aim has been threefold: first, to present a diverse array of interesting, authentic Kabbalistic writings spanning the centuries through our contemporary era. This approach reflects my view that the Kabbalah is not something existing only in the musty past like the legendary *golem* preserved in Rabbi Judah Loew's great Prague synagogue, but rather an energetic, ongoing tradition. Whether the names of rabbinic thinkers like Adin Steinsaltz, Jonathan Sacks, and David Hananiah Pinto will be celebrated for centuries like those of Abraham Abulafia, Isaac Luria, and Moses Chaim Luzzatto cannot yet be known. But it's essential to honor current-day contributions to the intergenerational transmission of this ancient system of knowledge.

Second, I've chosen selections representing some of the main features of Jewish mysticism as it pertains especially to daily life, including ethics, self-development, and interpersonal relationships including family life and friendship. In this respect, I've sought to balance the emphasis on remote theosophy and metaphysics dominant in previous Kabbalistic anthologies. Such a balance seems long overdue, especially because it's precisely how the tradition has been utilized by rabbinic leaders for centuries: to bring seemingly abstruse ideas, such as the ten *sefirot* and the Tree of Life, to everyday guidance and wellness.

Finally, I've deliberately included Kabbalistic selections from two broad historical sets typically ignored by earlier anthologies: the important body of Jewish religious rulings known as *halachic* responsa and the writings of Sephardic sages, who lived in the Middle East, North Africa, and neighboring areas. In the first instance, these works shed fascinating light on how rabbis have historically understood and applied mystical teachings to contemporary questions of Jewish life, and in the second, they help restore to rightful significance a long-standing, and still vibrant, tradition virtually unknown today to most diaspora Jews of East European origin. I confess my own ignorance in this regard until recent exposure in Israel to Moroccan-Jewish culture through my daughter-in-law, Ortal, who gently opened a doorway into the vast realm of Sephardic spirituality.

As Hebraic scholars nowadays correctly insist, the term *Kabbalah* is not truly synonymous with Jewish mysticism. That is, if we may loosely define mysticism itself as belief in a transcendent reality existing beyond the physical world, then the Kabbalistic current is a subset of that dazzling stream—arising in late medieval times in Mediterranean Europe and associated with particular beliefs, practices, and texts. However, outside the halls of academia, the term *Kabbalah* today has clearly come to signify more broadly what I call the visionary tradition of Judaism—focusing on such fascinating subjects as the nature of prophecy and personal development, dreams and higher consciousness, meditation and creativity in daily life, intuition and extrasensory knowledge, the immortality of the human soul, the messianic age, and unseen dimensions including the afterlife. Consistent with this perspective, I have therefore included in this anthology a variety of Jewish thinkers like Maimonides who inspiringly wrote about such topics for their contemporary audiences.

A NOTE ON THE TRANSLATIONS

The selections presented in this anthology were all originally composed in Aramaic or Hebrew—except for those by Rabbis Abraham Heschel, Jonathan Sacks, and Zalman M. Schachter-Shalomi, who wrote theirs in English, and Rabbi David Pinto, who wrote his in French. Except for the selections by Rabbis Simeon ben Zemah Duran, Tzvi Ashkenazi, Yair Bachrach, and Chaim Pinto, I have relied upon existing English translations and then rendered their English into a more contemporary style on an "as-needed basis" for improved readability. As we know from a famous letter to his own translator, Maimonides advised that translations always be guided by the principle of clarity rather than strict literalness. My intent has been to follow Maimonides' guidance.

The issue of translating gender terms is more challenging, in that Jewish law traditionally clearly differentiates between men and women. To a large extent, Orthodox Judaism in most variants today maintains these distinctions. Therefore, when presenting Kabbalistic views specifically on Jewish practice, I have maintained the existing gender construction. In all other instances—such as when these rabbinic thinkers wrote about ethics, prophecy, self-improvement, or mind-body health—I have tried to use gender-neutral phrasing. The house style of some Judaica publishers is to render "God" as "G-d"; throughout this anthology I have retained the style of the publisher from which the excerpt was taken.

ACKNOWLEDGMENTS

THIS BOOK WOULD not have been possible without the guidance of others. From her initial suggestion that I undertake this project through its completion, my editor Beth Frankl has been a valuable adviser. My oldest son, Jeremy, has been a fount of both enthusiasm and expertise while completing rabbinic training in Israel. I am particulary indebted to his conceptual contributions related to Kabbalah in the Sephardic community, both past and present.

I have enjoyed stimulating conversations with Guy Biran, Dr. Gerald Epstein and Rachel Epstein, Aaron Hostyk, Arthur Kurzweil, Rabbi Niles Goldstein, Rabbi Neal Kaunfer, Paul Palnik, and Rabbi Zalman M. Schachter-Shalomi, pertaining to diverse topics in this book. For his proficient Hebrew translation work and research advice, I am grateful to Dovid Bashevkin, rabbinic student at Yeshiva University; Phoebe Maltz at New York University also served ably as translator. For their research assistance, I also wish to thank Joseph Scherban and especially the cheerful and knowledgeable library staff of Yeshiva University.

Above all, I would like to thank my wife, Elaine, for her patience and unflagging support throughout this project.

INTRODUCTION

THE VISIONARY TRADITION of Judaism has a long and multi-layered history. Dating back to the Middle Ages, the term *Kabbalah* comes from the Hebrew root word "to receive"—with a double meaning: first, that this vast body of metaphysics and lore is viewed as divine in origins, that is, received by revelation rather than by reasoned analysis. And second, that each generation receives this wisdom in totality from its predecessor and teaches to its successor. From this long-standing perspective—which many scholars today broadly share—the Kabbalistic system has constituted an unbroken chain of transmission from its ancient inception.

Historians generally demark the primary phase of this recorded discipline as the Merkabah, or "Chariot," epoch. It spanned the length of the first century B.C.E through the tenth century C.E. and was centered in the Holy Land, ruled by a series of world powers. Reputedly shaped by some of the most renowned rabbis of the epoch, including Rabbi Akiva and his main disciple Simeon bar Yochai, it comprised a more or less cohesive body of knowledge, held together by an integrated set of doctrines and meditative techniques. Two main approaches dominated practitioners: *Ma'aseh Bereshit* (Act of Creation) and *Ma'aseh Merkabah* (Act of the Divine Chariot). The former was more theoretical and dealt with the world's creation and the first divine revelations. The *Ma'aseh Merkabah,* based on the Prophet Ezekiel's description of the celestial chariot, elucidates the soul's connection to God. Both of these paths were shrouded in mystery and kept secret to all but the most pious Jewish scholars. Many of the great sages who worked on the compilation of the Talmud (the major text of Judaic law, commentary, and Biblical exegesis, completed about 500 C.E.) were knowledgeable about this secret tradition, but not all desired to practice it.

The other major esoterica in Judaism during this era was more speculative—focusing on the structure of the cosmos and our relation to it. The most significant text was the *Sefer Yetzirah* (Book of Creation), composed anonymously during the third and sixth centuries while the Talmud was being molded into its final form. Offering a terse yet evocative description of the hidden workings of the universe, it highlighted thirty-two paths to God: ten *sefirot,* or primordial energy-essences, as they are termed, and the twenty-two letters of the Hebrew alphabet. All aspects of the cosmos, including the nature of space, time, and our interaction with them, are said to be upheld by the constant interplay of these vibrational forces. The concept of the ten *sefirot* became the foundation for the later Kabbalah, which developed this notion into a formalized system known as the Tree of Life.

With its precise and deductive style, the *Sefer Yetzirah* attracted considerable attention from Jewish visionaries from its first circulation in the sixth century. It provided the basis for later inquiry into our inner nature, as well as our connection to the energies in the universe around us. Over the years, many commentaries on the *Sefer Yetzirah* were promulgated, and it was perhaps the most widely studied esoteric Jewish work prior to the appearance of the *Sefer HaZohar* (Book of Splendor) in late thirteenth-century Spain.

THE EMERGENCE OF KABBALAH

The appearance of the anonymously written *Sefer HaBahir* (Book of the Clear Light) in Provence, southern France, around 1175, ushered in the true period of the Kabbalah. Like many Judaic works, it takes its title from the opening verse; its central premise is that there is a vast, unseen order beyond what we typically experience in everyday life. Perhaps reflecting their assessment of the oppressed Jewish condition in the Middle Ages, these early Kabbalistic works emphasized the hidden aspects of God. "People want to see the king," the *Bahir* metaphorically declares, "but do not know where to find his house. First they [must] ask, 'Where is the king's house?' Only then can they ask, 'Where is the king?'"

Comprising a dense treatise and manual for finding the glory behind the mundane world, the *Bahir* spread rapidly throughout the Jewish world. For the first time, esoteric conceptions began to reach a wider audience among Jews. By the year 1200, Kabbalists had acquired a distinct identity, especially in areas of southern France and Spain. They were not numerically significant, but the amassing of a movement was far from their aim; rather, their purpose was to enable individuals—not large groups—to rise beyond the travails so common to Jews of the time. Thus, in one of the earliest Kabbalistic texts, Rabbi Abraham ben David (Raavad) commented that all of these esoteric teachings were transmitted only from "one mouth to the next."

Undoubtedly, the most influential thinker of what came to be known as the Gerona school of Kabbalah was Isaac ben David of Posquieres, who lived in mid-twelfth- and early-thirteenth-century Provence and became revered as "Isaac the Blind." At roughly the same historical period, a somewhat parallel development occurred among Northern European Jewry. Around 1150 to 1200, a group known as Hasidim (not to be confused with the East European movement of the eighteenth century) exerted a long-lasting impact on German Jews. Focusing their speculation on the "mystery of God's unity," they combined esoteric interpretations of the Torah, dreamwork, and asceticism as the means to higher consciousness. The major literary work associated with this circle was *Sefer Hasidim* (Book of the Devout), a compilation of various writings from this time and locale.

MAIMONIDES AND NACHMANIDES

Maimonides was the most influential Jewish philosopher and rabbinic leader of medieval times. Born in Cordoba, Spain, and forced to wander with his family for much of his early life due to Islamic militancy, Moses ben Maimon eventually settled permanently in Fostat, near Cairo. There as a practicing physician, he completed his *Mishneh Torah* in 1180, a monumental codification of the Talmud, and later authored a variety of works. The most important of these was *The Guide for the Perplexed,* integrating traditional Jewish thought and Greek philosophy, especially Aristotle, to present a coherent view of human existence in a divinely created cosmos.

The *Guide* was not a Kabbalistic work in strict historical terms. It contained no references to concepts like the ten *sefirot* or to texts like the *Sefer Yetzirah* and the *Bahir.* Whether Maimonides had ever read these books is not even apparent from his voluminous writings, which included diatribes against healing amulets and astrology—practices commonly associated with "practical Kabbalah." However, his approach to prophetic consciousness inspired Jewish visionaries for centuries to come and exerted an encouraging influence on mystical study. For he clearly taught that personal revelation is not only possible in the postbiblical world but within reach through the right daily regimen of sacred study, emotional self-development, and right conduct. In this regard, he powerfully kept Judaism's door open for ecstatic seekers and visionaries to the present day.

Nevertheless, Maimonides' emphasis on finding God through rationality—epitomized by the Greek philosophers rather than through Jewish meditation and Torah study—aroused heated criticism in the decades following his death. Among the leaders of this opposition was Nachmanides, an ardent exponent of Kabbalah who lived in thirteenth-century Gerona. Fiercely rejecting Maimonides' embrace of classic Greek philosophy, Moses ben Nachman instead emphasized the ten *sefirot* and twenty-two Hebrew letters as the true pathways to divine knowledge. In the fourteenth and fifteenth centuries, such rabbinic leaders as Rabbi Joseph Albo and Simeon ben Zemah Duran sided with Nachmanides in his stance.

ABRAHAM ABULAFIA
AND PROPHETIC KABBALISM

Among the most influential of all Jewish visionaries was Abraham ben Samuel Abulafia. He had a major impact on the development of prophetic Kabbalism during his lifetime, and on the great flowering of the Kabbalah in the Holy Land three centuries later. Yet, Abulafia's name is rarely mentioned in most contemporary accounts of Jewish philosophy or history, undoubtedly due to his unique and controversial ideas. Born in Saragossa, Spain, Abulafia had little formal rabbinic training. Eventually settling in the city of Barcelona, he delved deeply into Kabbalistic writings as well as Maimonides' *Guide for the Perplexed*. Like many, he found its optimistic view of spiritual attainment to be immensely exciting. From Abulafia's own account, he gained spiritual enlightenment at the age of thirty-one, accompanied by various psychic gifts. Abulafia proclaimed his prophetic visions in several countries where he traveled, including Spain, Italy, and Greece. Though relying mainly on oral instruction to spread his methods for achieving higher consciousness, he also broke with Kabbalistic tradition by composing detailed manuals for personal development. In particular, he recommended utilizing the Hebrew alphabet as a meditative tool. "Concentrate on all the [letters]," he instructed, "in all their aspects, like a person who is told a parable, or a riddle, or a dream, or as one who ponders a book of wisdom." As part of Abulafia's influential system of higher development, he also prescribed yoga-like bodily postures combined with altered breathing and solitary contemplation.

Abulafia generated considerable antagonism from the rabbinic establishment of his day for his prophetic proclamations, including an attempt to convert Pope Nicholas III to Judaism. Abulafia and his band of disciples spent several weeks in intense preparation for their task. They prayed, fasted, and immersed themselves in secret meditative rituals involving the Hebrew alphabet. Even before Abulafia reached Rome, the pope condemned him to death, and the fire and stake were readied. When the impassioned visionary arrived at the city gate, he was informed that Pope Nicholas III had suddenly died during the night. The Franciscans held him in prison, but soon released him, apparently swayed by his charismatic personality.

THE *ZOHAR* (BOOK OF SPLENDOR)

During the era of Abulafia's bold prophecies and vehement battles with the rabbinate of his day, a remarkable volume of Jewish visionary lore appeared in Spain, in the 1280s or 1290s. Entitled *Sefer HaZohar* (Book of Splendor), it was circulated by Kabbalist Moses de Leon, and incredibly, bore the name of the revered second-century sage Rabbi Simeon bar Yochai, Rabbi Akiva's greatest student. Written in an exalted style of Aramaic, the *Zohar* contained a fascinating—and unprecedented—blend of metaphysics, transcendent cosmology, and esoteric psychology. It aroused immediate excitement among both Kabbalists and non-Kabbalists alike.

When asked how the exotic volume had come into his possession, Rabbi de Leon swore that it had arrived by special messenger, sent by the sage Nachmanides in the Holy Land, who had found it by accident. Today nearly all scholars believe that Moses de Leon wrote the *Zohar* himself in the early 1280s; a few years later, an anonymous author composed the last of the Zoharic books, namely, *Ra'aya Mehemna* (The True Shepherd) and *Tikkune Zohar* (Emendations to the *Zohar*).

The *Zohar* is a work that defies easy analysis; there is simply nothing like it in all Jewish history. It comprises a variety of parts, among which there is considerable overlap of material. Many of the sections, which vary tremendously in terseness and difficulty of symbolism, appear to record the conversations of Rabbi Simeon bar Yochai, his son Eliezer, and their colleagues. The ever-present backdrop is the Holy Land, then under oppressive Roman rule.

Filled with allusions to the ten *sefirot,* the nature of the human soul, ecstatic inner states, the mind-body unity and healing, and the afterlife, the *Zohar's* basic premise is that everything in the cosmos is in constant interplay, with an irreducible order underlying all. Nothing that happens to us is meaningless or haphazard. What we view as reality is merely one state of consciousness to which we have become habituated. "Man, whilst in this world," the *Zohar* declares, "considers not and reflects not what he is standing on, and each day as it passes he regards as though it has vanished into nothingness."

Despite its length and complexity, the *Zohar* spread rapidly. During the fourteenth century, it was carried from Jewish-Spanish communities outward, especially to Italy and the Middle East. Now that essential Kabbalistic concepts had appeared in the *Zohar,* numerous works were published before long, providing additional commentary and clarification upon the secret significance of Jewish law (*halacha*), ritual, and the quest for personal transcendence. The excitement that these works generated was sometimes so intense that its advocates argued that Judaism was barren without this exotic current.

After all, the *Zohar* stated plainly enough, "Woe unto those who see in the Law nothing but simple narratives and ordinary-words! . . . Every word of the Law contains an elevated sense and a sublime mystery." Much to the enmity of rabbinic authorities, some Kabbalists insisted that Judaism was but an empty shell without this dazzling, evocative tradition.

SAFED AND THE FLOWERING OF KABBALAH

Although the *Zohar* and other esoteric writings intrigued individual Jews and non-Jews for ensuing decades, it was not until the 1500s that the Kabbalah began to amass an international audience of important size. Historians agree that the catalyst was the rise of the Inquisition, followed by the Jewish expulsion from Spain in 1492 and Portugal five years later. Ironically, the tragic circumstances, among the most devastating of all Jewish experiences prior to the Holocaust, directly led to the greatest flowering of the Kabbalah in its entire history. For as it became clear that the exodus from Spain and Portugal would be accompanied by no immediate messianic intervention, the rigorous inward discipline of the Kabbalah suddenly had tremendous allure. With its promise of exalted joy and ecstatic visions for the devout, the esoteric tradition now appealed to many. Furthermore, political and social action against the Iberian kingdoms was essentially impossible and likewise helped propel certain Jews to the esoteric path.

The expulsion brought many from the Iberian Peninsula into the area around the Holy Land for refuge. Before long, the town of Safed in the Galilee region became known as the new center for Kabbalah. For both economic and political reasons, many Jews preferred this small town to the more biblically sacred city of Jerusalem. Safed also served as a magnet for spiritual reasons: the revered Simeon bar Yochai was buried there and his grave was a shrine for pious Jews around the globe. During the decades that followed the Spanish Expulsion, Safed attracted first one, then another, of the leading intellectual and spiritual giants of the period. These included Moses Cordovero, Joseph Karo, Solomon Alkabez, and Isaac Luria. Karo had been deeply affected by the Portuguese martyr Solomon Molko, a charismatic and messianic mystic burned alive by the Inquisition in 1532.

The most influential of the Safed Kabbalists was Isaac Luria, known as the "Ari" or Lion in Hebrew, in abbreviation of his title, the Ashkenazi Rabbi Isaac. An almost mythic figure in his own lifetime, he catapulted the Kabbalah into unprecedented importance. Luria wrote no books, and therefore, virtually all of what we know of his ideas comes to us through a filter: namely, his innermost disciples. In the few years the Ari lived in Safed before death took him in 1572, he succeeded in recasting Jewish historical experience in a completely new light.

Luria's major themes dealt with the basic questions of suffering and evil in the world. Not only are the Jewish people in exile from the Promised Land, but also the Divine Presence is itself separated from its Source, he declared. For in the very act of Creation, this cosmic exile was set into motion. In order for the material world to come into being, God contracted part of His Light—and divine "vessels" were readied to be filled with His essence. But unable to withstand the intensity of this energy, the "vessels" shattered—and confusion, or evil, was thereby introduced to the universe. The heavenly sparks from the Light were lodged in all things, Luria explained; it is each person's task to elevate them back to their primary source. When this finally occurs, the divine harmony will be complete once more. Confusion and evil will have vanished forever.

The task for recording the teachings of the Ari was seized by Chaim Vital, his chief disciple as well as biographer and scribe. Vital copiously recorded his mentor's nearly every word, or so he claimed in later years. After the Ari's death, Vital vied among several disciples for recognition as the only authorized interpreter of the master's discourses. Vital's works, including a diary, reflect the interests of the Safed group in such phenomena as meditation, altered states of consciousness, and parapsychology. Vital was especially intrigued by dreams, though it is unclear whether he was familiar with physician-Kabbalist Solomon Almoli's influential sixteenth-century work on this subject.

With its bold message of exile and redemption, death and rebirth, Luria's worldview spread with amazing rapidity throughout the Jewish world. His teachings gave a clear and comforting answer as to why such horrific events as the Inquisition and Spanish Expulsion had occurred, for he taught that the human soul has many lives here on earth, and each soul is here for a divine mission. Such ideas gave many Jews renewed hope and sense of purpose amidst a hostile Christian world. His message was carried first to Turkey,

Greece, and the Near East, then to Italy, Holland, and Germany, and eventually to Poland and Eastern Europe; among the most influential of early exponents of Lurianic Kabbalah was Rabbi Joseph Taitazak of Salonica, Greece, whose family had been expelled from 1492 Spain. Like Joseph Karo and Chaim Vital, Taitazak engaged in trance phenomena—which he taught to small groups of disciples—for achieving celestial communication.

For most Jews, Isaac Luria's teachings became familiar through popularizations in the late sixteenth and seventeenth centuries—mainly books designed to foster ethical conduct from a Kabbalistic viewpoint. These were strongly influenced by Cordovero's *Palm Tree of Deborah* and its anonymously written predecessor *Sefer HaYashar* (Book of Righteousness). New prayerbooks, derived from the meditative practices of the Safed community, also were freely circulated.

During this same "golden era" of Kabbalah, it became studied by growing numbers of educated Christians. For instance, in 1587 the landmark volume *Artis Cabalisticae Scriptores* was published in Rome. It comprised a variety of essays by Christian scholars on Kabbalistic works like the *Zohar,* and sought to prove, for example, that it affirmed the divinity of Jesus of Nazareth. In 1651, the French bibliographer Gaffarel published an index of the codices of the *Zohar.* Not long afterward, Knorr von Rosenroth translated some of its sections into Latin in a work that became standard for Christian theologians for centuries. Of particular interest to them was the *sefirotic* system, which they viewed as shedding light on their own exotic interpretations of the New Testament, such as the nature of the Trinity.

SHABBATAI ZEVI AND THE ANTI-KABBALAH BACKLASH

As the seventeenth century progressed, the teachings of the Safed visionaries inspired new generations of Jews. Then came the religious cataclysm of Shabbatai Zevi—and the Kabbalah was driven deeply underground. Judaic historians, such as Gershom Scholem, have insisted that it is impossible to understand all subsequent Jewish history—including both Hasidism and Zionism—without knowledge of the Shabbatai Zevi debacle.

Born in 1626 in Smyrna, Turkey, he showed early promise as a Talmudic scholar, and even more as a Kabbalistic adept. With a charismatic personality, he attracted supporters throughout the Mediterranean region, and by 1648 had amassed an ardent band of disciples. Like many Kabbalists, Shabbatai Zevi was interested in determining the advent of the messianic age—and more important, hastening it through arcane methods. Perhaps history would remember little of Shabbatai Zevi if not for his eventual partnership with another unusual figure: Nathan of Gaza. A brilliant young rabbinic scholar steeped in esoteric lore, Nathan of Gaza met Shabbatai Zevi in Jerusalem during the mid-1660s and convinced him that he was the Messiah. Joining forces, the two quickly aroused great excitement among Holy Land Jews, and then their coreligionists in Italy, Holland, Germany, and Poland. Thousands abandoned their livelihoods and homes to await the Day of Judgment. Even leading rabbis and sophisticated merchants in cities like Amsterdam and Venice were caught up in messianic frenzy—which abruptly ended with Shabbatai Zevi's forced conversion to Islam in 1666.

Though a few loyalists like Nathan of Gaza continued to insist that Zevi was the Messiah, the entire Jewish world suffered a tremendous loss of morale and hope. The long, long exile was still in full force. And if so, what had happened to the biblical covenant between God and the Jewish people? Did it even matter anymore? As a result of the Shabbatai Zevi affair, the rabbinate emphatically asserted that the Kabbalah could not be entrusted to ordinary Jews: it was simply too confusing and explosive. Key texts like the *Zohar* and those by Abraham Abulafia, Moses Cordovero, Chaim Vital, and others were rendered absolutely "off-limits" to everyone except the greatest Talmudic scholars. The orthodoxy's dictum became—and essentially still remains today in non-Hasidic circles—that pursuit of the Kabbalah is forbidden until one is over forty years of age, married, and has already attained a "full belly" of knowledge with the Talmud and other normative Judaic works. Though envicing great respect and even awe for the Kabbalah, rabbinic authorities regarded it as simply too dangerous for easy access. World Jewry, they reasoned, might not withstand another debacle like that wrought by Shabbatai Zevi.

Thus, for more than a century, the rabbinic establishment was quick to denounce and isolate any maverick rabbi who revealed Kabbalistic practices and built a following. For example, such was the fate of Moses Chaim Luzzatto, who in the 1720s and 1730s in Italy taught classes and organized a study group in his native Padua. Threatened with excommunication by Italian rabbinic leaders, he moved to more tolerant Amsterdam before relocating to the Holy Land, where he died in 1747. Rabbi Luzzatto was later revered for his inspiring books that focused on ethical living from a Kabbalistic perspective.

THE RISE OF HASIDISM

The last great flourishing of Kabbalah took place in Eastern Europe during the second half of the eighteenth century through the early nineteenth century. By all accounts, it originated in the charismatic activity and message of one man: Israel ben Eliezer, about whom few historical facts exist. The movement that he founded became known as Hasidism, as *Hasid* means "devout" in Hebrew. Born about 1698 in the Ukrainian village of Ukob in the Carpathian Mountains, he came from a family undistinguished by either scholarship or wealth, and as a young man, eked out a meager living in a variety of occupations while mastering the Kabbalah. According to legend, in about 1734, he revealed the full extent of his spiritual mastery. The first person to whom he openly confided was allegedly his brother-in-law, who immediately became a close supporter. He was a highly respected Torah scholar and Kabbalist, and would serve as a key link between the rabbinic establishment and the village folk in the burgeoning movement that Israel had begun to spark. Israel ben Eliezer became known as the "Baal Shem Tov" (Bearer of the Good Name) or "Besht" in abbreviation for his wonder-working reputation.

In effect, the Besht took the Kabbalah's abstruse notions concerning the human soul, and by charismatically incorporating them into parables and stories, made them accessible to the impoverished Jews of Eastern Europe. He stressed that Torah scholarship is fine, but ultimately useless unless wedded to the way of the heart. "No child can be born except through pleasure and joy," he is credited with saying. "By the same token, if one wishes his prayers to bear fruit, he must offer them with pleasure and joy." Furthermore, Israel ben Eliezer disseminated specific meditative techniques consistent with Isaac Luria's for attaining higher consciousness. Echoing the teachings of his predecessor, the Baal Shem Tov preached that it is each person's mission to liberate the countless fallen sparks in the material world. Even the seemingly smallest act, the Besht is reputed to have emphasized, if performed with the right intention or *kavana*, helps in the redemption of the entire cosmos.

Several years before his death in 1760, the Besht carefully chose and trained disciples who would succeed him in extending the Hasidic movement. Though some Hasidic leaders were well-recognized scholars, many were decidedly not—a situation that aroused the antipathy of Eastern Europe's rabbinic establishment. They eventually set in motion a countermovement known as Mitnaggedim (Opponents), who accused the Hasidim as heretical for minimizing Talmudic study and abandoning traditional Jewish practices of prayer, study, and kosher slaughtering. Especially in Lithuania—the stronghold of Talmudic study—opposition to Hasidism was fierce. In 1781, Elijah Gaon (Great Scholar) of Vilna issued an interdict which forbade pious Jews to marry Hasidim. In several towns, Hasidic writings were publicly burned by the Mitnaggedim, who felt the very future of the Jewish people was at stake. But the burgeoning movement could not be stopped. During the ensuing decades, Hasidism generated such influential rabbinic thinkers as Schneur Zalman of Liadi, Nachman of Breslov, and later, Mordechai Yosef Leiner of Isbitza and his disciple Yehuda Eiger.

It is crucial to understand that the dispute was *not* between Kabbalists or "mystics" versus "rationalist" exponents of Judaism. In the past, some scholars erroneously arrived at this view, since the Hasidim were enthusiastic Kabbalists. Rather, the Mitnaggedim were ardent Kabbalists, too—but viewed the visionary tradition as appropriate only for the erudite. For example, the Gaon of Vilna was so immersed in the Kabbalah that his writings on this subject alone surpass in volume all those of his Hasidic contemporaries combined. Even more intriguingly, this towering intellectual was also a trance medium. Like the revered Joseph Karo of the six-teenth century, the Gaon Elijah was reputed to have regularly ex-perienced paranormal trances since before the age of thirty.

Rather, the Mitnaggedim essentially looked upon the Hasidim as vulgarizers of an awesome and elite body of knowledge. Un-doubtedly, many Mitnaggedim also feared that Hasidism could erupt into the same type of disastrous messianism aroused by Shab-batai Zevi, precisely because Hasidim tended to extol their leaders or rebbes as infallible miracle workers. Eventually, the battle be-tween Hasidim and Mitnaggedim cooled considerably—and while never completely disappearing—reached a relatively civil truce.

For as Jewish assimilation and apostasy significantly increased during the first half of the nineteenth century, the two camps real-ized that they had more in common with one another than with their more secular coreligionists. Another reason for the eventual rapprochement between the Hasidim and their erstwhile opponents was the Hasidic downplay of their original Kabbalistic ideas. For instance, by the mid-nineteenth century, the techniques of Kabbal-istic prayer and meditation the Baal Shem Tov had taught were all but extinct among most Hasidim. His method for transforming dis-turbing thoughts during prayer was gradually minimized and later dropped altogether. This same pattern repeated itself for other tenets of the Hasidic founders, increasingly regarded as almost mythic supermen by later generations of followers. In general, the various Hasidic groups never eliminated the Kabbalah from their teachings, but like the Mitnaggedim, increasingly argued that such esoteric knowledge was better left to only the most learned Jews.

KABBALAH IN THE INDUSTRIAL AGE

While the religious battle raged between Hasidism and Mitnaggedim, much was happening in wider culture around them. The times were rapidly changing. With the advent of the revolutions in the American colonies and then in France, a new era of liberal democracy and political reform was dawning in the West. After centuries of having been systematically barred from university attendance and forced to live in cramped, demeaning ghettos, many European Jews were eager to join the general cultural advance.

The Jewish enlightenment or Haskalah movement first arose in Germany. Under the leadership of Moses Mendelsohn, a nucleus of Westernized disciples began to establish secular schools for Jewish children, the first in 1781 Berlin; the goal was to crush the superstition that Maskilim (Enlightened) felt enslaved by their less cosmopolitan brethren. Many Maskilim wrote diatribes against the Hasidic groups, accusing them of trying to drag Jewry into a perpetually medieval way of life. During the same era in Germany, the Reform Jewish movement was born. Backed by local governments, it succeeded in diffusing traditional rituals and prayers, and in 1801, the first Jewish Reform school was opened. Seven years later, philanthropist Reform leader Israel Jacobson issued a proclamation banning Kabbalah discussions from Reform synagogues, and in 1819, the long-favored Kabbalistic Sabbath prayer Lekha Dodi (Come, My Beloved) was replaced by a Lutheran choral in the newly published Hamburg Temple prayerbook.

Jewish involvement in the Kabbalah became increasingly negated by Maskilim at universities and Reform Jewish seminaries. Their influential leader was Heinrich Graetz, whose eleven-volume *History of the Jews* was published in Germany from 1853 to 1876.

Translated and often reprinted, it dominated Jewish historiography for generations with its derogatory, belittling view of Kabbalah— for example, ridiculing the revered *Zohar* as "curious, confused and chaotic" and the celebrated sixteenth-century Safed thinkers as "having an evil influence" upon Jewish civilization.

As for Hasidism, still thriving in Eastern Europe, Graetz contemptuously described its beloved founder as "ugly [with] a brain so filled with fantastic images that he could not distinguish them from real, tangible beings." Graetz's dismissal of Kabbalah as an aberrant stream of Judaism would eventually give way to the more insightful, respectful scholarship of Gershom Scholem and his protégés at the Hebrew University in Jerusalem and elsewhere.

But that development awaited more than a century in the future. Thus, by the mid-to-late nineteenth century in Western Europe and North America, the Kabbalah had become a relic to worldly Jews. At best, it was viewed an outmoded repository of once-relevant speculation. At worst, and this was by far the dominant appraisal, it was regarded as simply an embarrassing reminder of a medieval outlook that modern Jewry was eager to leave behind.

THE SEPHARDIC CONNECTION

It is important to realize that in modern times the Kabbalah has been embraced much more strongly by Sephardic Jewry, dwelling in the Middle East, North Africa, and neighboring areas. As late as the early twentieth century, in the old section of Jerusalem, a well-organized band of students continued to explore the *Zohar,* Isaac Luria's meditative techniques, and other Kabbalistic aspects. Based in the Beit El Yeshiva there, they served as the chief center for the visionary tradition throughout the Far East and North Africa.

More broadly, Sephardic Jews tended to be less influenced by secularism and scientism in their tightly-knit communities, and their rabbinic leaders were comfortable in applying mystical doctrines and practices openly with congregants. Yet, until the modern formation of the State of Israel, Sephardic culture, in near entirety, was almost wholly isolated from Western Judaism. For this reason, the names of historically renowned Sephardic Kabbalists such as Shalom Sharabi, Chaim Pinto, Chaim David Joseph Azulai (the Chida), Yosef Chaim of Baghdad (the Ben Ish Chai), and more recently, Yisrael Abuchatzeira (Baba Sali), remain obscure to Westerners. Fortunately, this situation seems to be rapidly changing as the Internet and high technology accelerate global interconnection. As a result, the historic Kabbalistic contributions of all Jews will come to be fully recognized.

PART ONE

The Seminal Period of Jewish Mysticism

ca. Fifth to Fifteenth Century

Sefer Yetzirah

The Book of Creation

THE SEFER YETZIRAH *is the oldest esoteric book in Judaism.
Though attributed by tradition to the patriarch Abraham of the
Bible, no actual historical evidence supports that view. The* Sefer
Yetzirah *first appeared anonymously during the third through sixth
centuries* C.E. *in the Holy Land, and was closely studied in small
groups for generations to come, generating many commentaries. Because of its brevity and succinct style, some scholars have viewed the*
Sefer Yetzirah *as a summary statement or syllabus, rather than as a
full text in its own right. Until the appearance of the* Zohar *(Book
of Splendor) in the late thirteenth century, the* Sefer Yetzirah *was
decisively the most important Kabbalistic work.*

The Book of Creation *(sometimes known in English as the*
Book of Formation) *sets forth the view that the cosmos is comprised
of thirty-two divine forces. These correspond to ten mysterious ema-
nations of God, called* sefirot, *and the twenty-two letters of the
Hebrew alphabet. The more we understand the nature of these
forces, the* Sefer Yetzirah *intimates, the better we comprehend ourselves and the entire universe. Over ensuing centuries throughout
the Jewish world, the* sefirotic *matrix and the Hebrew alphabet*

became the focus of metaphysical speculation and meditative tech-
niques. This excerpt from the Sefer Yetzirah *presents chapter 1 in*
its entirety, highlighting concepts in the five chapters that follow.

CHAPTER I

1. In thirty-two mysterious paths of wisdom did the Lord write, the Lord of Hosts, the God of Israel, the Living *Elohim*, and King of the Universe, the Almighty, Merciful and Gracious God; He is great and exalted and eternally dwelling in the Height, His name is holy, He is exalted and holy. He created His universe by the three forms of expression: Numbers, Letters, and Words.

2. Ten ineffable *sefirot* and twenty-two basal letters: three mothers, seven doubles, and twelve simple [letters].

3. Ten ineffable *sefirot,* corresponding to the ten fingers, five [over] against five and the only token of the covenant in the middle: word of the tongue and [the circumcision] of the flesh.

4. Ten ineffable *sefirot,* ten and not nine, ten and not eleven: understand with wisdom and apprehend with care; examine by means of them and search them out; *know, count, and write.* Put forth the subject in its light and place the Formator on His throne. He is the only Creator and the only Formator, and no one exists but He: His attributes are ten and have no limits.

5. The ineffable *sefirot:* their totality is ten. They are, however, without limits: the infinity of the Beginning and the infinity of the End, the infinity of the Good and the infinity of the Evil, the infinity of the Height and the infinity of the Depth, the infinity of the East and the infinity of the West, the infinity of [the] North and the infinity of [the] South; and only one Lord God, the trusty King, rules them all from His holy dwelling in all eternity.

6. Ten ineffable *sefirot:* their appearance is like that of a flash of

lightning, their goal is infinite. His word is in them when they emanate and when they return: at His bidding do they hasten like a whirlwind; and before His throne do they prostrate [themselves].

7. Ten ineffable *sefirot:* their end is in-their beginning and likewise their beginning is in their end, as the flame is bound to the burning coal. *Know, count, and write.* The Lord is one and the Formator is one and has no second (beside Him): what number can thou count before one?

8. Ten ineffable *sefirot:* close thy mouth lest it speak and thy heart lest it think; and if thy mouth open for utterance and thy heart turn toward thought, bring them back [to thy control]. Therefore, it is written: *"And the living creatures ran and returned"* (Ezekiel 1:14); and hence was the covenant made.

9. Ten ineffable *sefirot:* One—The spirit of the Living *Elohim,* His throne is erected in eternity, blessed and praised be His name, the Living God of ages, eternal and forever; Voice, Spirit, and Word: this is the Spirit of the Holy One. His beginning has no beginning and His end has no ending.

10. Two—Air from Spirit: He wrote and formed therein twenty-basal letters; three mothers, seven double, and twelve simple.

11. Three—Water from the Air: He wrote and formed therein twenty-two letters, from the formless and void—mire and clay; He designed them as a platband, He hewed them as a wall, He covered them as a building, He poured snow over them and it became earth, *even as it is written: "He saith to the snow: Be thou the earth"* (Job 37:6).

12. Four—Fire from Water: and He designed and cut thereof the Throne of Glory: Seraphim, Ophanim, the Holy Animals, the Ministering Angels; and with these three He founded His dwelling. *Therefore it is written: "He maketh His angels spirits and His ministers a flaming fire"* (Psalms 104:4).

13. He chose three of the simple letters, a secret belonging to the three mothers *Alef, Mem, Shin,* and put them in His Great Name and sealed them with six extensions.

Five—He sealed the Height stretched upward and sealed it with Yud-Hey-Vov.

Six—He sealed the Depth stretched downward and sealed it with Yud-Vov-Hey.

Seven—He sealed the East stretched forward and sealed it with Hey-Yud-Vov.

Eight—He sealed the West stretched backward and sealed it with Hey-Vov-Yud.

Nine—He sealed the (North) stretched to the right and sealed it with Vov-Yud-Hey.

Ten—He sealed the (South) stretched to the left and sealed it with Vov-Hey-Yud.

14. These are the ten ineffable *sefirot:* one—the Spirit of the Living Elohim; two—Air from Spirit; three—Water from Air; four—Fire from Water; Height; Depth; East; West; North; and South.

2

Sefer HaBahir

The Book of the Clear Light

APPEARING ANONYMOUSLY *in Provence, southern France, around the year 1175, the* Sefer HaBahir *aroused immediate interest. The Kabbalistic circle that first promulgated this evocative work attributed it to Rabbi Nechunya ben HaKanah, a beloved first-century sage deeply interested in the unseen world. Legend has it that when the Romans—who controlled the Holy Land at the time—issued a decree to execute the sages, he ascended to heaven to ascertain the divine purpose. The Talmud (*Megillah 28a) *relates that Rabbi Nechunya ben HaKanah lived to a ripe old age, and when his students asked him the reason, he replied: "In all my life, I never derived honor from the shame of a peer, I never went to bed before calming those who were angry with me, and I was generous with my money."*

Though the Bahir is a dense, highly difficult work to read casually, it expands considerably on concepts found in the Sefer Yetzirah, such as the ten sefirot *and the twenty-two Hebrew letters as divine forces acting ceaselessly in the physical world. The Bahir also presents several other notions never before appearing in a Jewish text— such as reincarnation and the existence of a life-energy flow throughout the human body. Despite many decades of modern scholarship, no specific source has yet been indentified to explain the appearance of these ideas in the* Bahir, *which strongly influenced subsequent Kabbalah.*

This excerpt presents the Bahir's *first five verses, which sets forth the broad metaphysics associated with this abstruse work. In equally terse fashion, the later verses focus on the issue of good and evil in the world as we perceive it.*

VERSE I

Rabbi Nehuniah ben Ha-Kana said: One verse (Job 37:21) states, "And now they do not see light, it is brilliant (*Bahir*) in the skies . . . [round about God in terrible majesty]." Another verse, however (Psalms 18:12), states, "He made darkness His hiding place." It is also written (Psalms 97:2) "Cloud and gloom surround Him." This is an apparent contradiction. A third verse comes and reconciles the two. It is written (Psalm 139:12) "Even darkness is not dark to You. Night shines like day—light and darkness are the same."

VERSE 2

Rabbi Berachiah said: It is written (Genesis 1:2), "The earth was chaos (*tohu*) and desolation (*bohu*)." What is the meaning of the word "was" in this verse? This indicates that the chaos existed previously [and already *was*]. What is chaos (*tohu*)? Something that confounds *taha* (people). What is desolation (*bohu*)? It is something that has substance. This is the reason that it is called *bohu,* that is, *bo hu*—"it is in it."

VERSE 3

Why does the Torah begin with the letter *bet*? In order that it begins with a blessing (*berachah*). How do we know that the Torah is called a blessing? Because it is written (Deuteronomy 33:23), "The filling is God's blessing possessing the sea and the south." The sea is nothing other than the Torah, as it is written (Job 11:9), "It is wider than the sea." What is the meaning of the verse, "The filling is God's blessing"? This means that wherever we find the letter *bet* it indicates a blessing. It is thus written (Genesis 1:1), "In the beginning *(be-reshit)*" *bereshit* is *bet reshit*. The word "beginning" *(reshit)* is nothing than wisdom. It is thus written (Psalms 111:10), "The beginning is wisdom, the fear of God." Wisdom is a blessing. It is thus written, "And God blessed Solomon." It is furthermore written (I Kings 5:26), "And God gave wisdom to Solomon." This resembles a king who marries his daughter to his son. He gives her to him at the wedding and says to him, "Do with her as you desire."

VERSE 5

How do we know that the word *"berachah"* [usually translated as blessing] comes from the word *"baruch"* (meaning blessed)? Perhaps it comes from the word *berech* (meaning knee).

It is written (Isaiah 44:23) "For to Me shall every knee bend." [*Berachah* can therefore mean] the place to which every knee bends. What example does this resemble? People want to see the king, but do not know where to find his house *(bayit)*. First they ask, "Where is the king's house?" Only then can they ask, "Where is the king?" It is thus written, "For to Me every knee bend"—even the highest—"every tongue shall swear."

VERSE 194

Rabbi Rahumai said: This I received [from the Tradition]. When Moses wanted to know about the glorious fearsome Name, may it be blessed, he said (Exodus 33:18), "Show me please Your glory." He wanted to know why there are righteous who have good, righteous who have evil, wicked who have good, and wicked who have evil. But they would not tell him. Do you think then that they did not tell him? Can one then imagine that Moses did not know this mystery? But this is what Moses said: "I know the ways of the powers, but I do not know how thought spreads through them. I know that truth is in thought, but I do not know its parts." He wanted to know, but they would not tell him.

VERSE 195

Why is there a righteous person who has good, and (another) righteous person who has evil? This is because the (second) righteous person was wicked previously, and is now being punished. Is one punished then for his childhood deeds? Did not Rabbi Simeon say that in the heavenly tribunal no punishment is meted out until one is twenty years or older? He said: I am not speaking of his present lifetime. I am speaking about what he has already been previously. His colleagues said to him: How long will you conceal your words? He replied: Go out and see. What is this like? A person planted a vineyard and hoped to grow grapes, but instead, sour grapes grew. He saw that his planting and harvest were not successful, so he tore it out. He cleaned out the sour grape vines and planted again. When he saw that his planting was not successful, he tore it up and planted it again. How many times? He said to them: For a thousand generations. It is thus written (Psalms 105:8), "The word that He commanded for a thousand generations." It is in relation to this that they said, "Lacking were 974 generations. The Blessed Holy One stood up and planted them in each generation."

3

MAIMONIDES

Moses *ben* Maimon

MAIMONIDES *has long been recognized as the greatest Jewish thinker of medieval times. Born in Cordoba, Spain, he was the son of a prominent rabbi-physician and showed scholastic brilliance at an early age. When the comparatively tolerant Islamic regime that ruled Cordoba was abruptly overthrown by the militant Almohads in 1148, he was forced into weary wandering with his family for nearly twenty years. Eventually finding permanent refuge in the bustling Egyptian city of Fostat near Cairo, Moses ben Maimon there gained an international reputation as a rabbinic scholar and Jewish communal leader, philosopher, and prominent physician to Saladin's royal court. In acclaimed works like* Commentary on the Mishnah *and his monumental* Mishneh Torah, *he organized centuries of Talmudic thought with brilliant precision—and influenced Jewish law and theology to the present day.*

But undoubtedly, Maimonides' most significant impact on Kabbalah came from his philosophical treatise, The Guide for the Perplexed. *Written late in his life, its goal was to integrate the Torah with classic Greek philosophy—especially Aristotle—to provide a complete picture of human existence. In this immensely*

*influential work, Maimonides dealt extensively with the nature
of prophecy—which he regarded as a definite state of human consciousness, attainable through systematic personal development
including study, piety, and emotional self-control. This excerpt has
inspired countless Kabbalistic practitioners for centuries with its
explication of dreams and higher consciousness.*

Prophecy is, in truth and reality, an emanation sent forth by the
Divine Being through the medium of the Active Intellect, in the
first instance to the individual's rational faculty, and then to his
imaginative faculty. It is the highest degree and greatest perfection
that one can attain. It consists in the most perfect development of
the imaginative faculty.

Prophecy is a faculty that cannot in any way be found in a person or acquired by someone through a culture of his mental and
moral faculties—for even if the latter were as good and perfect as
possible, these would be of no avail unless combined with the
highest natural excellence of the imaginative faculty.

You know that the full development of any faculty of the body,
such as the imagination, depends on the condition of the organ, by
means of which the faculty acts. This must be the best possible as regards its temperament and its size, and also as regards the purity of
its substance. Any defect in this respect cannot in any way be supplied
or remedied by training. For when any organ is defective in its temperament, proper training can in the best case restore a healthy condition to some extent, but cannot make such an organ perfect. But if
the organ is defective as regards size, position, or as regards the substance and the matter of which the organ is formed, there is no remedy. You know all this, and I need not explain it to you at length.

Part of the function of the imaginative faculty is, as you well
know, to retain impressions of the senses, to combine them, and
chiefly to form images. The principal and highest function is performed when the senses are at rest and pause in their action, for
then it receives, to some extent, divine inspiration in the measure
as it is predisposed for this influence. This is the nature of those

dreams which prove true, also of prophecy— the difference being one of quantity, not of quality.

Thus our sages say that dream is the sixtieth part of prophecy; and no such comparison could be made between two things of different kinds, or we cannot say that the perfection of man is so many times the perfection of a horse. In *Bereshit Rabba* (section xvii), the following saying of our sages occurs, "Dream is the *nobelet* (the unripe fruit) of prophecy." This is an excellent comparison, for the unripe fruit (*nobelet*) is really the fruit to some extent, only it has fallen from the tree before it was fully developed and ripe.

In a similar manner, the action of the imaginative faculty during sleep is the same as at the time when it receives a prophecy, only in the first case it is not fully developed and has not yet reached its highest degree. But why need I quote the words of our sages when I can refer to the following passage of Scripture: "If there be among you a prophet, I, the Lord, will make myself known unto him in a vision, in a dream will I speak to him" (Numbers 12:6). Here the Lord tells us what the real essence of prophecy is: that it is a perfection acquired in a dream or vision (the original *mareh* is a noun derived from the verb *raah*). That is, the imaginative faculty acquires such an efficiency in its action that it sees the thing as if it came from without and perceives it as if through the medium of bodily senses.

These two modes of prophecy—vision and dream—include all its different degrees. It is a well-known fact that the thing which engages greatly and enhances the individual's attention while he is awake and in the full possession of his senses forms during his sleep the object of the action of his imaginative faculty. Imagination is then influenced only by the intellect so far as it is predisposed for such influence. It would be quite useless to illustrate this by a simile, or to explain it fully, as it is clear, and everyone knows it. It is like the action of the senses, the existence of which no person with common sense would ever deny.

After these introductory remarks, you will understand that a person must satisfy the following conditions before he can become a prophet: The substance of the brain must from the very beginning be in the most perfect condition as regards purity of matter, composition of its different parts, size, and position, and no part of his body must suffer from ill health. Additionally, he must have studied and acquired wisdom, so that his rational faculty passes from a state of potentiality to that of actuality. His intellect must be as developed and perfect as human intellect can be, his passions pure and equally balanced, and all his desires must aim at obtaining a knowledge of the hidden laws and causes that are in force in the Universe. His thoughts must be engaged in lofty matters, his attention directed to the knowledge of God, the consideration of His works, and of that which he must believe in this respect.

There must be an absence of the lower desires and appetites, of the seeking after pleasure in eating, drinking, and sexual activity; and in short, every pleasure connected with the sense of touch. . . . It is further necessary to suppress every thought or desire for illusory power and domination: that is to say, for victory over others, increase of followers, acquisition of honor, and service from the people without any ulterior object.

On the contrary, the multitude must be considered according to their true worth—some of them are undoubtedly like domesticated cattle, and others like wild beasts, and they engage the mind of the perfect and distinguished person insofar as he desires to guard himself from injury in case of contact with them and to derive some benefit from them when necessary.

One who satisfies these conditions, while his fully developed imagination is in action, influenced by the Active Intellect according to his mental training—such a person will undoubtedly perceive nothing but things very extraordinary and divine, and see nothing but God and His angels. His knowledge will include only that which is true knowledge, and his thought will be directed only to such general principles as would tend to improve the social relations between human beings. . . .

Faculties of the body are, as you know, sometimes weak, wearied, and corrupted, and others are in a healthy state. Imagination is certainly one of the faculties of the body. You find, therefore, that prophets are deprived of the faculty of prophesying when they mourn, are angry, or are similarly affected. Our sages say: Inspiration does not come upon a prophet when sad or languid.

This is the reason why Jacob did not receive any revelation during the period of his mourning, when his imagination was engaged with the loss of his son Joseph. The same was true for Moses when he was in a state of depression through the multitude of his troubles—which lasted from the murmurings of the Israelites in consequence of the evil reports of the spies [he sent to reconnoiter the Holy Land], until the deaths of the warriors of that generation. He received no message of God, as he used to, even though he did not receive prophetic inspiration through the medium of the imaginative faculty, but directly through the intellect. . . . There were also persons who prophesied for a certain time and then left off altogether, something occurring that caused them to discontinue prophesying. The same circumstance—prevalence of sadness and dullness—was undoubtedly the direct cause of the interruption of prophecy during the exile . . . an evil state prophesied to us in the words, "They shall run to and fro to seek the word of God, but shall not find it" (Amos 7:12); "Her king and her princes are among the nations, the [Hebraic] law is no more, her prophets also find no vision from the Lord" (Lamentations 2:9).

This is a real fact, and the cause is evident: the prerequisites [of prophecy] have been lost. In the Messianic period—may it soon commence—prophecy will therefore again be in our midst, as has been promised by God.

4

NACHMANIDES

Moses *ben* Nachman

AMONG THE MOST IMPORTANT *Kabbalists of medieval times was Nachmanides. Born in 1194 in Gerona, Spain, he served for many decades as both a practicing physician and rabbinic leader—like Maimonides, with whom his name has often been linked antago-nistically in Jewish history. For though expressing great respect for Maimonides' personal piety, Nachmanides strongly insisted that revelation—not measured reason—is the true path for knowing God.*

For example, in influential books such as Sefer HaTemuna *(Book of the Image), Nachmanides described each of the twenty-two Hebrew letters as a particular manifestation of the divine, and also explained the various periods of world history in terms of those manifestations. Consistent with earlier Kabbalistic works, Moses ben Nachman wrote extensively about the sefirot as the "inner life" of the hidden, transcendent God.*

A key event in Nachmanides' life took place in 1263, known as the Disputation of Barcelona, when a fiery convert to Christianity named Pablo Christiani challenged him to publicly debate the truth of their respective religions. Granted in advance full freedom of

speech by King James I of Aragon, Nachmanides led the Jewish
delegation for the four-day spectacle before ecclesiastical and royal
officials. Unexpectedly, an admiring King James not only declared
Nachmanides the winner but also bestowed a financial reward. Un-
fortunately, this victory only magnified the enmity of the powerful
Dominican Order and Nachmanides was forced into exile. He
spent his final years in the Holy Land, helping to revitalize its be-
leaguered Jewish community—declaring that "even in this devasta-
tion, it is a blessed land."

Nachmanides is among the few Jewish thinkers historically to
discuss the nature of the afterlife. In this excerpt from Torat-Adam,
a treatise on mourning rites and burial customs, he devoted the final
chapter—entitled Shaar HaGemul—*to divine reward and punish-*
ment, resurrection, and related topics.

One may wonder why Moses [Maimonides] found it necessary to
adduce so many proofs and demonstrations showing us that in the
World-to-Come there are no bodies but only souls, since he believed that the World-to-Come is the place of human existence
immediately after physical death. The youngest Jewish student
knows that when a righteous person dies "his soul abides in prosperity," in the goodness of the higher world without any matter
or body whatsoever. Its good does not consist of eating, drinking,
anointing, or sexual activity, for these pleasures do not pertain to
the soul, but rather the soul is preserved only by virtue of the
splendor of the Divine Presence, as it said, "Your righteousness
shall go before you and the splendor of the Lord shall be gathered
unto you."

Even though the hidden meaning of these matters is known
only to an elite few and only the Lord, blessed be He, is able to
understand their full truth, their plain meaning is known to all.
Why, then, did the Master feel the need to write the following in
his *Essay on the Resurrection of the Dead*? "The life following which
there is no death is life in the World-to-Come, because there is
therein no body. For we believe, and it is correct according to all

men of knowledge, that the inhabitants of the World-to-Come are souls without bodies, like angels."

Now, since he believes that the explanation of the World-to-Come is that it is the World-to-Come for souls immediately after the death of the body, one may wonder why he needs these arguments. It is known by all that after the soul is stripped from the body of a dead person, the body is left to decay. Scripture testifies to this: "The dust returns to the earth as it was, and the spirit returns to God who gave it." However, it appears that the intention of the Master, of blessed memory, is that according to him, the [term] "World-to-Come" is used to denote all the worlds of the souls and all that occurs to [the souls] throughout all of eternity. Indeed, [the Master] truly believes that the meaning of resurrection of the dead—which is a fundamental axiom of the Torah—is that the soul will return to its body according to the will of the Creator.

The souls will exit from the World-to-Come and will return to their bodies in the days of resurrection. These privileged persons will derive pleasure from the goodness of this world during the Messianic Era, and they will merit therein a status higher than their original status. However, after this the Master, of blessed memory, decrees the death of the Messiah and of his generation. Their souls will exist in the goodness of the World-to-Come without bodies, as they had originally, but in a yet greater status since they merit [that status] by virtue of the commandments which they performed during the Messianic Era. They will exist for all eternity.

The Master, of blessed memory, goes to great lengths in making numerous statements in order to demonstrate that the inhabitants of the World-to-Come have no bodies for two reasons: First, he knows that the sages of our tradition believe that there is no death following resurrection of the dead on the basis of their explanation [of the verse] "He will swallow up death forever." They declared, "The dead which the Holy One, blessed be He, will revive do not return to dust." According to this opinion, the inhabitants of the World-to-Come will exist in that world with their bodies after the resurrection.

The Master negates this opinion with all his ability. Therefore, many of the wise men of these generations have disagreed with him concerning this, as is found in their statements. That the World-to-Come after death is [only] for the souls, no one disputes—whether wise or not. There is no need for the statements which the Master wrote in many places, for it is well known that the body has no share or privilege [in the World-to-Come after death].

Furthermore, the Master, of blessed memory, intended as a second purpose to strengthen [the concept of] the soul itself; that it is neither a body nor a force within a body, but is a transcendental intellect as are angels. Thus he said in the *Essay on the Resurrection of the Dead:* "The cause of all this is what occurs to the minds of the masses who believe that there is no existence other than the existence of the body. That which is not a body or an accident of a body does not exist in thought of these persons who are bereft of thought. . . . However, those who may be called truly wise . . . know demonstrably that anything which transcends the corporeal has a stronger and more enduring existence than that which has a body. It is not even correct to say 'more enduring,' rather transcendental existence is the true existence because it is not subject to change. They are wise to whom it has become clear by means of demonstration that the Creator is not corporeal and therefore His existence is the ultimate of duration. Similarly, the existence of every transcendental being—that is, angels and the celestial intelligences—is stronger and more enduring than any corporeal being. Therefore, we believe that angels are not corporeal and that the inhabitants of the World-to-Come are transcendental souls."

The Master, of blessed memory, states further: "How could one imagine that these foolish people would understand that angels transcend the corporeal since their very existence, that is, the existence of angels and inhabitants of the World-to-Come is thought by them to be known only by virtue of tradition on the basis of the Torah and that there is no mode of investigation which can prove the existence of angels or the continued existence of souls, etc.?"

This passage teaches you, on the basis of the statements of the Master, of blessed memory, the meaning of the World-to-Come:

namely, that it is the continued existence of the souls alone after death, and that it is a matter which became clear to [the wise] by means of proof and investigation and not by tradition, for the matter of the World-to-Come after resurrection, in truth, requires statements of the Torah and the explanation of tradition. Thus the belief of the Master, of blessed memory, in explaining the World-to-Come, as well as ours, has been explained.

In truth, one can find that some of the wise men of Spain, in their scholarly writings and in their prayer, agree with the opinion that the World-to-Come is the world of the souls. Rabbi Solomon ibn Gabriol, of blessed memory, says in his prayer: "Under your throne of glory is a stand for the souls of your followers and there they experience enjoyment without limit or end." This is the World-to-Come. Thus, he would pray, "At the proper time, take me out of this world; bring me in peace to the World-to-Come." But we are hearkened to, since we have stated the matter correctly, and we have brought proof from the statements of our rabbis. I later found that Rabbi Saadia Gaon, in his commentary on the Book of Daniel, explains the World-to-Come as we have explained it. It is the tradition of the early [generations]; you should not forget their teachings. In any event, there are only semantic differences between us. Everyone agrees with regard to the [nature of] resurrection of the dead and the existence of that era both in general and in its details as I have explained, except [for] the opinion of the Master, Rabbi Moses, of blessed memory, who imposes a limit on the period of the resurrection and [claims that] everyone returns to the world of the souls, as we have mentioned above. However, we maintain that those resurrected exist forever from the era of resurrection to the World-to-Come, which is an eternally long world. May the Master of mercy cause us to merit the goodness which He has hidden for those who fear Him and has made for His servants according to His compassion and His mercies. Amen and amen.

5

ABRAHAM ABULAFIA

BORN IN SARAGOSSA, SPAIN, *in 1240, Abraham Abulafia is among the most intriguing figures in Judaism. Though he exerted a profound influence on the Kabbalah that exists through the present day, his name is rarely mentioned in books on Jewish history or theology—undoubtedly due to his unconventional life, marked by ceaseless wandering. His first journey was to the Land of Israel at the age of twenty, and soon after he devoted himself to intensive study of esoteric Judaic texts and Maimonides'* Guide for the Perplexed.

A disciple of the prominent philosopher-physician Hillel ben-Samuel of Verona, Abulafia was an enthusiastic teacher and wrote extensively on Kabbalistic, philosophical, and linguistic subjects, succeeding in attracting many devoted students. While living in Barcelona, he immersed himself in the Sefer Yetzirah *and its commentaries, and gradually came to espouse its perspective on the Hebrew letters as divine forces. Abulafia also began to write books of prophecy based on visionary experience. After his incredible attempt to convert Pope Nicholas III to Judaism in 1280, Abulafia was forced to wander Italy and other regions before vanishing completely from historical record in 1291.*

*More than any other Kabbalist, Abulafia stressed the path of
"knowing God through the twenty-two letters of the Hebrew alphabet," as he poetically declared his method, still practiced today
around the world. These excerpts from Abulafia's writings present
a reminiscence of his spiritual odyssey and several of his specific
guidelines for inner development.*

SELF–REVELATION

When I was thirty-one years old, in the city of Barcelona, God
woke me from my sleep and I studied *Sefer Yetzirah* with its commentaries; and the hand of God [rested] upon me, and I wrote
some books of wisdom and wondrous books of prophecies, and
my spirit was quickened within me, and the spirit of God came
into my mouth, and a spirit of holiness moved about me, and I saw
many awesome sights and wonders by means of these wonders and
signs. And among them, there gathered around me jealous spirits,
and I saw imaginary things and errors, and my thoughts were confused, because I did not find which of my people would teach me
the way by which I ought to go.

Therefore, I was like a blind man groping at noon for fifteen
years, and the Satan [stood] by my right hand to accuse me, and I
was crazy from the vision of my eyes which I saw, to fulfill the
words of the Torah and to finish the second curse [of] the fifteen
years which God has graced me with some little knowledge, and
God was with me to help me from the [Hebrew] year 5001 to
5045, to save me from every trouble; and at the beginning of the
year 5046, Elijah the Prophet [sent from God] had favor in me and
brought me to his holy tabernacle.

COMPELLED TO PROPHECY

Know that every one of the early prophets was forced to speak
what they spoke and to write what they wrote, so that one finds
many of them who say that their intention is not to speak at all
before the multitude of the people of the earth—who are lost in the

darkness of temporality—but that the divine influx which flowed upon them forces them to speak, and that they are even subjected to shame, as in the saying of the prophet, "I gave my back to the smiters and my cheek to those that plucked; I hid not my face from shame and spitting" while another prophet said, "The Lord God will help me, who shall condemn me?" And many other similar [sayings] in the way of the chastiser.

THE POWER WITHIN

It is known and conspicuous to all the sages of the Torah who are Kabbalists, nor is it concealed to the true philosophers, that every man is given a choice without any compulsion, and without any force, but there is a human power within man, and it is called the Stirring Power (*koah ha-me'orer*) and it is that which arouses his heart to do or not to do [anything]. And after this, a man finds in his heart one who forces him between these two opposites, and whichever of them shall be victorious over him will activate the limbs to perform actions for good or for evil; and this principle shall return, of man always struggling and warring against the thoughts of his heart, the two former motivating all of the aspects of his many thoughts, as it is written in *Sefer Yetzirah*, "The heart in soul [i.e., within man] is like the king in a battle."

And a man possesses these two forms—called impulses or powers or angels or thoughts or comprehensions, or whatever you wish to call them. For the intent of them all refer to one thing, but the main thing is to apprehend His reality and to recognize their essence in truth, by proofs which are based upon tradition and reason, and to distinguish between two paths of reality which they have, and to know the great difference between them in degree.

STRENGTHENING THE INTELLECT

One who enters the path of combination [of letters], which is the way that is close to knowledge of God in truth, from all the ways he will at once test and purify his heart in the great fire, which is the fire of desire; and if he has strength to stand the way of ethics, close to desire, and his intellect is stronger than his imagination, he rides upon it as one who rides upon his horse and guides it by hitting it with the boots to run at his will, and to restrain it with his hand, to make it stand in the place where his intellect will wish, and his imagination is to be a recipient that he accept his opinion. . . . The man who possesses this great power, he is a man of truth.

LETTER COMBINATION

And begin by combining this name, namely, YHVH, at the beginning alone, and examine all its combinations and move it and turn it about like a wheel returning around, front and back, like a scroll, and do not let it rest, but when you see its matter strengthened because of the great motion, because of the fear of confusion of your imagination and the rolling about of your thoughts, and when you let it rest, return to it and ask [it] until there shall come to your hand a word of wisdom from it, do not abandon it. Afterwards go on to the second one from it, *Adonay*, and ask of it its foundation (*yesodo*) and it will reveal to you its secret (*sodo*). And then you will apprehend its matter in the truth of its language.

Then join and combine the two of them (YHVH and *Adonay*), and study them and ask them, and they will reveal to you the secrets of wisdom, and afterwards combine this which is namely *El Shadday,* which is tantamount to the Name (*El Shadday* = 345 = ha-Shem), and it will also come in your portion. Afterwards combine *Elohim,* and it will also grant you wisdom, and then combine the four of them, and find the miracles of the Perfect One, which are miracles of wisdom.

SPEAKING TO THE DIVINE NAME

Direct your face toward the Name, which is mentioned, and sit as though a man is standing before you and waiting for you to speak with Him, and He is ready to answer you concerning whatever you may ask Him, and you say "speak" and he answers. . . . And begin then to pronounce, and recite first "the head of the head" [i.e., the first combination of letters], drawing out the breath and at great ease; and afterwards go back as if the one standing opposite you is answering you, and you yourself answer, changing your voice, so that the answer not be similar to the question. And do not extend the answer at all, but say it easily and calmly, and in response recite one letter of the Name as it actually is.

MEDITATION AND THE BODY

Again, go and mention the head of the middle of the Name. You already know that you ought to pronounce [the names of] the organs from what I have said—that there are, so to speak, three spots on your head: the inside, which is the head of the head, the middle, which is the inside of the head, and the behind, which is the end of the head. And likewise imagine as if there are three points on your torso, which is the place of your heart: the head, which is the center of the middle, the middle, which is the middle of the middle, which is but one point in its center, and the behind, which is the end of the end. And likewise imagine that there are three points in your belly: the front, which is the point of your naval, the middle, which is the point of your entrails; the middle of the end, and behind, which is the point of the end of your spine, which is the place of the kidneys where the spinal cord is completed, the end of the end.

DETACHMENT FROM THE WORLD

Be prepared for thy God, O Israelite! Make thyself ready to direct thy heart to God alone. Cleanse the body and choose a lonely house where none shall hear thy voice. Sit there in thy closet and do not reveal thy secret to any man. If thou canst, do it by day in the house, but it is best if thou completest it during the night. In the hour when thou preparest thyself to speak with the Creator and thou wishest Him to reveal His might to thee, then be careful to abstract all thy thought from the vanities of the world.

When you wish to recite the Names of seventy-two letters, following the preparation we have mentioned, you must arrange to be alone in a special place, to pronounce the secret of the Ineffable Name, and to separate and isolate yourself from every speaking creature, and from all vanities of [the world, so as not to view them as] attributes [of God]. Also so that there not remain in your heart any thoughts of human or natural things, of either voluntary or necessary [matters], as if you are one who has given a writ of divorce to all forms of the mundane world, as one who has given a testament in the presence of witnesses in which he orders [another] to take care of his wife and his children and his property, and has relieved himself of all involvement and supervision and transferred it from himself and one away.

6

Sefer HaZohar

The Book of Splendor

THE BOOK OF SPLENDOR, *or* Zohar *as it's typically known, is the bible of Kabbalah. It was first circulated by Rabbi Moses de Leon in late thirteenth-century Spain, who claimed, astoundingly, that it had been sent to him by Nachmanides in the Holy Land and had been written by the revered second-century sage Simeon bar Yochai. Deceased for several years, Nachmanides was in no position to re-fute this assertion, one which traditionalists continue to accept as true. However, modern Judaic scholars are united in insisting that linguistic analysis reveals that Rabbi de Leon composed it himself in the 1280s—though he may certainly have been influenced by esoteric oral traditions dating back millennia.*

In a manner that has no parallel for any other Kabbalistic book, the Zohar *eventually gained exalted status among worldwide Jewry—ranking alongside the Torah and the Talmud as a sacred work, transmitted by the divine to guide earthly life. Though this unique historical development may be attributable, in part, to the* Zohar's *presumed author, undoubtedly its remarkable content has also played a vital role. For with powerful poetic imagery, it depicts*

human existence as a mysterious and wondrous adventure in a
dazzling cosmos—where joy is our key link to God.

Structured loosely on the portions of the Pentateuch, the Zohar
presents the conversations and experiences of Rabbi Simeon bar
Yochai and his colleagues as they roamed the Holy Land. The
mood is usually surrealist as flying scrolls appear out of nowhere
and small children utter words of profound wisdom.

In a highly nonlinear way, teachings about such traditional
Kabbalistic subjects as the ten sefirot *and the letters of the Hebrew*
alphabet are explicated—together with fascinating commentary
about dreams, ecstatic states of consciousness, mind-body diagnosis
and healing, extrasensory experience, and many other topics. This
excerpt provides a vivid depiction of another prominent theme in
the Zohar: *the nature of the human soul and the afterlife.*

There is, besides, in the center of the whole of the heavens, a door
called *G'bilan*. Underneath that door are seventy other doors, with
seventy chieftans keeping guard, at a distance from it of two thousand cubits, so that no one should come near it. From that door,
again, there is a path mounting higher and higher until it reaches the
Divine Throne. The same door gives access to all quarters of heaven
as far as the gate called *Magdon,* where is the end of the heaven
that extends over the Land of Israel. All the seventy doors that are
inscribed on the door called *G'bilan* are called "gates of righteousness," being under the direct control of the Divine Throne, and no
other power. It is through those gates that the Holy One provides
the Land of Israel with all that it needs—and it is from the resi-
due of that provision that the Chieftans take and transmit to all the
lower chieftans.

In connection with the firmament that is above the lower Paradise there are sublime mysteries. When the Holy One was about to
make the firmament, He took fire and water out of His Throne of
Glory, fused them into one, and out of them made the lower firmament, which expanded until it reached the area of the Lower Paradise, where it halted. The Holy One, blessed be He, then took from

the holy and supernal heaven fire and water of another kind—such as both are and are not, are both disclosed and undisclosed—and of them He made a further expanse of heaven, which He spread over the lower Paradise where it joins the other firmament.

That expanse of heaven, above the lower Paradise, displays four colors: white, red, green, and black, and correspondingly contains four doors in its four sides. These four openings form a passage for four light-radiations. On the right side, two lights shine forth through two doors, one through the door of the right and one though the opposite. Within the light-radiation on the right, a certain letter stands out with scintillating effulgence—that is, the letter *Mem*. That letter moves up and down continually without ever resting at one point.

Within the opposite light-radiation, there similarly stands out with a scintillating effulgence the letter *Resh,* which on occasions, however, assumes the shape of the letter *Beth*. This similarly moves forever up and down, at times being revealed and other times hidden.

When the soul of a righteous person enters the Lower Paradise, these two letters emerge out of the midst of that radiation and appear above that soul, where they continue to rise and fall. Then out of the same two doors there emerge from on high two legions, one under the command of Michael the great prince, and the second under the great chieftan called Baeel, who is the noble minister called Raphael. These legions descend and pause above the soul, which they greet with the words: "Peace be your coming; he enters into peace, he enters into peace!"

The two letters then return to their place and become absorbed within the radiation that passes through those two doors. Similarly, through the other two doors—that are on the left and on the west—there pass two light-scintillations, that is, a *Gimel* and a *Nun*. When the two previous letters return to their own place, these two flaming letters emerge from the midst of their surrounding illumination and appear above that soul. Then again, emerging out of the other two portals, there come forth two other legions—one under the command of the great chief Gabriel and the other under that of the great chief Nuriel. These fix themselves above the soul while the letters return to their place.

After that, these two legions enter into a certain hidden Palace in the Garden, called *Ahaloth* [literally, "aloes"]. Therein is the hidden storage of the twelve varieties of sweet spices that Scripture enumerates: "Spikenard and saffron, calamus and cinnamon . . ." (Song of Songs 4:14). Therein is also the repository of all the garments wherewith human souls are invested, each according to its desert. On each garment all the good works that a person did in this world are inscribed, and in each case, a proclamation is made, saying, "This garment belongs to such a one," after which the soul of the righteous in Paradise is clothed therewith, so as to become a replica of the individual's personality whilst in this world.

This takes place not less than thirty days after the person's death, inasmuch as for the first thirty days every soul must undergo correction before entering Paradise, as already stated elsewhere. After purification, it receives its garment, in virtue of which it is then assigned to its appropriate place. All the letters and legions then disappear.

Now the firmament over the Lower Paradise revolves twice a day under the impetus of the other firmaments that are attached to it. That firmament, moreover, is inwrought with all the letters of the [Hebrew] alphabet in various colors, each letter distilling the heavenly dew over the Garden. It is in that dew that the souls bathe and recuperate after their previous immersion in the *Nehar dinur* (river of fire) for purification. That dew descends from no other source but from the midst of the letters that are graven in the firmament, these letters containing in miniature the whole of the Torah, and that firmament forming the esoteric part of the Torah, since it is made out of the fire and water of the Torah itself.

Hence they drop their dew upon all those in this world who give themselves up to the study of the Torah for its own sake. The very words of their studies are inscribed in Paradise, where they mount up to that firmament where they receive from those letters that dew on which the soul of the good person is nurtured. So

Scripture says: "My doctrine shall drop as the rain, my speech shall distill as the dew" (Deuteronomy 32:2).

In the center of that firmament there is an opening directly facing the opening of the supernal Palace on high and forming the gateway unto the Higher Paradise, by way of a pillar that is fixed in the Lower Paradise reaching up to the door on high. There is, moreover, a column of light—formed of a combination of three lights of so many different colors—radiating upward from the opening in the center of that firmament, and thus illuminating that pillar with a many-hued light. Thus that firmament scintillates and flashes with several dazzling colors.

The righteous are illumined by the reflection of that supernal resplendency, and on each New Moon, the glory of the *Shekinah* as revealed in that firmament transcends that of other times. All the righteous then approach and prostrate themselves before it. Happy is the portion of whoever is found worthy of those garments wherein the righteous are clad in the Garden of Eden. Those garments are made out of the good deeds performed by a person in this world in obedience to the commands of the Torah. In the Lower Paradise, the human soul is thus sustained by these deeds and is clad in garments of glory made out of them. But when the soul mounts up on high through that portal of the firmament, other precious garments are provided for it of a more exalted order—made out of the zeal and devotion that characterized his study of the Torah and his prayer.

For when that zeal mounts up on high, a crown is made out of it for him to be crowned with, but some of it remains as the person's portion—out of which garments of light are made for the soul to be clad in when it has ascended on high. The former garments, as we have said, depend on his actions, but these depend on his devotion of spirit, so as to qualify their owner to join the company of holy angels and spirits. This is the correct exposition of the matter as the Holy Lamp [Rabbi Simon ben Yochai] learned it from Elijah. The garments of the Lower Paradise are made of a person's actions; those of the celestial Paradise of the devotion and earnestness of his spirit. . . .

The river that goes forth out of the Lower Eden is a mystery known only to the initiated, and is alluded to in the words (Isaiah 58:11), "and he will satisfy your soul in dry places with brightness." The soul that departs this dark world yearns for the light of the upper world. Just as the thirsty person yearns for water, so does the soul thirst for the brilliancy of the light of the Garden and the firmament. The souls sit there by that river that flows out of Eden. They find rest whilst clad in ethereal garments. Without those garments, they would not be able to endure the dazzling light around them. But protected by this covering, they are in comfort and drink their fill of that radiance without being overwhelmed by it. It is the river that renders the souls fit, and able to feast on and enjoy that radiance.

7

SIMEON BEN ZEMAH DURAN

AMONG THE MOST CELEBRATED *sages of pre-expulsion Spain was Simeon ben Zemah Duran. Born in 1361 on the island of Majorca, he studied under leading rabbinic teachers before mastering astronomy, mathematics, science, and philology to become a practicing physician. Then came the persecutions of 1391. An estimated fifty thousand Spanish Jews were massacred by Christian mobs in a matter of months. Entire communities were destroyed, including Rabbi Duran's in the capital city of Palma. He thereupon left Majorca for Algiers, where he eventually became chief rabbi. He accepted the post on the bold condition that approval by the Algerian rulership not be involved—as he insisted that the position was purely an internal Jewish matter. In contradiction to Maimonides' influential view, Rabbi Duran made it lawful for rabbis to accept a salary so that they could devote full attention to communal matters. Over the course of his long lifetime, he became revered both as a scholar and a wonder-working Kabbalist.*

Rabbi Duran's most famous work is known as the Tashbetz *(an acronym of the book's title,* Teshuvah Shimon ben Tsemah*). Comprising approximately eight hundred responses to diverse*

Jewish legal questions he received, the Tashbetz *offers fascinating light on the condition of Spanish and North African Jewry in that era. Among the wide-ranging religious queries presented was one brought by Amram Merevas Ehorati of Oran. A fellow Jew had a recent dream in which the whole Jewish community would be excommunicated unless all fasted: was everyone therefore obligated to fast? Rabbi Duran's responsum (2:128) was influential in affirming and promulgating the longstanding rabbinic perspective on dreams—one that combined both a rationalistic and mystical viewpoint.*

Regarding a dream that was dreamt, which indicated that if the community does not fast on a certain day they will all be excommunicated. The Rabbi of that community concluded that they are all obligated to fast as a community, and he also maintained that they should make a special blessing during the Mincha service, and he assembled a quarry of ten people to rescind the excommunication.

I was silent for a moment in contemplating this story, for it seems that whichever way the incident is analyzed it seems the community erred. . . .

And what is fitting to consider regarding this incident is the issue of dreams in general as presented in the Talmud. The general categories of knowledge must be considered before explaining the specifics of the applied knowledge. And we find in several places that our rabbis of blessed memory were concerned for the contents of dreams, yet in other places they appear to be unconcerned. And therefore it is fitting to consider the underlying reason for this (i.e., nature of dreams), for the knowledge of something in its essential foundation is a complete understanding, and without knowledge of the fundamentals it is not true knowledge but rather speculation. . . .

It seems, however, that the place in Talmud where the Rabbis were concerned for the contents of dreams was in regards to the circumstances of the aforementioned incident, and that is, in regards to excommunication within a dream which is mentioned

first in tractate *Nedarim* (8a) in addition to several other places,
such as towards the end of tractate *Brachos* (55a). . . . However, the
places where the rabbis were clearly not concerned for the contents of dreams appear in tractate *Sanhedrin* (30a), for which they
say there that there was a man who was aggravated regarding
money which was designated as tithes which his father had left for
him in his will. The keeper of dreams appeared to this man in a
dream that the money which his father left for him is in "such and
such" a place. Regarding this incident, the Talmud states, "The
words of dreams cannot elevate an item in status or descend an
item from its status" (i.e., they have no import).

Clearly there is here a contradiction.

Perhaps it would seem possible to explain that in truth there is
no contradiction by explaining that in truth one may always rely
on a dream which one dreamt, whether it relates to oaths, tithes, or
other issues; however if someone else had the dream which has
implications for another, such should not be relied upon at all.
Thus we could interpret the passage in *Sanhedrin* that "the keeper"
of dreams is really a third party who dreamt this answer (and that
is the reason why it must be disregarded). And thus the community
erred in fasting, since the dreams of one person should not impact
another. However, since the Talmudic passage concludes with the
blanket statement, "The words of dreams cannot elevate an item in
status or descend an item from its status," the aforementioned dis-
tinction is not tenable. . . . If so, we are left with the original difficulty, why were they concerned [for the content of the dreams]
regarding excommunication, and similarly rely on them in many
cases [even though the passage in *Sanhedrin* seems to blanket reject
the significance of dreams].

And I say that what will heal the difficulty of this question is one
passage in Talmud tractate *Brachos,* that it is said there: Rava contrasted the verse which states, "Dreams speak falsehood" (Zechariah 10:2), and it also states, "Through a dream I will speak with
him" (Numbers 12:6). (Rava explained.)

There is no contradiction, here [the verse in Numbers] discusses a dream which is related through an angel; here [the verse in Zechariah] deals with a dream related through a demon.

Clearly we see that our rabbis of blessed memory were actually aware and saw that there are certain dreams which are apt to rely on; there are other types which cannot be relied upon. Some dreams are related through an angel, and an angel does not lie, while others are related through demons who speak like a cloudy morning which has no light.

And this Talmudic passage was vindicated by the philosophers in this place. And even though the words of the rabbis are words of pure Torah which don't need any justification, it is still worthy to substantiate their words with philosophical works in order that they (the words of the rabbis) are better understood, and to appreciate that no secret escaped them.

It is known from the roots of secular wisdom that certain dreams are correct and some are incorrect. And those dreams which are correct are those which are formulated through the active imagination while it is healthy of complexion and formation and content. There should be no infiltrations of bad mental chemistry from foods which create bile of black and red hues mixed together. And when the dreams are dreamt in a correct state, they will be produced through the clear active mind which creates true dreams.

And it has already been stated that one of the great wonders of divine providence is the knowledge bestowed (on few) to know the future, in order that the man should be protected.

And that is what the rabbis meant that correct dreams are relayed through angels, and the meaning of the Talmudic statement that dreams are one sixtieth of prophecy. . . .

And the dreams which are incorrect are those which are produced through the power of imagination when it is unhealthy, or inherently the person has bad composition and dispositions, or because of fatty foods which create black and red bile and burden the mind; these dreams are composed of sensory perceptions which have no basis or validity. Regarding these dreams it is stated (*Yoma* 83b). That is what is meant that incorrect dreams are related though demons, for the phrase "demons" in this particular passage is a term used to connote bad internal spirits which harm and belabor a person. All of these [incorrect dreams] are made of nothing and implications are meaningless, they have no basis whatsoever, and there is no need to be concerned for them.

8

Sefer HaYashar

The Book of Righteousness

THOUGH AN INFLUENTIAL *ethical text for more than five hundred years,* Sefer HaYashar *(Book of Righteousness) is shrouded in mystery. Like many major Judaic works, its author is unknown. Some past traditionalists attributed it to Rabbi Zerahiah HaYevani, a Greek-Jewish thinker who lived in the Byzantine empire during the thirteenth or fourteenth century. However, most contemporary scholars believe that it was composed anonymously in thirteenth-century Spain by a Kabbalist who wished to conceal his identity because, like other texts from that era, it presented potentially explosive esoteric ideas couched in muted philosophical language.*

Over the centuries, an added source of scholarly confusion has been that many different Judaic works have been called the Book of Righteousness, a title derived from two mysterious biblical verses. Thus, we read in Joshua 10:13 concerning the miracle of the sun standing still, "Is not this written in the Book of Yashar?" And, in Second Samuel, we have the lament of David for King Saul and Jonathan: "Behold, it is written in the Book of Yashar."

Despite its author's anonymity, Sefer HaYashar *seems to have been a popular Jewish ethical work from the time of its appear-*

ance—and was first printed in 1520 in Constantinople. With the growth of the musar *(ethical) movement in nineteenth-century Eastern Europe,* Sefer HaYashar *gained renewed interest—and especially among Hasidim, it was read in home study groups.*

Written in an inspirational style, Sefer HaYashar *begins by urging, "Let us praise our God and bless our Maker who created us and summoned us to do that which will improve our souls." As these excerpts show, this time-honored book presents such topics as self-reckoning and right conduct, emotional development and wisdom, faith and the nature of the afterlife, from an optimistic and action-oriented perspective.*

RIGHT OUTLOOK

My soul, my soul. Lift up your eyes to the heavens and contemplate their awesome wonders, luminaries, and their dominions, the mountains and their foundations, the lands and their inhabitants. Set your heart to know Who created them and ordered them wisely. After that, consider the secret of their creation from that which was not and to what end they were created.

Seek to understand the events and occurrences of the world and its happenings, as well as the benevolence of the Creator, His goodness and compassion. Seek to understand the events of this transitory world, which is like a gourd which appeared and perished overnight.

Set between your eyes His being, His worth, the ordeal of His judgment, the retributions of His just decree. Set these things before you so that they will not be swerved from your attention. Then your soul will be aroused so as to stand upon the path of wisdom, hope, and dread.

Let love and reverential fear draw you toward the worship of the Creator. Both of these will enable you to attain your utmost goal and desire, while each will serve to preserve you from the pit of confusion. If you dwell upon them with diligence, they will open to you the gates of hope and salvation, and save you from the depths of sin. They will serve you as tokens of remembrance.

If you forget they will remind you, if you sleep they will awaken you, if you err they will warn you. With this in mind, you will then find a bountiful reward for your effort. You will not lose your just reward. Just as this work will help you, it will help everyone whose provisions are like yours and whose position is like yours. Although the wise and pious may not need this work, perhaps a wanderer from the true path might find help therein if he meditates upon it.

UNDERSTANDING LIFE

An apple will not grow from a nut-bearing tree, nor will almonds grow on it, for that is not found in its root. Only that which is found in its root can come forth from its branches. There can come forth only nuts from a nut-bearing tree. If there were such a power in the roots of the tree, such a power would bring forth apples or almonds, it would be evident in its fruit. For as they came up from the earth, there would be seen in them the form of nuts. For there cannot grow forth from the branches anything except that which is found in the roots.

Thus, we can understand that everything which is found in this world comes from the strength of the other world, for the upper world is like a root. This world is like its branches, and therefore, through the mysteries of the lowly world, we can understand the secrets of the upper world. . . .

Every outflowing seeks and strives to return to its source.

An example of this is that when we take a stone from the ground and hurl it upward with the power of our hand, the stone rises by the power of this throw, and when it leaves the apex of its ascent through the power of the hurler, it then returns, by its very nature, from the place where it was taken. So it is with water. If we throw it upward, it will reach the maximum limit proportionate to the power of the thrower, and then it will return, by its very nature, to the place below.

Thus it is with air. If you cause it to enter into an inflated bag by blowing into it, and you stop up the openings, it will be contained therein by force so long as the bag is closed. But when the bag is opened, the air will quickly rush out and return to the place of its origin. Thus it is with fire. When the flame ascends, we see the flame is striving to ascend to the heights, to its source. But when the flame is bound to the wood which is being burned, it cannot ascend completely. When the flame is able to separate itself from the wood, it goes upward to its place. Thus the soul, when it is taken from Heaven and joined to the body, is like the flame of fire that is bound to the wood and cannot separate itself from it until the strength of the body which holds life is spent. Then the soul can return to its source and to its place far above.

ELIMINATING ANGER

Another quality which interferes with the true worship of God is anger. It is one of the evil qualities which can destroy the worship of God. For the worship of God cannot dwell in the heart of one who is wrathful. At the time of his anger, he pays no attention to anything he does, but instead he multiplies oaths, profanes the name of Heaven, kills his friend, and harms his companion. It is possible that as his wrath grows fierce, he will go and worship idols or commit suicide. Therefore, a person should not trust his worship of God if he cannot subdue his wrath.

The healing of wrath is this: we should know the forces that stir up wrath and we should reverse them. And we say that the causes of wrath are too little reflection, the folly of the one who is angry, the lack of companionship of the wise and the intelligent, who could teach him to subdue his anger, and the companionship of fools and wicked people. He does not recognize what an ugly quality anger is. Nor does he recognize how many good qualities there are in forebearance and patience.

For no one who is patient will ever regret it, nor will he need to do anything for which everyone who hears of it will reproach him and shame him. But let all of his deeds be in quietness and gentleness, as it is said in Proverbs 16:32, "One who is slow in anger is better than the mighty; and one who rules his spirit is better than one who takes a city." Know that the pious sages would, at the very outset of the condition of their worship, put upon their souls this condition: to subdue their anger and not to be wrathful or hate, but that their mind would be broad enough to accept the deeds of humanity whether they be good or bad. If a vile person were to injure them, their soul should be too precious to profane their honor by entering into a dispute with him and repaying him according to his desserts. If an honored person were to injure them, they would patiently bear his words and restrain themselves.

Therefore, if a true servant of God wishes to remove wrath from his heart, he must accustom his soul to subdue the hardness of his heart, and he should swear not to be angry. He should place between his eyes the symbol of his nobler quality and the remembrance that he, himself, is but dust and ashes. Then his heart will be humble. If a person should injure him, he will avoid a quarrel with him by a soft answer, or he will make silence as a bridle for his mouth and consider that such a person cannot be called wise if he cannot govern his spirit. When he brings his soul into a sincere covenant and oath that he will not be angry for a certain number of days, it will be for him like a healing—bitter as wormwood—which he knows will restrain him from a difficult and formidable disease.

Let him, therefore, swear always to eat of this bitter medication. If he does this for only two months, he will see all sorts of occasions for anger that passed him by, yet he bore them all with a pleasant countenance, and he will recognize in himself that he will be strong and wise.

CULTIVATING SELF-DISCIPLINE

Therefore, I would say that he who accustoms his soul to the service of God ought not begin with difficult matters, but with simple ones. If he cannot do them even if they are simple, let him do a part of them, and as he continues, let him add to them. If he sees that he is annoyed or uncomfortable, let him lessen his task and do a part of them, but let him not abandon everything, as I have previously explained.

The easy matters are, for example: prayer, greeting, helping the poor according to one's ability, visiting the sick, accompanying the dead. It is different with difficult matters, such as: fasting, withholding oneself from all desire that happens to come; guarding oneself from cheating, robbery, oaths, anger, jealousy, and from forbidding what is permitted and permitting what is forbidden. In these matters, a person must train and accustom himself, just as a father accustoms his son in teaching him worldly things, for he must at first teach him the easy matters that do not involve effort and exertion.

As he goes on, let him add to them, and then the son will not grow impatient with him. For if the father teaches his son difficult matters at the very beginning, the son will grow impatient with him, and this may cause him to reject everything and not return to it. Therefore, there is nothing that the sensible person can utilize to subdue his evil inclination that compares with reminding the soul of the good things and the joys that are inherent in the service of God and the evils that come to those who do not serve God.

GO SLOWLY IN INNER DEVELOPMENT

It is necessary for the intelligent person at the very beginning of his service to accustom himself slowly so that he will not grow impatient in his service. When love enters the heart to fulfill some good deed, one must hurry to do it. . . . [And] when [one] sees that hatred has entered his heart and he is impatient with his service, he should not abandon the thing entirely, and he should not say, "I will lay the matter aside for the present and afterward I will return to it." For if he abandons everything, his power to fulfill the commandment will be lost. But if he clings to a part of it, his power to fulfill the commandment will not be lost. It is similar to a person who has one of his limbs cut off. If the limb is entirely cut off from the body, there is no remedy, and there is no healing. But if the limb is still joined to the body, there is a remedy, and the limb will be restored to its former strength when they heal it.

APHORISMS

The wise person is drawn to the companionship of the wise, the fool is drawn to the companionship of fools.

Wisdom and knowledge cannot be destroyed, but they exist forever.

9

JOSEPH ALBO

AMONG THE LEADERS *of late medieval Jewry was Rabbi Joseph Albo, born in the Spanish kingdom of Aragon in around 1380. Few details are known about his early life, though he claimed having studied with Barcelona's illustrious Talmudic philosopher Hasdai Crescas. By middle age, Rabbi Albo had gained sufficient stature among Spanish Jews to help serve as a chief defender in the notorious Disputation of Tortosa in 1413–1414, in which rabbinic delegates were forced to debate the validity of Judaism against an antagonistic apostate before the royal and ecclesiastical court. This was the longest and historically most important confrontation initiated by the Catholic Church against Jewish practitioners, and involved the Antipope Benedict XIII, recognized in Spain, as an active participant.*

Over the twenty-month session, the Jewish delegation was openly threatened with death by the Inquisition if it replied too strongly, and forced conversions abounded in several towns. After this harrowing event, several Jewish leaders decided to write books explicating the essentials of their religion, among them Rabbi Albo, whose Sefer HaIkkarim *(Book of Principles), composed in 1424, became the most popular and influential. With a lucid and engaging style, it presented the basic teachings of Jewish theology drawing upon diverse sources.*

In Rabbi Albo's view, Jewish belief can be reduced to three primary "roots"—the existence of God, the reality of revelation, and divine reward and punishment for human conduct. In this regard, he eliminated as secondary several of Maimonides's long-accepted thirteen tenets, such as belief in the coming of the Messiah and resurrection. This selection presents Rabbi Albo's view of prophecy, which he regarded, like Maimonides, as a real and comprehensible phenomenon. This outlook has influenced Kabbalists through the present day.

The divine inspiration which we said was necessary in order that we may know through it what things are acceptable to God and what things are not, man cannot acquire without divine consent. For it is not natural that the spirit of an intellect devoid of matter should rest upon a material thing. For this reason, all the ancients thought it impossible that the divine spirit should rest upon man, and that the latter should prophesy by means of a supernatural power and foretell the future. And therefore the ancient peoples used to make images and burn incense and offer prayers to the stars to bring down the spiritual influence of some star upon one of their images, in order that through it the spirit of a star residing in the body of the star should rest upon man, who is a corporeal being, so that the latter might foretell the future through the spirit of the star exerting an influence upon the person. This is the meaning of divination. . . .

The prophets had indeed also this power of foretelling the future as a secondary consideration, as a testimony to the truth of their prophetic teaching, in order that persons may believe them. Accordingly we find that all the prophets admonish us constantly to observe the Torah and carry out all the commandments. The main purpose of God in inspiring the prophets was that through them, man may attain to his perfection by doing those things which are acceptable to God and not in order to give humanity a knowledge of the future, as is the case with diviners. These foretell the future by certain practices which strengthen the power of imagination in a natural way, and not through the spirit of God, as the prophets do; unless, indeed, we say that prophecy is also a function of the imagination, as is the opinion of some of our wise men who follow the Philosopher. They hold that prophecy is a natural phenomenon, pertaining solely to the power of imagination, like dreams. They go so far as to say that it is an unusual thing if a person does not prophesy being wise and prepared thereto: that is, if his imagination is prepared for prophecy.

This is, however, contradicted both by our senses and our reason. The argument from the senses is that we never find the gift of prophecy in any one of the philosophers, though they were wise men in theoretical speculation; whereas we do find the gift of prophecy among the Jewish people. This shows that it is not a natural phenomenon associated with theoretical speculation. For if it were so, why should this gift have been kept from the other nations, so that their wise men despite their perfection of intellect and imagination are devoid of the prophetic inspiration? There is no doubt, therefore, that prophecy is a divine inspiration which comes by the will of God upon the rational power, either through the medium of the imagination or without it, as will be explained.

The argument from reason is that the diviners, the image worshippers, those who consult ghosts and familiar spirits, and those who indulge in other practices in order to strengthen the power of imagination so as to know the future, cannot determine the things which are acceptable to God, because they have no means of knowing this, seeing that it is above nature and the spirit of uncleanness and the powers of the spheres, from which they obtain all their information. And for this reason, they are not always correct in their prognostications.

And this, for two reasons: First, because the power of imagination is necessarily deceptive from its nature, for not everything that is imaginable is possible, as is known to those who are familiar with the nature of that faculty. And second, because God can destroy the power of the constellations and bring out the opposite of that which they determine. Therefore astrologers are necessarily liable to deception, as the Bible says: "Let now the astrologers, the stargazers, the monthly prognosticators, stand up and save you from the things that shall come upon you" (Isaiah 47:13). The Rabbis comment upon the expression "from the things," as meaning that they save from some of the things, but not from all the things. They cannot foretell truly all that has been determined for they are necessarily liable to error for the two reasons mentioned, either by reason of the nature of the imaginative faculty, or because God can nullify by His will that which is determined by the stars.

The prophet is the opposite of all this. His inspiration comes from God and is due to the will of God, and not to the powers of the spheres. Moreover it descends primarily and essentially upon the rational power. Hence there cannot be any error in it. The Bible testifies to this effect concerning Samuel, "And did let none of his words fall to the ground. And all Israel from Dan even to Beer-Sheba knew that Samuel was established to be a prophet of the Lord" (1 Samuel 3:19). The meaning is that the true character of his prophecy was known from the fact that none of his words fell to the ground, unlike the diviners and magicians.

So Baalam says to Balak, "For there is no enchantment with Jacob, neither is there any divination with Israel. Now it is said of Jacob and of Israel: what has God wrought!" (Numbers 23:23). The meaning is: Do not think that the good which is promised to Israel can be nullified in any way, as those things are nullified which are determined by the stars. No, it cannot be, for they know what is determined, not by means of divination and enchantment, but through prophecy do they know "what God has wrought"—that is, what God has decreed that He would do. Therefore, it cannot be nullified in any way.

For God has the power to destroy all the constellations and the work of the diviners and the magicians as well as the results of their science, for He is "God who brought them forth out of Egypt, He is for him like the lofty horns of the wild ox" (Numbers 23:22). The word *lo* [literally "to him"] refers to the people of Egypt, though it is in the singular, as in the expression, "Egypt said: 'let me flee from the face of Israel' (Exodus 12:31). 'Shall Egypt be like women'" (Isaiah 19:16). The meaning is that though the people of Egypt had knowledge through diviners and magic, and great strength like the horns of the wild ox through the constellations, nevertheless God took Israel out of their power and punished their gods.

From all this, it is clear that it is impossible to know all the things that are acceptable to God in any way except through the will of God: that is, through the medium of a special inspiration coming from Him for this purpose. Accordingly the definition of prophecy from this viewpoint is that it is an inspiration coming from God to the rational power in man, either through the medium of the power of imagination or without it, by virtue of which information comes to him through an angel or otherwise concerning matters which a man cannot know rationally by himself. The purpose is to lead him or others to happiness, so that humanity may attain the human purpose.

In defining prophecy as coming through the medium of the imagination or without it, our purpose is to embrace all degrees of prophecy. For there are prophets to whom, in the beginning of their career, prophecy comes through the medium of the power of the imagination. For this reason, they see extraordinary images in their prophetic visions by reason of their inferior status as prophets. Thus some see forms of women, as Zechariah said, "And, behold, there came forth two women, and the wind was in their wings; for they had wings like the wings of a stork" (Zechariah 5:9). Others see angels with great and fearful bodies, as Daniel said, "His body was also like the beryl, and his face as the appearance of lightning, and his eyes as torches of fire" (Daniel 10:6). And there are other instances of images named by the prophets when the inspiration of the rational power came through the medium of the imagination.

Some prophets remain in that stage, while others ascend to a higher stage, some reaching so high that their prophecy comes to them without a medium. That is, the inspiration of the rational power is not associated with the activity of the imagination at all. This was the status of Moses at all times after the first revelation, when an angel of God appeared to him in a flame of fire out of the midst of the burning bush. Thereafter the Bible says, "With him do I speak mouth to mouth," (Numbers 12:8) that is, without a medium.

PART TWO

The Iberian Expulsion: Safed Era

ca. Fifteenth and Sixteenth Century

10

Solomon Almoli

Dreams have fascinated *Jewish visionaries since biblical times—and the author of the most influential dream book was Rabbi Solomon ben Jacob Almoli. As is true for many other Kabbalists, few details of his life are known to historians. He was born in Spain before 1485 and eventually settled in Constantinople, most likely after Jews were expelled from Spain in 1492. In Turkey, he conducted both rabbinic and medical work, enjoying a high reputation in both fields. In later years, Rabbi Almoli seems to have acquired wealth, for he self-published poetry and numerous books on subjects including both Hebrew grammar and Kabbalah.*

Among Rabbi Almoli's Kabbalistic works was Sha'ar HaShem HeHadash *(Gate of the New Name), a treatise on the immortal human soul. But far more influential was his* Pitron Halomot *(Interpretation of Dreams), first published in Salonica, Greece, in 1515. It soon became the most important Judaic book ever written on dreams, and was cited by both Sigmund Freud and Carl Jung nearly four centuries later in their respective psychological works. In full or abridged form,* Pitron Halomot *has been republished at least a dozen times in Hebrew, twice in Yiddish, and twice in Persian translations.*

In essence, Rabbi Almoli's goal in Pitron Halomot *was two-fold: to explain authoratively how dreams should be interpreted, and how to prevent evil dreams. As these excerpts reveal, he drew upon both Talmudic and Kabbalistic sources in presenting dream-work as a coherent process, involving specific principles for individual attainment.*

FULFILLMENT OF DREAMS

A righteous person is given advance notice of coming events in order to allow him time to prepare to work toward the dream's fulfillment, and for this reason, the fulfillment is often delayed. However, it would be wrong to inform a wicked person of coming events in time to allow him to plan an appropriate course of action, and so he is informed close to the time of fulfillment. This rule applies to everyone, each according to his [spiritual] level.

This point is also made in the *Zohar.*

If a person is meritorious, his soul ascends Above and sees whatever it sees, but if not, it is seized on that side and is informed of false matters or matters which will soon come to pass.

Scripture, too, verifies this rule, for we see that the dreams of the wicked come to pass quickly, while the fulfillment of the dreams of the righteous is delayed.

THE PRACTICE OF DREAM INTERPRETATION

After all this, it should be evident that our Sages' statement that "all dreams follow the mouth" does not mean that an interpreter can nullify the implications of a dream by giving an interpretation that opposes the dream's true meaning. Rather, this statement can be explained in one of the following three ways:

The first interpretation proceeds from the first axiom: that the interpretation of dreams follows the inquiries of the one who makes the request. Therefore, he should make his affairs known so that an accurate interpretation may be made, in keeping with the interpreter's imaginative faculty. . . .

The second interpretation is as follows: Every dream has several implications, as noted, and no one, no matter how well versed in this science, can understand them all. Instead, he will understand and interpret one or two, and leave the rest. The dreamer will take note only of the interpretations he has been given, and when they come to pass, he will recognize those parts of his dream that have been fulfilled. He will not recognize the fulfillment of those parts of the dream which have *not* been interpreted. . . . [This illustrates] the matter of the twenty-four dream interpreters in Jerusalem, each of whom recognized one specific implication of the dream.

The third interpretation proceeds from the third axiom, "Do not be wise in your own eyes, do not rely on your own understanding" to interpret your own dreams according to whatever occurs to you. Know that a dream can bring awareness only after it has been interpreted; otherwise the dream is meaningless and as though it had not been dreamed.

UNDERSTANDING DREAM SYMBOLS

As the wise know, while two persons may have the same dream, the interpreter must apply his knowledge of the dreamers and not interpret the dreams identically. For example, a horse may represent either wisdom or strength. Thus, if a wise man dreams that he manages with great difficulty to cross a river while riding a horse, this indicates that he will overcome great obstacles by using his wisdom. However, if the dreamer is not a wise man but a strong and valiant one, we should interpret the horse as representing strength rather than wisdom.

Likewise, if a highway robber dreams he is being hanged from a palm, the interpretation will not be the same as it would be for a young scholar who dreamed the same thing, for each interpretation follows the situation of the dreamer: in one case the dreamer will be hanged, in the other, rulership is indicated, as is explained at the end of tractate *Yoma:*

> Rabbi Hanina dreamed that Rav was being hanged from a palm in Babylon. Now, tradition has it that one who is hanged on a palm will become a leader; thus he concluded that Rav would become a head [of a yeshiva] and therefore sent him to Babylon to establish a yeshiva there.

This principle is hidden from fools who claim knowledge of the science of dream interpretation, but really know nothing about it.

BE CAREFUL WHO INTERPRETS YOUR DREAMS

There is no alternative but to say that an interpreter, if he so wishes, can change a dream's outcome from what he knows to be its true meaning. . . . How is this so? For example, if a dreamer has a dream intended to reveal the good fortune in store for him, but goes to an enemy to have it interpreted, the enemy will very probably give the dream a negative interpretation. Since the dreamer, as a result, will be unaware of the good in store for him, he will not try to bring it about; moreover, misguided by the enemy's false interpretation and thinking it true, he will try to delay the fulfillment of the dream. While his efforts to delay the dream's fulfillment will be in vain, this is still a serious defect.

However, if one goes to a friend to have the dream interpreted, whether for good or ill, in order to speed the fulfillment of the dream, it is clear that his friend will interpret it truthfully. It is for this reason that the *Zohar* suggests that one consult with a friendly interpreter.

ADVICE FOR DREAM INTERPRETERS

The proper course of action for an interpreter—when a person comes to have a dream explained—is to give the truth as one sees it. If the interpretation is unfavorable, let him advise the dreamer to try to distance himself from it and seek God's mercy; if favorable, one should encourage the dreamer to aid in its fulfillment.

11

Meir ibn Gabbai

THOUGH THE DETAILS *of Rabbi Meir ibn Gabbai's life are obscure, he is today acknowledged as his generation's greatest systematizer of Kabbalah—the intellectual precursor to both Moses Cordovero and Isaac Luria in the Safed renaissance. His ability to apply cogently classic Kabbalistic doctrines—such as the* sefirotic *array and the nature of God (the* Ein Sof *or "Infinite") to traditional Jewish components like prayer, ritual, and Sabbath observance had enormous influence. Especially to those seeking a revitalized Judaism after the cataclysm of 1492, ibn Gabbai's works gained an enthusiastic following.*

Born in 1480 Spain, ibn Gabbai probably immigrated east with his family during the Great Expulsion. He composed his first Kabbalistic work, Tola'at Ya'akob, *at the age of twenty-seven. Held in high regard, it served as the foundation for his magnum opus,* Avodat HaKodesh *(The Work of Holiness), completed in 1531. Several years later, Rabbi ibn Gabbai completed a treatise on the* sefirotic *system, in which he extolled the* Zohar *for its insights on the human soul's lofty, and inextricable, connection to the divine.*

The first selections that follow are taken from Sod HaShabbat
*(Mystery of the Sabbath), the most systematic explication of the
Sabbath in classical Kabbalah. Comprising a section of* Tola'at
Ya'akob, *it brought together many disparate strands from classic
esoteric texts. The last selection is from* Avodat HaKodesh,
dealing with human existence amidst good and evil.

MYSTERY OF THE SABBATH

The Holy One, blessed be He, has given us the Sabbath as our
inheritance and it is equal to the entire Torah, as it is said: "And You
came down upon Mount Sinai. . . . And You made known to them
Your Holy Sabbath (Nehemiah 9:13–14). This passage teaches us
[via parallel structure] that the Sabbath is equal to the entire Torah.

There is a hidden meaning in the fact that Shabbat is sometimes
treated as a masculine form and sometimes as a feminine form:
namely, to hint at the "Two Faces," the mystery of "Remember"
and "Keep." As [an allusion] to this mystery both terms are included in the Ten Commandments, for the entire Torah is included
in these two; the *mitzvot* of commission are contained within "Remember" and the *mitzvot* of omission are contained within "Keep."
And so, Sabbath esoterically represents the entire Torah.

Know that during the six days of Creation, the six levels of the
[Divine] Structure were engaged in their activities, turning all
things from potential into actual, until the twilight of the seventh
day. When the seventh day arrived, they all rested. This was *shebitat
ha'olam,* the cessation of the world from creative labor. Thus, the
seventh day was called *Shabbat,* Cessation.

Know that each level causes the cessation of the preceding one.
For example, the Light that emanated the first level of the Structure
ceased after it had completed actualizing its potential. And the same
was true through the seventh level, at which point, they all rested.

Regarding this mystery, we read in the Talmud's tractate *Shabbat,*
chapter "A Great Principle" (69b):

Said Rabbi Huna: "If one is traveling in the wilderness and does not know when it is the Sabbath, he must count seven days and observe that day as the Sabbath."

The reason [that any of the days may be treated as Shabbat] is that they are all called "Sabbaths of the Lord" (Leviticus 23:38).

The hidden meaning of keeping a dream-fast on the Sabbath

We read in the first chapter of tractate *Shabbat* (11a):

Rabba bar Mehasseya said in the name of Rabbi Hama bar Gurya in Rav's name: "Fasting is as potent against an [ominous] dream as fire against straw." Rabbi Hisda said: "Providing it is on that very day." And Rabbi Joseph added: "And even on the Sabbath."

We read in tractate *Berakhot,* chapter "One should not stand" (31b):

Rabbi Yohanan said in the name of Rabbi Yose ben Zimra: "If one keeps a fast on the Sabbath, a decree of seventy years standing against him is annulled: [turned] from evil to good."

Rabbi Nahman ben Isaac said: "Yet all the same he is punished for neglecting to make the Sabbath a delight. What is the remedy? Let him keep another fast to atone for this one."

Out of God's love for him, a person is alerted in a dream. Through it, he may turn in *teshuvah,* so that compassion may be sought for him, on high. Woe to the person who is not warned. Of him it is said: "One who rests satisfied and is not visited [in a dream] is evil" (Proverbs 19:23).

[Rabbi Hisda stated] "*Providing it is on that very day,* and not thereafter. For the dominion of a day does not extend to another.

A day can only request compassion on behalf of that which occurred on it. Therefore a day does not leave until the [dream]'s
decree has been annulled, through fasting thereon. However, *"a
decree of seventy years"* cannot be abrogated [through fasting] except
on the Sabbath.

The reason the text states: "And even on the Sabbath" is that one
is attended to by Providence more closely on that day, and the
[dream-faster] more so than other people. For on the Sabbath, rest
and joy fill the world; on this day, even the sinners in Gehinnon
rest. So when this one sits in sorrow, all those on high inquire after
him, asking "why is this one grieving when the whole world is
rejoicing?" This one's prayer ascends to the Compassionate One,
who annuls the decree which had been approved by the celestial
court, the mystery of the seventy places. For when the supernal
light is disclosed, the gates of compassion open and the entire cosmos is gladdened. Those forces of *din* cower before Him.

To what may this be likened? To a king who married off his son
and enjoined all his subjects to rejoice. All were indeed joyous except for one man who was bound in chains and was sad. When the
king arrived to regale his son, he saw that everyone was rejoicing.
But when he lifted his eyes, he saw that sad-faced man bound in
chains. The [king] said: "All my subjects are rejoicing in my son's
time of joy, while this one is bound in chains." Immediately, he ordered that the man be released. Thus, the [Gemara] states: *"A decree
of seventy years standing against him is annulled,"* esoterically referring
to the seventy supernal years, the mystery of the celestial court.

*"Yet all the same he is punished for neglecting to make the Sabbath a
delight."* Why? Because the portion [of the spirit] that descends to
experience pleasure with Israel, below, is not properly completed;
it ascends less fulfilled than [the portion partaking of] the Supernal
Delight. Because the portion below is not completed, neither is the
one above, for the one depends on the other. Since this person
causes a diminuation on high, he is subject to punishment. Thus,
the Gemara continues, What is the remedy? Let him keep another
fast to atone for this one. . . .

Therefore, one must fast immediately [after Shabbat], on Sunday, when the profane spirit holds sway. Since the aspect of good was not enhanced, neither should the aspect of evil. This [second fast] provides healing, as is indicated in the verse, "He shall restore that which he took away by robbery" (Leviticus 5:23). Thereafter, no further punishment may be exacted. . . . But the Holy One [may] punish him in this world and in the next.

Guard your speech on the Sabbath

Concerning mundane speech, it is written: "Not finding your own affairs, nor speaking your own words" (Isaiah 58:13). Our rabbis of blessed memory gave the following interpretations:

> Your speech on the Sabbath should not be like your speech on weekdays. (*Shabbat* 113a–b)

The reason for this is that there is no uttered word that does not have a "Voice." Now a [profane] Voice ascends on high and rouses that which is called *hol,* Profane. When the Profane is roused on the holy Sabbath, it is a great denigration. He who does so "separates friends" (Proverbs 6:28). The Holy One, blessed be He, and the Community of Israel ask: "Who is this who seeks to break up our union?" For the Supernal Holy One does not dwell amidst the profane.

This matter contains a deep mystery. As the [profane] entity is aroused on high, "It defiles the sanctuary of the Lord" (Numbers 19:20). Now if this occurs because of an insignificant word, it would certainly occur in the case of a more serious deed, which defiles the upper and lower [worlds].

"Thought [about mundane matters] is permitted" (*Shabbat* 113b), for a thought has no Voice. But [beneficially] should a person utter words of Torah, words of holiness, a voice is produced. It rises up and arouses the holy entities. Concerning this [event], it is written: "Go forth, daughters of Zion" (Song of Solomon 3:11).

AVODAT HAKODESH

The first Adam was created in the image of God, and he transgressed because the serpent led him astray. And if he had not contained within himself any part of the *Kelippah,* [the serpent] would not have had the power to cause him to sin. It is indeed within the choice of all people to either repair or to ruin; and although all are drawn after the animating soul (*nefesh*) and [each] *nefesh* is drawn according to its root; yet, with learning and habituation, one may either improve or deteriorate. And, it is possible for a person to change [one's predisposed *nefesh*] with regard to its attachment to the inner and outer attributes. One has the ability to increase wickedness and evil.

So too with regard to the good, as our sages (*Hagigah* 15r) have commented on the verse, "God made one as well as [i.e., in parallel contrast to] the other (Ecclesiastes 7:14). He created *zaddikim* and created the wicked. Each and every person possesses two portions: one in Eden and one in Gehenna. If one merits and is a *zaddik,* one takes his portion and the portion of his neighbor [who is wicked] in Eden. If one is culpable and wicked, he takes his portion and the portion of his neighbor [who is righteous] in Gehanna.

All this is in accordance with [the direction to which] one is drawn, be it after the good or after evil, in conjunction with the portions that caused their influence to be felt in him. For certainly the higher levels and their celestial halls and "branches" and "wings," as well as their *kelippot,* are bound to us through our forms, which are effused by the Tree of Knowledge of Good and Evil, by the One who begins and ends all things, and [the one whose] name is included within Him [that is, the angel Metatron], who fastens diadems for his Master.

12

JOSEPH TAITAZAK

FOR REASONS THAT REMAIN *historically baffling, beginning in the middle decades of the fifteenth century, and increasingly during the sixteenth century, Jewish visionaries often relied on mediated divine revelation. In this highly esteemed Kabbalistic practice, an apparent messenger from heaven—known as a* maggid *(literally, "sayer")— appears before the adept and reveals divine secrets. In most cases, practitioners reported hearing a voice without an accompanying image, while in other instances, they described a clear apparition. A related phenemonon elicited by Kabbalists particularly during that era involved "automatic writing," in which the adept would evoke a meditative trance and then initiate a spontaneous outflow of writing. Typically it would involve discourses on exalted subjects such as the hidden nature of the human soul, the afterlife, and reincarnation.*

Among the most influential Kabbalists in this regard was Joseph Taitazak. His family was among the many Jewish refugees from Spain who settled in Greece and Turkey after the Great Expulsion. Though the details of his life are scanty, it is clear that he was re-vered as both a rabbinic expert on halacha *and a master of applied*

Kabbalah. While living in Salonica, Greece, he mentored several figures, including Joseph Karo, who later became prominent in the Safed community.

This selection is representative of the various revelations given to Rabbi Taitazak by his reported maggid. It should be noted that these encompassed detailed instructions on how to receive celestial secrets.

You shall now hear the wonders of the living God about this subject—the secret of the celestial writing, without a hand, without a foot, without ink. You shall then know of your own knowledge that the spirit of God has been flourishing in you, when you understand the secret of the celestial ink and the celestial pen, because it is a wondrous secret. It is the same secret by which the Tablets of the Covenant were written, with the finger of God. You shall then know the secret of the celestial finger and the celestial hand, and understand the secret of the hand of Daniel. When these subjects will be clarified and written in a book, you shall realize that your knowledge of this wisdom originated and was caused by God, and you shall understand the secret of celestial writing and celestial ink. The [celestial powers] write their messages in brief, in headlines, in order to exhaust the subject in a short note, because writing long passages is characteristic of lowly writing, while brief headlines represent the supreme stage. Many scholars in Israel have learned this wisdom in the past, so that their words will be believed by future generations.

Now, after I have informed you of this, I shall tell you who is the one who writes this wisdom and who is the celestial scribe. Gabriel is the one who writes, and Michael the angel is the scribe. These two angels have the power, derived from their station, to write, if you invoke them, and they write without ink, which is a wonder—how can they write and preserve the writing. The writing is in Assyrian letters which is written with the adorning crowns and rounded. The secret meaning of "hand" is that for the time being, the writing is observed on the wall or in the air or on paper, if you request this, and it is made of linen sheets.

Now I shall go deeper into the subject of this wisdom in order to explain it well, so that you shall understand, because this wisdom is deeper than the sea. Many [scholars] in Israel have fathomed it, and so do Joseph and me, we have learned it with great effort and toil....

I have sworn in the name of the living God of Hosts, that immediately a [secret] angel will descend downward, in order to write, without a hand, without a foot, without a pen. This is what you should say after reciting [the holy names of God of twelve and seventy-two letters], "may there be the will of God," and every time you read the names, say the following: "I hereby invoke you by the explicit names which I have mentioned, that you should immediately show your power and your writing in the lower world, in this paper or this book or this wall or this air. Right now, at this time, [show] it and subjugate it by the secret of the celestial ink, whatever it is that I wish, in abbreviated words and the letters and the vocalization marks above, and you should announce it, the meaning of the words, what each word means. I am invoking you with all the power of the letters which I have mentioned that immediately, at this time, you should write and engrave and imprint in fire these letters in paper and that the divine fire will not burn the paper, and that the writing will be visible to every eye, even that of Christians and Jews and Muslims, so that all will know and recognize that this is a divine phenomenon, when they see that there is no ink in it.

I am invoking you, the princes of the celestial writing and the princes of the divine writing with the finger of God. I am invoking you with all the power in the sanctity which I have mentioned and which I intended, that you should immediately demonstrate your power and your writing down here, without delay and without any hindrance. I invoke you with the full power of "one God whose name is one" and with the full power of the sanctity which is hidden in the secret of every point and the full power of the secret of his fire and its color, and in the power and secret of the point, and in the power and secret of the hidden thought, and in the full power of the two halves of a ball and the full power of "one God whose name is one" which is connected to the supreme point, that immediately your power and your fire will come down and will immediately write this thing which I demand on this paper which I have placed in a certain place, a true thing, or on the wall if it is white.

You shall then mention the wall or the air or the place you wish them to write and imprint the writing. You shall then use four kinds of *ketoret* [incense] three times with a smoking paper, and in order to give it the needed strength the paper should be treated by smoke before that, and after it is smoked, you should enter a room clean of any *tumaah* [religious impurity], and you should recite the names which I have instructed you, forward and in reverse.

After you have recited it seventy times with the invocation every time, immediately the secret of Gabriel and Michael will descend, their whole stature and their power, and they will write what you ask them to, or what you wish to know whether it is true or not. I am swearing in the name of God, blessed be He, that it will happen exactly as I am telling you. And then, when you envision this celestial writing, you shall know that there is a God in Israel, you and everyone else who observes this, and they will believe that there is a God in Israel, and the spirit of God will inhabit you.

I shall now explain this in detail. The secret of this supernal writing is the secret of the descent of the power of God in his glory, and the people of the world call it "a written question." The secret included in this writing should be believed by everyone, like the one who had written it originally, for it is real prophecy and will come true fully. This is the secret of the supernal writing. With this power, you can achieve the ability to write whatever you wish, be it a great deal or just a little.

You shall understand the secret of the *writing Name,* guided by an angel, whenever you wish it, and everything written in this way you should believe to be true as if it were done by God himself. . . . With this secret, there is nothing you cannot achieve, like actual prophecy itself, and this is one of the greatest wonders of the living

God. A person who reaches this stage, after he has observed the process in his own eyes, will render praise and thanks to God, and will receive everything he wants in the celestial realm, and he will be like a member of the [heavenly] household, he who has mastered the secret of the supernal writing. . . . Do not hesitate to try it alone or in any way you wish, only the room should be clean and pure of any unclean thing, and this you should observe.

13

SOLOMON MOLKO

THROUGHOUT THE KABBALAH'S *long history, its visionaries have been fascinated by dreams. Some, like the anonymous author of the Zohar and Rabbi Solomon Almoli, presented ideas and methods to enhance dream comprehension; others kept detailed dream diaries or journals to advance their own inner development. Among the most intriguing of all such figures was Solomon Molko, whose brief life undoubtedly contained more religious drama than that of countless contemporaries combined. Certainly for this reason, he has been the subject of several historical novels.*

Molko was born in 1500 Lisbon as Diogo Pires, the son of prominent conversos (forced Portuguese-Jewish converts to Christianity). He undoubtedly received an excellent secular education, for by his mid-twenties, he was serving as an important secretary at the court of King John III. A promising, wealthy career lay before Pires, when suddenly in 1525, a strange, charismatic Jew bearing letters from the pope appeared before King John's court. His name was David Reubeni, and he claimed to be a prince from a far-off Jewish kingdom called Habur—seeking King John's military support to take back the Holy Land from the Turkish Empire.

Scholars today vigorously debate Reubeni's true identity and origins, though his plan never materialized and he apparently died in a royal prison several years later. More historically important, though, was his impact on Pires, who became seized with Jewish messianic fervor. Changing his name to Solomon Molko, he nearly died while engaging in self-circumcision, and then fled Portugal to study the sacred works of Judaism including Kabbalah. He wandered the Mediterranean region for several years: studying intensively with Rabbi Joseph Taitazak in Salonica, personally inspiring young Rabbi Joseph Karo, and gradually gaining a reputation as a charismatic Kabbalist seeking to hasten the messianic age. Except for composing an abstruse book of lamentations about the Jewish exile, he presented his message in fiery public speeches. Molko was apparently so impressive that Pope Clement V granted him several private meetings whose purpose remain unclear, but not even the pope was able to save Molko from a martyr's death at the hands of the Inquisition in Mantua, Italy, in 1532.

This selection is from Molko's dream diary and was penned after his near-fatal self-circumcision.

I saw a venerable elder, his beard very long and its appearance as snow, white. And he said to me, "Come with me to a ruin amidst the ruins of Jerusalem." So I went there with him. It seemed to me that I was a long time on the road. I saw three trees along the way, all of them come forth from a single root, their branches divided toward every direction. Upon their branches, I saw many white doves, and among them other doves of an ashen color, and they were more numerous than the white ones. The color of the ash that was upon them seemed not to be their original color, but that they were first white and became the color of ash. I saw other doves, black ones, fewer than the white ones.

Nearby the white doves was a great square field, and through its midst passed a great river. On its other side there was a multitude of people—warriors and knights on horseback bearing many weapons, including swords, bows, and instruments of iron for hurling iron and fiery balls. It was the aim of this force to cut down the trees, and I heard it said, "These trees are from our region, so let us cut them down and fell them to the earth."

Then they attacked the ashen doves and black ones as well, and they would fall at once to the earth. And large birds came and ate their flesh until not one of them remained. As I looked upon this great assault against the black and ashen doves, some people came near to me and said, "What is this?" And I replied, "This people has struck those doves, which have fallen to the earth, and now they seek to attack the white doves as well, which are very beautiful and which fill the tree that it might not wither."

And the people said to me, "Let us make a high wall around them and a barrier to defend them." And I replied, "Let us do so." Then the elder and I hastened toward them to make for them a barrier of timber and dirt beside the river. The warriors, however, did not cease from killing the doves, and when they saw the barrier that we had erected, they destroyed it with weapons of fire and struck some of the people who were with me as well. Then the large birds descended to eat their flesh as they had of the doves.

Then I was struck in my chest by an iron ball from a weapon of fire. The ball came through my back, and I struggled mightily and with difficulty not to fall to the ground, but I had not enough strength and I fell down. As I fell, I said, "Woe is me, for the birds will eat my flesh as they did the flesh of the people who were with me, and I will not be buried with my brothers."

Yet, I was calm and saw great visions. I said, "It is true what was said to me while I was alive, that one sees greater things after death than in life." And I saw the white doves that had been in the tree, some of them having become ashen, and also some of the ashes ones, white. Then the people who remained alive and were standing beside me brought a woman to heal me. I was asked, "Who is this woman?" And I was told, "This is the woman so-and-so, the wife of so-and-so," as I have not yet been given permission to reveal her name from my dream.

The woman pleaded deeply to God, praying that I be healed,

and the people mourned for my condition. All the while, the number of doves diminished and many changed their color. And while the woman was praying, I saw an apparition like that of a man. His clothes were white as snow and his appearance was liken unto God. I saw another man facing him, and his appearance was much more awesome than that of the first man and his clothes were whiter and finer and splendid.

He held large scales in his hand and sought to set them straight and even, and he began to walk along the way of the first man whom I had seen. The second man—who was bigger than the first—walked toward him through the air until both drew near to me. The first man asked the people standing with me, "Has any bird descended upon this one?" And they answered, "We have not allowed the birds to touch him." At once, he sent the people far away so that not even one could be seen anymore in the field.

The two of us remained together—the great man and I—and the second stood over us in the air. Suddenly, the first man fell upon me and put his mouth on my mouth, his eyes on my eyes, his palms against my palms, and spoke words to me in the name of God. He repeated them several times, and then stood me upright and said, "Have you understood the appearance of the doves and the changing of their colors, what they are and what they mean, and these non-Jews who attack and kill them, what that is?"

I replied, "My lord, your servant has not yet understood this thing, but I feel pity for the doves and for my companions. I have compassion for them and my heart burns for them, yet I do not know what they are nor do I know their troubles."

And he said to me, "Look up at all the armies and you will comprehend their end and you will know what the doves are." Then he blew out upon the hordes and they became a heap of dust. The man had not crossed the river to attack them; he had been on the other side, where the doves were. Then he blew out upon the doves that had changed their color, and they all became white. None among them were different from any other. Then the water in the river increased from what it had been, and trees suddenly appeared on both of the river banks, and also many fruits of different kinds.

Then I said to the man, "Let my lord tell his servant what these wonders and miracles are, if I please you." And he replied, "You cannot know the things now, but it will not be hidden from you." And I bowed down before him and said, "Let my lord speak to his servant so that I may be certain of what all these things mean." Then he blessed me.

I awoke from this apparition and understood nothing. Thereafter, I saw the appearance of the first aged man whom I had seen as the first apparition. He explained everything to me. I do not yet have permission to make public any of what he explained. When the Holy One, blessed be He, brings me in peace to the land of Edom [Rome], I will write out at length with a clear explanation of all that I have seen, and send it from there to those who fear God and esteem His name.

14

THE RAMEK

Moses Cordovero

AMONG THE MOST *influential Kabbalists in Safed was Rabbi Moses Cordovero, known as the Ramek (an acronym of his name). Contemporary scholars believe that his family fled Cordoba, Spain, during the Great Expulsion, and that he came to Safed, in the Holy Land Galilee, as a young man. There he studied with leading rabbinic exponents of Kabbalah including the brilliant legal scholar Joseph Karo and the poet Solomon Alkabez, who became the Ramek's brother-in-law.*

Although Rabbi Cordovero initially studied philosophy, he re-jected its analytic methodology because "philosophers are not versed in the Kabbalistic approach." Strongly conceptual in his approach to Jewish esoteric thought, Rabbi Cordovero composed several highly complex theosophic works—beginning with Pardes Rimonim, *which focused on the ten* sefirot. *His commentary on the* Zohar, *entitled* Or Yakar, *is sixteen volumes long and exists only in manuscript.*

Eventually establishing a study center in Safed whose students included young Chaim Vital, the Ramek emphasized the unity of Kabbalah and traditional Jewish ritual observance; in this respect, he shared a common outlook with his Safed colleagues. He also viewed the Land of Israel as possessing uniquely transcendent, holy qualities. Until the arrival of Rabbi Isaac Luria in Safed in 1570, the Ramek was regarded as the foremost Kabbalist of his time. He was revered for both his piety as well as his esoteric knowledge, and for example, the Ari admiringly referred to him as "our master and teacher."

The first selections come from several of Rabbi Cordovero's theosophical texts including Pardes Rimonim, Or Yakar, *and* Or Ne'erav. *These illustrate his approach to the ten* sefirot *and the Hebrew letters, meditation, and "sacred wanderings" through the Holy Land. The final selection represents the Ramek's chapter in its entirety on how to cultivate* chochmah *(wisdom), from* The Palm Tree of Deborah, *his most influential work—emphasizing ethical development from a Kabbalistic perspective.*

THE TEN *SEFIROT*

Everyone knows that all Kabbalists unanimously agree that there are ten *sefirot*. We know about the *sefirot* from *Sefer Yetzirah*, attributed to Abraham our father. There are some who attribute it to Rabbi Akiva, but there is no consensus on that. The text of *Sefer Yetzirah* is highly esoteric and remains obscure in spite of the numerous commentaries that have been written on it. Nevertheless, I will try to explain its text as best as I can with my limited knowledge.

It says in *Sefer Yetzirah* (1:3): "Ten *sefirot* of nothing, the number of the ten fingers, five opposite five, and the single covenant is in between, as in the circumcision of the male organ and the circumcision of the tongue." . . . The author begins by saying "ten *sefirot*," implying that since they are numbered, they are subject to a certain degree of limitation and corporeality.

What is meant by "of nothing"? The author means that, in reality, the *sefirot* are intangible. Although we speak of them in terms of the number ten, we firmly believe that they are "of nothing." That is, they have no substance. This means that the *sefirot* have no essence that can be understood by the human mind because they are above physicality. And something that has no physicality can be perceived only by Jewish visionaries, like prophets. . . . The word *sefirot* is related to *mispar* (number), to indicate that although they are "of nothing" [and intangible], nevertheless they can be counted.

To establish the fact that there are exactly ten *sefirot,* the author says, "the number of ten fingers." [Everything in this world has its counterpart in the higher world. In the physical world, there is the human individual who has ten fingers, and his counterpart in the higher world is G-d, in whose image he was created.] Speaking of the Creator, Scripture says: "When I behold your heavens, the work of Your fingers" (Psalms 8:4). The passage implies that the creation of heaven and its legions of stars came about through G-d's "fingers," which is a metaphor for the *sefirot.* Since the human individual has ten fingers, it follows that G-d created the world through ten *sefirot.*

Each place which is engaged by words of Torah receives holiness and I sanctified . . . ; when a *zaddik* engages in words of Torah in a known place, that place is sanctified by him and the holiness emanates from his very soul. . . . And when the holiness of the *zaddik* is empowered at known times, he should take note of and visit the places which were sanctified by him, since it is as if the spark of his soul resides there, awaiting him to come and relight it from time to time. And even should he engage there in other words of Torah [that is, words not directly associated with either the deceased *zaddik* or the specific time of visitation], he still attaches sanctity and illuminates one with the other—leading his added sanctity to awaken the earlier one, which in turn awakens the soul of the deceased *zaddik* and illuminates it. And should [the living *zaddik*] engage the exact idiom or words that he [the deceased *zaddik*] had once innovated in that [exact] place, he further ties holiness with holiness and [the soul of the deceased] *zaddik* shall hasten to that place, for now he is rejuvenated since his lips [never ceased] to utter words [of Torah] in the grave, and his soul awakens, hastening to the place of its renewal and attaching to those who have caused him to awaken.

The first [stage] pertains to *Mikrah* [Torah study], a virtue devoid of [dceper] measure, for even as one invokes words with his mouth and they in turn ascend upward, they still do not draw esoteric measures of Torah, since Torah is measured by the secret imbued within its letters. Therefore, he who shakes its words below does not draw new measures but affects the same ones repeatedly and unifies them. It is, however, not sufficient a unification, since he neither draws nor renews measures on high. Indeed, *Mishnah* is a rewarded virtue since it is "a Torah by heart" and therefore transcends [the grip] of letters. He who engages on such a level both measures and assesses its greatness.

It is therefore superior to *Mikrah,* for [now] he measures and assesses. By doing so, one rectifies the Shekinah and prepares the limbs by which she may accept her male companion [the *sefirah* of *tiferet*] and one is rewarded, for she is a vessel into which rewards from above are poured. Indeed, *Talmud* is the finest level, for it affords one the ability to innovate and strike [words] against each other in order to birth solutions to inquiries, truly breaking shells and ascending beyond measure. And should one reach such mastery as to assume the teaching of others, one truly draws new measures and joins the esoteric [shaking the gates] of the King.

It is certainly easy for a person to study throughout the day. However, the optimum time for gaining profound wisdom is the long night, from midnight onward, or on the Sabbath day, which is [itself] a factor. Thus, also the eve of the Sabbath commencing at noontime and on holidays, particularly on *Atzaret* [festival of Shavuot]. I have tried this many times and found it to be a marvelously successful day. Also, there is great success [in studying] on Sukkot in the Sukkah. These times I have mentioned I have tried. I am speaking from experience.

If one wishes to take pleasure in the understanding of his Creator, let him concentrate according to the accepted premises which he has learned and let him look at a particular physical form, so he may learn from it that which is alluded in the spiritual worlds, and he will see the detailed organs of it, and the varied matters and its lights. And from thereon, he will gradually fathom the innermost secrets of the spirituality of that form, and he shall attain *devekut*. Such was the way of Adam in the Garden of Eden. Now, if the *cherubim* were physical-spiritual beings, he may gaze at them and come to contemplate and to apprehend from what is pictured here, in terms of the visual, that which makes sense to the mind—[proceeding] from the physical to the spiritual.

Each letter has an awesome spiritual form emanating from the *sefirotic* essence, wherein each [letter] becomes a shrine for the spiritual potency of its respective *sefirah*. And when a person mentions and shakes either word, the breath of his mouth configures its holy form, which in turn ascends and connects to its root in the emanated realm. By striking the potencies of letters against each other with the hammering soul, the breath of one's mouth is spiritually uplifted, as an angel who ascends and connects to his root.

Another extremely important method is explained in the *Zohar*. A person should exile himself, wandering from place to place for the sake of Heaven, becoming a chariot for the exiled Shekinah. He should think to himself, "Behold, I am in exile but I have all my implements with me. But what about the honor of the Supreme One, since the Shekinah is exiled without any implements, for they were lost in the wake of the exile?" For this reason, he should manage with as little as possible, as the verse states, "make yourself implements for exile"—and let the exile humble his heart, while he binds himself to Torah. Then the Shekinah will be with him.

He should also impose an "expulsion order" upon himself, always banishing himself from the comforts of home, just as Rabbi Simeon bar Yochai and his comrades banished themselves to toil in Torah. Better still, he should weary his legs by trudging from place to place without horse or wagon. Concerning such a person, it is stated in Psalms (146:5) "his hope is with the L-rd his G-d." And [the *Zohar*] explicated its derivation from the word *breaking*—for he breaks his body for the honor of the Supreme One.

PALM TREE OF DEBORAH

How should a person train himself in the attribute of *chochmah*? Although it is hidden and exceedingly exalted, the attribute of *chochmah* Above is spread out over all creation. As it is written, "How many are Your works, O L-rd; You have made them all in *chochmah* (*Tehillim* 104:24). Similarly, a person's *chochmah* should pervade all his actions, and he should be ready to benefit and influence others with his *chochmah*—according to their capacity—letting nothing prevent him.

Now, the attribute to *chochmah* Above has two aspects: The higher aspect faces *keter* and does not face downwards; rather, it receives from above. The lower aspect faces downwards, overseeing the other *sefirot,* to which the attribute of *chochmah* extends.

Likewise, a person should have two aspects: The first aspect should be communion in solitude with his Creator in order to increase and perfect his *chochmah;* the second should be to teach others the *chochmah* with which the Holy One, Blessed Be He, has endowed him. And just as the attribute of *chochmah* Above extends to each *sefirah* according to its measure and needs, one should disseminate his *chochmah* to each person in the measure his intellect can grasp, according to what is proper for him and his needs. One should take care not to give more than the mind of the recipient can contain, lest harm result, for the Supernal *sefirah* does not go beyond the limits of the recipient.

Moreover, it is the nature of *chochmah* to oversee all of existence, for it is the Supernal Thought, which contemplates everything that exists. Of *chochmah,* it is said: "For My thoughts are not your thoughts" (Yeshayahu 55:8), "and He gives thought so that he who is exiled is not banished forever (II Shemuel 14:14), and "For I know the thoughts I think of you (the House of Israel) says the L-rd, 'thoughts of peace and not evil, to give you hope for the future'" (Yirmeyahu 29:11).

In the same way, man should keep a watchful eye on the conduct of the nation of G-d in order to benefit it. His thoughts should be concerned with bringing near those who have strayed and thinking well of them. Just as the Divine Mind contemplates the benefit of all existence, he should contemplate the benefit of his fellows, taking counsel with G-d and His people regarding both individual and communal matters. And concerning one who has strayed from the good path, he should guide him to proper conduct, serving as his advisor and counselor and directing and leading him to good and forthright behavior, just as the Supernal Thought guides the highest worlds.

Furthermore, *chochmah* gives life to all things. As it is written: "...chochmah gives life to those who possess it." (*Kohelet* 7:12). Likewise, one should instruct the entire world in the ways of life, helping others attain life in this world and in the World-to-Come and providing them with the means to live. In general, one should give life to all beings.

In addition, *chochmah* is the source of all existence. As the verse states: "How many are Your works, O L-rd; You have made them all with *chochmah*" (*Tehillim* 104:24). Thus, everything lives and exists due to that source.

In the same way, a person should act as father to all G-d's creatures, particularly Israel, for its holy souls emanate from that source. At all times, he should pray for mercy and blessing for the world, being like our Father Above, Who has compassion for His creatures. And regarding those afflicted with suffering, he should constantly pray for them as if they were his own children and he had formed them himself, for this is what the Holy One, Blessed Be He, desires. As Moshe, the faithful shepherd, said: "Did I conceive this nation . . . that You say to me, 'Carry it in your bosom . . . '?" (*BeMidbar* 11:12). In this way, a person should carry all of G-d's people "as a nurse carries an infant" (ibid.). He should "gather the lambs in his arm, lifting them to his bosom, and lead the little ones" (Yeshayahu 40:11). He should take care of the desolate, seek out the young, heal the broken, nourish the needy, and return the lost. One should have compassion for Israel, bearing its burdens cheerfully, just as the Merciful Father bears all. One should not tire or hide or despair, leading each person according to his needs. These are the qualities of *chochmah*: a father who is merciful to his children.

Furthermore, one's compassion should extend to all creatures, and he should neither despise nor destroy them, for the *chochmah* Above extends to all of creation—inanimate objects, plants, animals, and humans. For this reason, our sages have warned us against treating food disrespectfully. Just as the Supernal *chochmah* despises nothing, since everything is created from there—as the verse states, "You have made them all with *chochmah*" (*Tehillim* 104:24)—a person should show compassion to all the works of the Holy One, Blessed Be He. That's why Rabbi Yehudah the Prince was punished: He had no pity on a calf that tried to evade slaughter by hiding behind him, and he said to it, "Go! For this purpose, you were created," suffering—which derives from the aspect of severity—came upon him, for compassion shields against severity. Thus, when Rabbi Yehudah the Prince had mercy on a weasel, quoting the verse, "His mercies extend to all His deeds" (*Tehillim* 145:9), he was delivered from severity, for the light of *chochmah* spread over him, and his suffering disappeared.

Similarly, one should not disparage any creature, for all of them were created with *chochmah*. Nor should one should one uproot plants unless they are needed or kill animals unless they are needed. And one should choose a noble death for them, using a carefully inspected knife, in order to maximize his compassion.

This is the general principle: Having pity on all beings and not hurting them depends on *chochmah*. However, if one intends to raise them higher and higher—from plant to animal, and from animal to human—then it is permissible to uproot a plant and slaughter an animal, taking away from them in order to benefit them.

15

CHAIM VITAL

AMONG THE MOST *intriguing leaders of the Safed Kabbalists—
and the only one born there—was Rabbi Chaim Vital. His wide-
ranging interests included dreams, ecstatic states of consciousness,
and celestial communication. Throughout his fifty-year career, he
zealously promulgated the Jewish esoteric tradition, initially in the
Holy Land—and then in Syria, where he later resided for decades.
Though close with both Joseph Karo and especially Rabbi Moses
Cordovero, he is best known for his association with Rabbi Isaac
Luria. For when the Ari arrived in Safed in 1570, Rabbi Vital
became his foremost disciple and scribe soon after the death of his
longtime mentor, the Ramek.*

*As Rabbi Vital related, Rabbi Moses Cordovero susbsequently
appeared to him in a dream, and so the former earnestly asked:
"Tell me the truth, whose Kabbalah is studied in paradise—yours
or the Ari's?" And the Ramek replied: "Both approaches are true.
However, my approach is the simple one, suitable for beginners,
whereas the teachings of your teacher [Rabbi Luria] are deeper and
are the primary approach. I, too, in the Heavenly Academy study
only according to your master's approach."*

Following Rabbi Luria's death after only two years in Safed, Rabbi Vital seized the role of chief expounder. He compiled his mentor's Kabbalistic teachings in a highly influential book entitled Eitz Chaim *(The Tree of Life), and wrote subsequent works such as* Sefer HaGilgulim *(Book of Transmigrations),* Shaarai Kedushah *(The Gates of Holiness), and* Sefer HaLikutim, *an anthology of Torah thoughts. In these writings, Rabbi Vital presented Lurianic concepts of theosophy including reincarnation and soul journeying, as well as practical methods for attaining exalted mental states. These excerpts come from* Shaarai Kedushah—*and focus on the way to prophetic consciousness.*

GATE 4

Here, greatly condensed, are the conditions for prophecy: It has already been stated that there are dents which damage the vegetative soul and there are those that damage *Chaya* [the transcendent soul], and so forth. All this must be refined. Therefore, first of all, one must do *teshuvah* and turn away from all trespasses or vices, never to relapse into them. Then one must carefully keep all of the 248 *mitzvot* which apply to our times. This too has already been stated in part 1. One must take special care to set permanent times aside for the study of Torah both day and night, so that not even one day be wanting. Then you must pray with perfect intentions, each of the three daily prayers, and perform the benedictions and the grace after meals with their particular intentions. One must honor the Sabbath in all its details, and love your neighbor as yourself with a perfect heart, and read the *Shma,* the prayers, and observe the *mitzvot* of the *tzizit* and *tefillin.* One must also be guarded to keep the 365 negative commandments, especially those which bring with their transgressions either the death penalty by a court of humanity or heaven, or excommunication, and so with any "thou-shalt-nots" even in details of *halacha.* Special watchfulness is necessary against tale-bearing, slander, empty talk, and mockery, or of lustful gazing, all kinds of accidental seminal emissions, all kinds of approaches to menstruous women, and of oaths even to swear the truth. The keeping of the Sabbath is the most important of them all.

You must also be guarded from all vices, for they defile the elemental soul. Remove yourself to the very extreme from the vice of pride and liken yourself to the very lowest threshold upon which all step. The virtue of humility must become a second nature in you, so that you will feel neither joy in being honored nor pain in being defamed, so that both will be equal to you. Be guarded from anger, even if you be smitten on the cheek. There is no greater obstacle to *Ruach HaKodesh* than anger and irritability. You must refrain from such, even unto the very extreme, even before members of your own household. So also must you guard yourself from melancholy. Prophecy does not rest on even the most deserving one who is melancholic. Be glad in your portion even at such times when you are beset by suffering. As it is said, "Love the Lord thy G-d with thine whole heart." Then study the Torah for Her sake with all your strength, intend to do this only to give pleasure to your Creator. Be extremely gladsome when busy with the Torah and the *mitzvot,* as it is said, "I rejoiced over Thy word as one who finds great treasure." By doing so, you will draw great power to flow down into all the worlds. The root of all is the awe before Him, be He blessed, which you must generate at every moment in yourself in order not to sin. This you can achieve by visualizing the [divine] Name before your eyes, as it is written, "I have YHVH facing me." Intend to adhere your mind to Him, not to be separated even for a moment. This is the mystery of "Cleave unto Him."

GATE 5

The concept of prophecy can be understood in that man, when he has purged himself of all sin and the defilement of the *yezer hara,* can by preparing himself to adhere to a particular supernal root of this being, realize it in full. However, even if you have become worthy of this, you need to divest your soul completely and totally from all things of matter and the senses. Only then will you be capable of adhering to and realizing the spiritual root. However, this divestment which is written about in many books, is not a complete divestment from action, in which the soul leaves the body—that is sleep and what is realized in it is a dream. The presence of *Ruach HaKodesh* in man is in the waking state when his soul is in his body, not when it has left him. What is meant by this divestment is a complete removal of thought. In thought, there resides a power of *M'dammeh* (association, fantasy, and illusion), which makes for conceptualization. This *M'dammeh* comes from the elemental animative soul. This *M'dammeh* must be halted and cut off from association, from weaving thoughts and mental rehearsal of worldly cravings, as if one's soul has left the body.

Only then you turn the *M'dammeh* into the direction of one of the upper worlds, into the direction of one of the roots of your soul, and proceeding from one to another until your describing will attain to your Supernal Source. There you will become impressed by the thought forms of the Lights, which will form themselves according to your ability to receive them in the very same quality of apperception which you have for things in this world and which are not before your eyes. Then think and intend to receive Light from the Ten Spheres from that point which is tangential to your soul. There you intend to raise the Ten Spheres up to the Infinite, so that from there an illumination will be drawn down to them—to the very lowest level.

When this light is drawn down to them, they rejoice and become more luminous from that light which was drawn down unto them by the root of the soul which has its hold on them—in the measure that it deserved. Then you intend to lead it downward step-by-step so that the light will reach the intellective soul, which is in the body. From there and then, it will reach the animating soul and its associative powers where the content becomes construed in material thought forms in your association. Then you will understand them in the same manner as if you had seen them with the eye of flesh. At times, this light becomes construed in the form of an angel which addresses you, where you either behold him or hear him, or sense him. There a displacement and projection occurs toward the outer periphery of the sensorium which is part of the animal soul as is well known. Thus you see, hear, smell, and speak with your physical senses, as it is written, "The spirit of God spoke in [through] me and this word was on my tongue." For the Light has become materialized and it took on form through the physical senses. At other times, your prophecy will be only with the spiritual senses through the power of *M'dammeh* alone. But all this comes only as a result of diverting the physical *M'dammeh*.

In this way, prophecy can be compared to a dream in which the rational soul has left the body and ascended, rung-by-rung, and arriving there, it beholds and espies, and then returns and descends, and draws with itself the Light to the animating soul and its power of *M'dammeh*, where the things become construed and take on further shape. But after the soul has left the body, this does not apply.

There are two different kinds of prophecy: (a) The prophecy of all sorts of prophets whose feat of prophecy is like a trance. For they achieve to Light which flows downward to the rational soul and from these is drawn to the animating soul, where it becomes shaped into projections of the five inner senses and their associating power. But with such seers, their outer senses became so overwhelmed, they fell to the ground and had no strength to contain all this Light in themselves and made it gross enough for the physical senses to perceive. This kind of prophecy is called "dream," although we do not mean actual dream but rather a trance. (b) The second prophecy is a perfect prophecy, in which the senses are not overwhelmed but in it all assumes its proper shape, and this is the prophecy of the quality of Moses. The cause of this is that he had so fully clarified and refined the substance of this body which had so completely changed by the holiness of his actions that it had attained to the level of soul. The defilement had passed away from it, and remained so pure and good to prove that his body was never confining for the powers of his soul.

It was already explained that the soul has many roots in the worlds above, depending on the level of its origin and depending on that is also the level from where the prophet will draw forth his prophecy. Consequently, if the root of the soul originated in a higher place, the person will have need to amend all the other rootlets which are below it—so that he should be able to draw down from there to influence his prophecy. Otherwise, he will be able to draw forth prophecy only from a level which he has already rectified. Thus, you will understand why there are so many levels of prophecy that their number is infinite. You realize, therefore, that it is the desire to be raised to the higher levels which opens the channel for the influence of the thoughts to be attained, as well as intelligence being attained, to become united with the soul and to be drawn downward. Consequently, you will realize that [its] content is truly a Light and substance of the spiritual, which comes down to the mind and through the rational soul. This influx and very real Light is what is called "thought."

When you realize it fully, you will see what this means in terms of the prayer intentions and the good thoughts of man—and also the reality of evil thoughts, which mean a cleaving onto evil with one's mind. Thus, you realize that prophecy is a gift which by necessity is given to each person who attains to holding onto the end of the tree's branch. He who is capable of shaking a branch of the tree is capable of moving the entire tree. But the only way in which the upper branches will be moved is if that person has merited to draw on himself the supernal Light, and then with his thought, he is able to drawn down even these supernal and sublime Lights. One that has not so merited and purified himself will not find himself capable of drawing down supernal Light, for up there he will not be reckoned with it at all. These Lights will not agree to come to him and become incorporated in his thought. Vanity is developed without purification, and this is no help.

16

Joseph Karo

THE FASCINATING LIFE *of Joseph Karo exemplifies the historical reality that Kabbalah and traditional Jewish law have hardly been adversaries, but in truth, close allies. For this revered legalist and codifier of* halacha *was also a trance medium for decades. Like his mentor Joseph Taitazak in Salonica, Rabbi Karo purported to channel a* maggid. *According to Rabbi Karo, this celestial being was none other than the "Spirit of the* Mishnah," *who transmitted arcane teachings on such topics as the hidden nature of God, Torah, and the cosmos, the subtleties of reincarnation, and the afterlife. The fact that the author of the definitive legalistic work known as the* Beit Yosef, *and its abridgment the* Shulkhan Arukh, *could function with great admiration in both realms of Judaism highlights their historical unity.*

Rabbi Karo was quite a cosmopolitan figure for his era. Born in 1488 Spain, he sojourned in Constantinople and Salonica, and was strongly influenced by contact with the impassioned Solomon Molko, burned alive by the Inquisition in 1532. A few years thereafter, Rabbi Karo permanently immigrated to Safed, where he served as head of its communal council, directed a yeshiva of approximately two hundred students, and mixed with leading esoteric thinkers such as Moses Cordovero, Isaac Luria, and Chaim Vital. Rabbi Karo's mystic visions, written in a breathtaking literary style, were preserved in an extraordinary diary originally entitled Sefer HaMaggid *(Book of the Preacher) and later* Maggid Mesharim. *Inspiring his contemporaries, it gained him a devoted following as a seer, and undoubtedly enhanced his rabbinic reputation as an un-equalled commentator on Judaism's legal tradition as well. This selection, taken from* Maggid Mesharim, *presents his* maggid's *advice for inner development.*

Know that if you see garments torn in a dream, it means that there is something wrong with our deeds. It is a dream that Gabriel brings about. He extends throughout the world, among all the nations. If you will ask: Why is it that a person grieves over a calamity seen in a dream more than over one which befalls him while he is awake? It is because in a person's waking life the soul is clothed by the body. No sense of urgency is experienced, because the body acts as a shield. But the harm seen in a dream oppresses the naked soul so that it experiences far greater anguish. This will help you to under-stand the verse (Genesis 41:8), "And his spirit was troubled." Keep yourself from eating too much meat, for this flaws the soul. As for drinking wine, you have no idea how much harm it does and how great the flaw in the soul it causes. Be far, therefore, from these and be very careful. The masses imagine that this world is all it appears to be, so that there is no one to see when they eat and drink in order to satisfy their evil inclination. Woe to them. For they are fooled by the world. The hand writes it all down up above and they are obliged to pay for it severely. Therefore, it is written, "What will you do on the day of visitation?" Happy are you in that you have been warned. Reveal it to your friends, and they, too, will wake up. . . . If you will improve your behavior, I shall reveal to you the mys-teries of reincarnation. I shall show you the previous incarnations of all your friends and relatives, and you will witness wondrous things and be astonished.

Thus it has been decided in the Heavenly Academy and the Holy One, blessed be He, together with the members of the Academy, has sent Me to tell you new things hitherto unrevealed. All the sages of the generation, when they hear these things coming from your mouth, will praise you.

Gaze at all the great love and goodness the Holy One, blessed be He, has wrought for you. He created you out of nothing to bring you into this world. Even though you have sinned, He caused you to be reincarnated again and again until he brought you into this age. And He held your right hand even when you sinned. You returned to Him in those days, but then you became lax in repenting. But now that you have drawn near to the fear of Him, I have come to take delight with you—to speak in your mouth, not in a dream but as one speaks to his neighbor. Hold fast to me, therefore, and give up bodily pleasures. Drink no wine during the day and eat no meat. At night drink only one cup of wine and eat meat but not a great deal, only enough to keep you in good health. You are permitted to drink wine on the Sabbath and on festivals but yield not to your evil inclination to drink, as you wish to do, a great deal, except for the festival of Purim when you may drink limitless quantities. If you do this, forsaking bodily pleasures so that your heart and mind become a constant nest for the Torah and if you never cease from thinking on the Torah, then the Holy One, blessed be He, will take delight in you. Busy yourself constantly with rendering decisions in Jewish law and with the Talmud, the Kabbalah, the Mishnah, the *Tosefot* and Rashi, as you are doing. For you combine them and fit one to the other, bringing the hooks into the loops. Because you do this, the Holy One, blessed be He, loves you. At the time when you arise to offer your prayers and to study—the time when the Holy One, blessed be He, delights with the saints in the Garden of Eden at midnight—He takes delight in you, too, and extends over you a thread of mercy that kisses you with loving kisses and embraces you.

And the *Shekinah* converses with you, and you become attached in such a way never achieved by even one in a generation, nay, by one in many generations. From it you can see how great is the love the Holy One, blessed be He, bears for you. He has stretched out His right hand to receive you as you repent. These days in which you have repented now shine for you. Your glory is upon them and theirs upon you. You will be worthy of being burned for the sanctification of God's Name. Then will your sins be completely erased, all the dross and rust being purged by fire. You will be clothed in a robe of light when you ascend to Heaven. There you will be among the saints of the highest degree. You will no longer be obliged to return to earth in a new incarnation, for here you will rest—as it was said to Daniel, until the resurrection of the dead, when you will rise again together with the saints. Be strong, therefore, in separating yourself from your bodily pleasures. For [the demon] Samael and the serpent try to prevent you, their desire is to overcome you, but you will prevail over them, to reject and subdue them, and the Lord will be at your right hand. If they entice you to eat more meat and drink more wine than you should, whether on weekdays or on the Sabbath and festivals, pay them no heed. Also, when they entice you with base thoughts, as they do, rebuke them and subdue them. Busy yourself constantly in the study of the Torah, for when you analytically examined the opinions of the Rambam [Maimonides] yesterday, the two views you expressed are correct and the Rambam is pleased that you have succeeded in uncovering his full meaning and that you always quote his opinions and discuss his views analytically. Your words are right except in the few instances I shall show you. When you die, the Rambam will come out to meet you because you have defended his decisions, and even now, he pleads on your behalf. And he is among the saints, not as those sages who say that he has been reincarnated. For let it be that so it was decreed because of certain heretical views he expressed, but that the Torah he had studied protected him as well as his good deeds. For he was a master of good deeds, so he was not reincarnated . . . and he is now among the saints.

PART THREE

Early Modern Thinkers

ca. Sixteenth to Eighteenth Century

17

THE MAHARAL

Judah Loew ben Bezalel

THE MOST FAMOUS *Kabbalist in Western history is undoubtedly Rabbi Judah Loew, for his legendary creation of a* golem *in late sixteenth-century Prague. The tale is strictly a modern European invention, but the Maharal, as he was popularly known—in Hebrew, an abbreviation of "Our teacher, Rabbi Loew"—was indeed a celebrated figure in his time. He was revered for great piety, as well as his knowledge of philosophy, science, and the hidden Torah—so much so that occultist Emperor Rudolph II summoned him for a private meeting in 1592, presumably to discuss such esoterica as alchemy and the Kabbalah. During his lengthy career, the Maharal served as chief rabbi of Poland and later of Prague. As a yeshiva director, he was a reformer in Jewish education, and urged, for example, that Talmudic learning be implemented more flexibly, taking into better account the emotional maturity of students. Though Rabbi Loew valued the emergence of scientific investigation such as astronomy, he also insisted that it had no bearing on Judaic study. The Maharal was a prolific writer who often presented abstruse Kabbalistic concepts in philosophical garb—whether writing about the afterlife, the messianic age, or biblical events like Exodus. In this regard, he is credited with significantly influencing Hasidic thinkers like Rabbi Schneur Zalman of Liadi, as well as their opponents, including Rabbi Elijah "Gaon" of Vilna. These selections are taken from the Maharal's major works* Tiferet Yisrael *and* Gevurot Hashem. *They reflect his wide-ranging writings on such topics as the capabilities of the human soul, and the centrality of the Torah for the Jewish people.*

COMPLETION

Every human being longs for completion. Every soul yearns for an inner feeling of fulfillment. When one finds his soulmate and gets married, he feels a certain level of completion. When one finds a reliable source of income and is able to support his family comfortably, he also feels a sense of completion. Yet, the human soul is not easily satisfied. There is always a part of man that is searching for new and deeper levels of fulfillment. What is the source of this longing for completion? And why does it seem to be such a fundamental part of the human condition? "Completion" is the point where a living thing or an entity can no longer be added or improved upon. It is the point at which anything added is either superfluous or negative. When God created the world, he made "finished products," entities that were complete in and of themselves. Fish and birds, trees and flowers, were created with all the parts necessary for their survival and the fulfillment of their function in Creation. Man, however, is different. Man's defining characteristic (that which elevates him above the animal kingdom) is his intelligence—his ability to think, express his thoughts, and apply his thoughts to action. For man to be complete, then, his intelligence would have to reach a point where it can no longer be added to. But is this possible? Can man ever reach a point where his understanding and knowledge cannot grow? Seemingly not. How, then, can he ever reach completion? Through the Torah. The Torah is the blueprint of all existence. It encompasses all the knowledge and wisdom in the world, and cannot be added to. God gave the Torah to man to learn and internalize. As much as man inculcates the Torah into himself, he will be complete. God gave man the potential for completion just as He gave it to every other thing. But in man, the completion is not inherent; he must find it in, and obtain it from, the Torah.

THE PRODUCT OF THE SOUL

In creation, we find that many entities produce things attributable only to themselves. For example, the sun provides sunlight, heat, and solar energy. The earth provides the growing ground and the nutrients for vegetation. Water provides basic sustenance for all life. What product does man create that is attributable only to him? There are three aspects of man that are capable of production: his body, his speech, and his soul. The products of his body (based on the decisions of his intelligence) are his physical actions and his intellectual achievements. The product of his speech is his communication, in words and in song. The products of man's soul, his component closest to God, are the *mitzvos* that he does. *Mitzvos* are spiritual deeds that regulate man's actions. They are almost always done without personal gain, and reflect the ambitions of man that transcend his physical needs and desires.

ABRAHAM

One of the basic tenets of Judaism is that everything in the world exists only because God wills it to exist, and that every event that occurs does so because God wills it to occur. Another fundamental fact is that the Torah is the book in which God reveals His will to the Jewish People—who in turn are entrusted to transmit His will to the nations of the world.

MA'ASEI AVOS SIMAN LABANIM

Since the phenomenon and occurrences in the world express God's will, and the Torah expresses God's will, then the world and the

Torah are intrinsically connected. Each and every detail of all that exists, as well as each and every detail of all that has ever occurred, must be contained somewhere in the Torah. The Talmud (*Sotah* 34a) alludes to this in the words *ma'asei avos siman labanim*—"The lives of the fathers [patriarchs] are a prototype of the destiny of the sons [the Jewish People]." Not only does all of world history lie encoded within the words of the Torah, but even more specifically, the history of the Jewish People is encapsulated in the lives of three patriarchs, Avraham, Yitzchak, and Yaakov. In very general terms, the Jews have experienced three eras in their national history:

1. The Egypt and Sinai Desert Experience. The Jews began their history as slaves in Egypt, where they suffered bitterly for many years. They were finally redeemed by God and brought to Mount Sinai, where they received the Divine Torah. Then, they spent forty relatively peaceful years in the desert, during which time they incorporated the lessons they learned at Sinai into their national consciousness.

2. The Mishkan [Tabernacle] and the Temple Era. After crossing the Jordan River and settling in the Land of Israel, the Jews, for the most part, enjoyed a vibrant and thriving life, governed by the laws of the Torah. This continued for hundreds of years, until the destruction of the First Temple. After a seventy-year exile in Babylonia, they built a Second Temple and again enjoyed a spiritual life. Although this period was not nearly as great as the period of the First Temple, the Jews were still able to offer *korbanos* (sacrifices) in the Second Temple and live on their own land. This era came to a close at the end of the Second Temple period, when anarchy set in and civil war broke out. It was then that the Romans succeeded in destroying the Temple.

3. The Diaspora Experience. With the destruction of the Second Temple, the Jews were dispersed and exiled to countries in many different parts of the world. For nearly two thousand years, they have survived as a people estranged from its land, lacking a Temple and the governance of Torah....

These three experiences are mirrored in the lives of our patriarchs. . . . The Torah's description of the lives of our patriarchs thus spells out Jewish identity: *ma'asei avos siman labanim*.

Yet, there is one more bit of information that relates to our sequence. The Talmud (*Ta'anis* 5b) says: "Our patriarch Yaakov never died. . . . Just as his descendants live on, so too he lives on." This is the final message to the Jewish people. True, Jewish history in the diaspora will be a story of one struggle after another, but, nonetheless, the Jewish People will reach a time when "they will live forever." The long diaspora will give way to an era when the Jews will live without troubles and without suffering, and will experience only pure spiritual bliss.

TO EACH ONE AN ANGEL

At Mount Sinai, when the Jewish People accepted God's offer of the Torah, they called out, *"Na'aseh venishma," "We will carry* out [God's will] and [only then will we] heed [understand] *everything"* (*Shemos* 24:7). The Jews committed themselves to fulfilling the *mitzvos* even before they knew what those *mitzvos* would be. The saying *na'aseh venishma* was a tremendous merit for the Jewish People, as it indicated their belief in the goodness of God. The Talmud (*Shabbos* 88a) tells us of the great reward the Jews received: Each Jew received two crowns from God, one for *na'aseh* and one for *nishma*. A separate angel was dispatched to give out each crown, because the Midrash (*Bereshis Rabbah* 50:2) teaches, "One angel cannot do two missions simultaneously." Yet, wasn't the act of giving the crowns to the Jews one general mission? Why were separate angels needed for each person, and for each crown? The answer lies in appreciating the importance of each person in the Jewish Nation. If a population of no less than six hundred thousand persons (or family units) was needed to form our identity as a nation, then each individual in that group was clearly an indispensible part of that nation. Clearly, each member added his own dimension to the national character. Each Jew is immeasurably unique. Therefore, each statement of "we will do and we will hear" was said from a unique perspective and outlook. Each reward, then, would have to be unique, too, to correspond exactly to the action done. Thus, no angel could give more than one crown to each person, as the giving of each crown was indeed a different mission.

18

CHACHAM TZVI

Tzvi Ashkenazi

LIKE MANY EARLIER *Kabbalists, Rabbi Tzvi Ashkenazi, of Polish birth, was a master of both the normative and esoteric Judaic traditions. Holding important rabbinic posts in Sarajevo, Amsterdam, Hamburg, and Lemberg from 1686–1718, he was revered as an outstanding scholar and Talmudist. Yet Chacham (Sephardic for "rabbi") Tzvi, as he was admiringly known, was also an ardent Kabbalist drawing upon ancient theosophic texts like the* Sefer Yetzirah *for insights about human existence—and Jewish life in particular—in the contemporary world. His piety was sometimes costly, for historians today report that a major reason for Chacham Tzvi's frequent relocations was his tendency to antagonize prominent, wealthy congregants by showing more respect for their poor but learned peers.*

Rabbi Tzvi Ashkenazi is best known for his collection of halachic *responsa, some of which may have been republished many times. Among these is an intriguing Kabbalah-borne issue that he posed and answered (responsum #93): Can a* golem *be considered part of a* minyan *[Jewish prayer quorum]? Not only has Chacham Tzvi's ruling fascinated Jews for centuries, it has also become a chief basis for determining whether a "virtual" gathering, such as an Internet chat room, might constitute a valid minyan in the eyes of Jewish law. Such is the process by which the Torah is seen to maintain its timelessness and universality. The second excerpt is an addition the Chacham Tzvi wrote in a later response, additions #46.*

I was unsure if a being which was created through the *Sefer Yetzirah* (Book of Creation), as is mentioned in tractate *Sanhedrin* 65b that Rava created a man, and as has been testified that my grandfather—the great Eliyahu, the head of the rabbinical court in Chelm—likewise did so, if such a being can be counted in a *minyan* [religious quorum]: for example, for the recitation of Kaddish and Kedusha. Do we conclude that since it is stated (regarding the source for the requirement of ten men for a religious quorum, see tractate *Brachos* 21b), "And I will be sanctified among the sons of Israel" (Leviticus 22:32), that such a being *cannot* be considered for such a quorum (since he is not *halachically* considered of the sons of Israel). Or, perhaps, since it is stated in tractate *Sanhedrin* 19b that whoever raises an orphan in his own house the Torah treats it as if he birthed the child, so here too since this being is a product of the [Kabbalistic] handiwork of the righteous the being can be considered part of "the sons of Israel"—for the handiwork of the righteous is, in many senses, considered their offspring. It appears to me, that since we find that Rabbi Zeira (tractate *Sanhedrin* 65b) stated after encountering such a creation), "You are the work of my colleagues, return to your dust!" it seems he killed the creation. And if it would be that such creations could be used for such a lofty purpose, such as being counted in a religious quorum, Rabbi Zeira certainly would not have removed the being from this world. Even though it is clear that there is no formal prohibition in killing such beings—for the verse describes specifically those human beings who are created in the womb of another human being (see tractate *Sanhedrin* 57b based upon Genesis 9:6), thus it is specifically a human which develops from a fetus which is underneath the formal prohibition of murder. This dictum therefore excludes the creation of the like which Rava made, which is *not* birthed through the womb. Therefore, had such a creation been able to serve a purpose, it surely would have never been killed, it seems certain that one cannot consider such a being for use in a religious quorum.

I have seen in the book authored by Rabbi Moshe Cordovero, in the *Sha'ar Heichalos* chapter 10, after citing the aforementioned Talmudic passage about Rava, Rabbi Cordovero writes: "Such beings that appear in the form of man do not have a spiritual soul, a lower soul, or any human spirit, but rather comprise the most basic form of life." This passage by Rabbi Cordovero provides a substantive basis for my earlier conclusion—that since such beings do not even have a human soul, it is certain that they cannot be of any relevance to matters which require a religious quorum of ten or three Jews. . . . Therefore, it is clear that such beings cannot be considered for any religious quorum of ten which are composed of people who are obligated in the commandments. . . . Even those rabbinic opinions who allow a baby in its cradle to be counted for such religious quorums—that is only because in the future the child is destined to be a grown man. This dictum excludes Kabbalistically-created beings, who will never become full-fledged Jews.

19

SHALOM SHARABI

AMONG THE LEADING *Sephardic Kabbalists of the eighteenth century was Shalom Sharabi. Born in 1720 Yemen, he worked as a peddler-boy after his father died, to help support their impoverished family. According to legend, Shalom eagerly studied Kabbalah while a young traveling merchant in Aden, Baghdad, Bombay, and Damascus before settling in the Holy Land. Upon reaching Jerusalem, he went to the Beit El Yeshiva—founded in 1737 as a center of Kabbalistic study—and asked to be hired as janitor. Its renowned director, Rabbi Gedalia Hayoon, agreed, and Shalom listened to the lessons in his spare time. Before long, he became recognized as the most brilliant student of all, and when Rabbi Hayoon died in 1751, Rabbi Sharabi was appointed as his successor.*

Under Rabbi Sharabi's leadership, the Beit El Yeshiva gained a worldwide reputation, particularly for its emphasis on the meditational and prayer techniques of Rabbi Isaac Luria, as disseminated by his chief disciple, Rabbi Chaim Vital. In this capacity, Rabbi Sharabi developed a prayer book with extensive Kabbalistic commentary—known as the Siddur HaKavvanot—*still used internationally today for prayer, meditation, and advanced study. Rabbi*

*Sharabi's esoteric writings, extremely dense and abstruse, are re-
garded as meaningful only to accomplished Kabbalists. The selection
that follows is a signed agreement or "bill of association" composed
by twelve Beit El participants, including Rabbi Sharabi, to forge a
spiritual fellowship of uncompromising loyalty, friendship, and
brotherhood.*

Since the Lord desires the return of those who do *teshuvah,* the
spirit took hold of us—the young ones of the flock—the undersigned, to become as one man, companions. This is all for the sake of
the unification of the Holy One, blessed be he, and his *Shekhina,* in
order to give satisfaction to our Creator. For this purpose, we have
made a pact and the following conditions are completely binding
upon us. First, we the undersigned, twelve of us, corresponding to
the number of the tribes of Judah, agree to love one another with
great love of soul and body, all for the purpose of giving satisfaction
to our Creator through our single-minded association, although
we are separated. Each man's soul will be bound to that of his companion so that the twelve of us will be as one man greatly to be
admired. Each one of us will think of his companion as if the latter
were part of his very limbs, with all his soul and all his might, so that
if, God forbid, any one of us will suffer tribulation, all of us together
and each one of us separately will help him in every possible way.

The main principle is that each of us will rebuke his companion
when, God forbid, he hears of any sin the latter has committed.
This embraces the obligation of the undersigned to bind ourselves
together in the mighty bond of love. We take it upon ourselves
from now onward, even after we have departed this life and gone
to the World-to-Come, that each one of us will endeavor—both in
this world and the next—to save, perfect, and elevate the soul of
each one of our circle to the best of his ability, and with every kind
of effort to do everything possible for the others' eternal bliss. Each
of us agrees to save his companion in the event it has been decreed
in heaven, God forbid, that one of us should receive the goodness
that belongs to his neighbor, on the basis of the idea that there are

occasions when a man receives both his portion in Paradise and that of his neighbor who has sinned. In return for the advantage each of us has received from the others, we hereby resolve to participate in that companion's tribulations, may they never come. With firm resolve, we take upon ourselves the obligation—with all the formulae required to make it binding—both according to the laws of men and according to the laws of heaven, to relinquish that goodness that is to come to us for the benefit of that companion for whom it has been decreed that it be taken from him. We shall have no benefit from it and "every man's hallowed things shall be his" (Numbers 5:10), as our master the Ari [Rabbi Isaac Luria] of blessed memory said when commenting on the passage in the liturgy: "And let our portion be with them." Following this idea, we have taken the above-mentioned obligation upon ourselves. . . . We take it upon ourselves the obligation never to praise one another, even if it is clear to everyone that one companion is superior to another both in age and in wisdom. None of us will rise fully to his feet before any other companion, but we shall merely rise a little as a token of respect and we shall not say much about it. We shall conduct ourselves as if we were one man, no part of whom is superior to any other part. Though we have eyes of flesh, our heart knows our own worth and the worth of our companions, and there is no need to give expression to it in words. We further take upon ourselves the obligation never to reveal to any creature that we have resolved to do these things. We further take it upon ourselves never to be annoyed with one another in any way, whether because of his rebuke to us or because of anything else, and if one of us offends his companion, the latter will forgive him at once with all his heart and with all his soul. All this we have taken upon ourselves under the penalty of the ban and by an irrevocable resolve in accordance with the laws of our sages of blessed memory. We are resolved to keep these things, and we give them the full force of all the regulations that have been issued from the days of Moses our teacher, on whom be peace. And let the pleasantness of the Lord our God be upon us, and establish thou the work of our hands upon us: yea, the work of our hands establish thou it. As an indication of our sincerity, we hereby sign this in the holy city of Jerusalem, may it be speedily rebuilt and established, on the week of the *sidrah* (Torah portion): "Behold, I give unto him my covenant of peace" (Numbers 25:12). May the Lord bless His people with peace. All this is lasting and firm, the thing is right, true, and established.

Shalom Mizrachi di-Ydi'a Sharabi, pure Sephardi

Yom Tov Algazi

Samuel Alhadif, pure Sephardi

Abraham Belul, pure Sephardi

Aaron Bacher Elijah ha-Levi, pure Sephardi

Menachem ben Rabbi Joseph

The Young Chaim Joseph David Azulai, Pure Sephardi

Joseph Samanon, pure Sephardi

Solomon, son of my master and father Bejoash

Jacob Biton

Raphael Eliezer Parhi, pure Sephardi

Chaim de la Roza

20

YAIR CHAIM BACHRACH

A DESCENDENT OF *the Maharal, Rabbi Yair Chaim Bachrach*
was born into an esteemed family in 1638 Germany. Showing early
brilliance, he produced a variety of scholarly works including a
forty-six-volume encyclopedia on many topics. Yet, to Rabbi Bach-
rach's coreligionists, his life served as an important cautionary
tale—for as a Kabbalistic devotee, he and his rabbinic father, Sam-
uel Bachrach, vigorously supported Shabbatai Zevi as the Jewish
Messiah. More than merely hopeful supporters, Yair and Samuel
were German rabbinic leaders in the movement that brought thou-
sands of frenzied Jews from North Africa to Northern Europe to
ruin. As modern scholars confirmed, the Bachrach home in Worms
served as an international center for news of the latest activities and
speeches of Shabbatai Zevi and his "prophet," Nathan of Gaza.
For example, both Bachrach rabbis kept up an enthusiastic corre-
spondence with Rabbi Isaac Deggingen—head of Amsterdam's
Jewish-German community—who sent laudatory accounts of the
letters arriving there daily with news of the miracles performed in
the south. Events had reached such a fever pitch that a special
prayer for Shabbatai Zevi—joyously proclaimed as the King

*Messiah—was being offered at local synagogues there. Rabbi Yair
Chaim Bachrach even organized a fellowship of thirteen Talmudic
scholars in Coblentz, pledging to sanctify themselves by pious study
to prepare themselves appropriately for the imminent Redemption.
Rabbi Yair Chaim Bachrach was only twenty-eight years old during
the Shabbataian cataclysm of 1666, and went on to a distinguished
career spanning some thirty-five years. But the debacle never disappeared from his ensuing outlook on Jewish belief and practice. Thus,
when earnestly asked by a correspondent about the importance of
learning Kabbalah for leading a worthwhile religious life, what follows was his heartfelt and influential reply (from responsa* Havvot
Yair *210).*

[Regarding learning the secret wisdom of Kabbalah], behold I
will speak with trembling and concern. What I shall say will be
concise, but nevertheless I will respond, due to the great honor of
the questioner.

I shall begin with an analogy for those who are willing to listen
to my words. That the study of the Holy of Holies [that is, the Kab-
balah] is comparable to the obligation to travel to the Holy Land,
which even Moses and Aaron did not merit, the land which God
seeks and is His abode. . . . Even a maidservant who dwells in Israel
and one who walks four cubits in the land merits life in the World-
to-Come. And the Midrash (*Bereshit Rabbah* 16:4) states that there
is no wisdom like wisdom received in the Land of Israel. The Talmud (*Bava Batra* 158b) also states that the Land of Israel makes one
wiser. Additionally, there are myriads of commandments which can
only be fulfilled in Israel, and there is no question that praiseworthy
is the one who merits to live in the land and acquire completion in
Torah and the commandments. Nevertheless, you have seen what
the *Tosafist* (*Ketubot* 110b) write in brevity—that Rabbi Chaim
writes that nowadays it is not obligatory to live in Israel for there are
many commandments (which the masses are ignorant of and will
stumble upon and derive punishment) and there are great dangers
for those traveling on the road to Israel. Furthermore, I found it

written that one who will not be able to financially sustain himself in the Holy Land, it is better that he remain outside, lest by settling in Israel his poverty will prevent him from learning Torah and fulfilling God's commandments. . . . Here too [in regard to involving oneself in the esoteric works of Kabbalah], who would ever deny or belittle the greatness of this wisdom which is exalted over all else in quantity and quality? But one can only involve oneself with certain conditions, such as the following: that he has an exalted soul, and he merits to learn from a master of Kabbalah who himself has an accredited tradition. . . . And only one in a thousand merit these conditions. Go forth and learn from the Talmudic story of the four sages who entered *Pardes* (the esoteric "fields" of learning). They were the greatest rabbis in their generation, yet only one of them was able to enter and leave in serenity (Talmud *Chagigah* 14b). Who among you wishes to enter, yet is not dreadfully concerned that he will not leave in peace? And Rabbi Shimon bar Yochai has stated (*Succah* 45b): I have seen men of transcendence and they are few. . . .

And my beloved—who is like a brother—consider the aforementioned analogy. The long road to the place of God is difficult for the seeker, and the object for which he is in search is of great depth, and there are many different signposts along the road. . . . Specifically in regards to this wisdom, that is, the Kabbalah, there are many aspects which prevent true understanding. Firstly, in terms of the difficult language, as is evident in the *Zohar*. Secondly, in terms of lengthy passages. Thirdly, in terms of the depth of the matters. And fourthly, in terms of the many printing mistakes and errors which have crept into the texts of many Kabbalistic works—for since there are so few people who master these works, they have not been sufficiently corrected and these stumbling blocks have not been removed. And moreover, the greatest concern, is the matter of one's sins, which create a partition between the mind and what it wants to apprehend. The weakness of the traveler on the long road to Israel, can be compared to the weakness of the mindset of the masses on the "road" towards the wisdom of Kabbalah. And the lack of a clear pathway to Israel, and the concern that one may get lost on the way, is comparable to those who think they understand the Kabbalah, yet in truth they do not understand. The speculations of man in this area of wisdom are meaningless and empty. On the road to Israel, there are many different signposts which seem to guide the traveler in many different directions in order to find the land; this is comparable to the words of the Kabbalists, and sometimes the words of the *Zohar* itself, which oftentimes appear contradictory. Even if a later Kabbalist were to come and attempt to reconcile these contradictions, in our generation there is no one truly fit to explain such matters. . . . That there are many dangers such as poisonous snakes, scorpions, robbers, and murderers on the road to Israel, this is comparable to the dangers to the soul, the spirit, and the body which the study of Kabbalah poses. For the study of Kabbalah can damage one by leading him on a treacherous path in understanding piety, and one may come to invent in his mind false conceptions.

And now, what leaves from the essence of my words is that: certainly, to separate completely from the wisdom of Kabbalah is like separating oneself from the essence of life. All of the praises upon praises which have been attributed to those who discover and master its words are true and correct, so long as there is a direct oral tradition from one expert to another . . . all the more so those who have merited to hear from the exalted holy Kabbalists. This, however, is not what we see in our generation where we do not learn with a clear oral tradition, but rather from books. Certainly not all books written on the matters of Kabbalah are equal, and they should not all be grouped together in determining from which of them it is fitting to learn. This concern is not, God forbid, in terms of the knowledge of the authors or their holiness, for I am not fit to determine which scholars are suitable and to grant honor and to bestow and detract honor from one author or another—even though there are certainly differences among the different Kabbalistic scholars. I, with my limited knowledge, will not contemplate such distinctions.

21

THE RAMCHAL

Moses Chaim Luzzatto

THE LIFE OF RABBI *Moses Chaim Luzzatto vividly reveals the hardship of being born in the wrong historical time and place. For though he came from a wealthy, educated Jewish family in 1707 Padua, this brilliant, charismatic teacher of Kabbalah encountered swift suppression from Italy's rabbinic establishment. The motivation, of course, was to prevent even the slightest recurrence of the Shabbatai Zevi disaster, whose memory still burned among many Jews in the early eighteenth century. Faced with the threat of excommunication in 1729, the Ramchal, as he came to be known (a Hebrew acronym of his name) eventually settled in Amsterdam, and then finally immigrated to the Holy Land, where death took him soon after.*

In historical irony, he become elevated to revered status posthumously in the Orthodox Jewish world, through the circulation of his ethical books, including The Knowing Heart *and* The Way of God, *which drew masterfully upon Kabbalistic ideas. A gifted poet and playwright, Rabbi Luzzatto wrote in a beautifully clear style, very different from the dense tomes typical of many earlier Kabbal-*

ists. An iconoclastic figure who practiced maggidism *(trance medi-
umship) until rabbinic authorities ordered him to stop, the Ramchal
was scornful of contemporary Judaism in the absence of Kabbalah.
"How many masters of the study halls exclaim loudly, day and
night, regarding the difficulties of the Talmud," he caustically wrote
in his* Treatise on Redemption. *"But none endeavor with their
Torah to remove the Shekinah from exile, to unite her with her
spouse." This selection is from* The Way of God, *and presents a
lucid depiction of human existence from the esoteric perspective.*

INDIVIDUAL PROVIDENCE

It is necessary to realize that the Highest Providence takes account
of everything associated with each detail, whether it precedes it or
follows from it. In dealing with each element, its ultimate effect on
the whole is calculated, taking into account the manner in which
every element is interconnected with every other one in the structure of creation as a whole. Thus, when an individual is judged,
Providence takes account of his state and level with respect to what
precedes him, what follows him, and what is associated with him.
Each person is thus judged in relation to his forebears who pre-
ceded him, his descendants who follow him, and the people of his
generation, city and community who are associated with him. After
all this is taken into account, he is then given his particular mission
and challenge, as well as a specific responsibility in serving God. It
is important to realize, however, that this is true only for one's judgment in this world. It is for this reason that we have specified that
what is decreed is one's mission: that is, the state in which he will
exist in this world. His responsibility will then depend on that state.
In the World-to-Come, however, the state in which a person finds
himself depends completely on his own deeds. The prophet Ezekiel
(18:20) thus said, "The son shall not bear the sin of his father."

Thus, for example, if it is decreed that an individual be worthy
of great riches, then his children will also be born wealthy, and

unless their situation is changed, they too will have wealth and status. Wealth such as this is therefore merely the result of one's parentage. The same can also be true of poverty.

Our sages therefore teach us that a parent can endow his children with five things. It is thus possible that one be born with good as a result of his parentage, and it is likewise possible that he should later attain good as a result of his parents' merit.

It is likewise possible that [one attains good because of his children. Thus, for example,] success and other good may be granted to an individual in order that his children be born with these advantages. In a similar manner, it is possible that good or evil befall a person because of the place where he lives or because of the group with which he is associated. . . .

A single soul can be reincarnated a number of times in different bodies, and in this manner, it can rectify the damage done in previous incarnations. Similarly, it can also achieve perfection that was not attained in its previous incarnations.

The soul is then ultimately judged at the end of all these incarnations. Its judgment will depend on everything that took place in all its incarnations, as well as its status as an individual in each one.

When an individual has a reincarnated soul, it is possible that he will be affected in a particular manner as a result of his deeds in a previous incarnation. The situation in which he is placed may follow from this, and this situation may bring with it the special responsibility given to him, as discussed earlier.

God's judgment of each individual is extremely precise, depending on every aspect of his nature and including every detail of his exact situation. But in the World-to-Come, which is the true good, no individual is required to sustain a liability which is not the result of his own doing, but a result of his mission and responsibility in this world, as parceled out by the Highest Wisdom. In cases such as these, the individual is judged accordingly.

There are many details in the concept of reincarnation, involving the manner in which an individual is judged according to one incarnation, and how this judgment depends on previous incarnations. The crucial point, however, is the fact that all is truly fair and just, as the Torah states (Deuteronomy 32:7), "The Creator's work is perfect, all His ways are justice."

From this entire discussion, we see that there are many different and varied reasons for everything that happens to an individual in this world, whether it is for good or otherwise. It is important to realize, however, that this does not mean that every event is always the result of all these causes. These are merely all the *possible* causes, but things can sometimes result from one and sometimes from another.

The Highest Wisdom, however, perceives and knows what is best to rectify all creation. In its profound design, it weighs everything together, and directs each individual element of creation accordingly.

[Although creation is arranged to follow a cause-and-effect Relationship], every cause does not always necessarily have the same effect. Many causes are almost always involved, and in many cases one will contradict the other.

Thus, for example, the merit of one's parents may entitle an individual to wealth and prosperity. His own deeds, however, may require that he be poor. His place in the general scheme may furthermore exert an influence in determining whether he is granted wealth or made poor.

The same can also be true with respect to the individual's own actions. He may have done one deed that should result in his attaining something good. At the same time, however, he may have also done something else that would require that he not receive this very same good.

Because of these many conflicts, the Highest Wisdom must balance and decide every factor, creating situations which are products of the various combinations of these causes with respect to each individual. Occurrences may thus be the result of one or another of these causes, but ultimately at least one of the causes that we have discussed must be involved.

The details of this judgment are beyond the grasp of human

understanding. But to know its general concepts and categories is to know much, as we have explained earlier.

One must also realize that things can happen to an individual both as an end in itself and as a means toward something else. Thus, when it is appropriate that something happens to an individual as a result of one of the above causes, then it is said to be an end in itself. Other things may happen to an individual, however, which are merely means ultimately to achieve some other end completely.

With regard to such means, the prophet Isaiah (12:1) said, "I will thank You, God, though You showed me anger." Our sages explain that this refers to a situation where someone's cow broke its foot and fell, and as a result, he found a buried treasure. They likewise apply it to a case where one escapes from a calamity as a result of something that he may initially have considered a grave inconvenience. The example given is that of a person who wanted to embark on an ocean voyage, and was detained and missed his ship. The ship then sank [and a result of this inconvenience, his life was saved].

Means such as these can be destined to affect the individual himself or to influence others. Something can thus happen to a person in order to bring good or evil to someone else.

The Highest Wisdom, however, determines what should befall each individual, and in this same manner, determines the means through which this should come about. Everything is ultimately decreed with the utmost precision, according to what is truly best.

22

THE BAAL SHEM TOV

Israel ben Eliezer

THE GREAT EXPANSION *of the Kabbalah in the second half of the eighteenth century was due to the charismatic fervor of a single figure: Israel ben Eliezer. Arising from obscurity in a Ukrainian village called Okup, the Baal Shem Tov (Bearer of the Good Name), or Besht (the Hebrew abbreviation by which he was admiringly known), founded and led the Jewish revivalist movement known as Hasidism. Within seventy-five years of his birth in about 1698, half of the Polish and Russian Jewry had embraced the Hasidic way of life; these comprised the major populations of world Jewry at the time. Initially attracting mainly poor and unschooled Jews through his inspiring aphorisms, parables, and tales that emphasized joy as a rightful path to God, the Baal Shem Tov eventually won over major rabbinic scholars, who unequivocally viewed him as a master of Kabbalah and a holy visionary.*

Unlike most influential Kabbalists, however, with the notable exception of Rabbi Isaac Luria, the Besht composed no books or treatises. Indeed, the only document in existence directly attributable to his hand and that historians regard as authentic is a single letter that he wrote late in life. Its intended recipient was his brother-in-law, Rabbi Abraham Gershon Kitover, then living in the Holy Land. However, the Baal Shem Tov's courier—Rabbi Jacob Joseph of Polnoye—changed his plan to make the arduous journey from Eastern Europe, and so the letter was never delivered. It remained with the Besht's inner circle for over twenty years before it was first published in Ben Porat Yosef, *a collection of Hasidic discourses by Rabbi Jacob Joseph.*

This remarkable letter, excerpted here, shows the strong Kabbalistic foundation of the Besht's outlook on Judaism and his mission on its behalf.

To my dear friend and brother-in-law, whom I love as my own self, wondrous Rabbi and Hasid, renowned in knowledge of the Torah and fear of God, his honor our teacher, Rabbi Abraham Gershon, may his light shine. Greetings to all and to his modest wife, mistress Bluma, and all their offspring. May they all be blessed with life. Amen. Selah.

I received the letter written by your holy hand at the Lyck fair in the year 5510 [1750] which you sent by the hand of the envoy from Jerusalem. The letter was very brief but you state therein that you have written to everyone in letters sent by the hand of a man who was traveling from Egypt. Unfortunately, these lengthy letters never arrived and I am greatly distressed not to have had the lengthier epistles written in your holy handwriting. For our sins, the reason for it is, undoubtedly, the confused state of communication among the countries. The epidemic has spread to all lands, reaching near to the place where we reside: to the holy communities of Mogilev and in the lands of Volhynia and the Tartar lands. You also remark that the new ideas and mysteries I recorded for you by the hand of the scribe, the rabbi and preacher of the holy community of Polnoye, did not arrive. Over this, too, I am greatly distressed, for you would undoubtedly have derived much satisfaction from them. Now, however, I have forgotten many of these matters, yet I shall write to you very briefly those details I do recall.

For on the day of the New Year of the year 5507 [September 1746], I engaged in an ascent of the soul, as you know I do, and I saw wondrous things in the vision that I had never before seen since the day I had attained to maturity. That which I saw and learned in my ascent it is impossible to describe or to relate even from mouth to mouth. But as I returned to the Lower Garden of Eden, I saw many souls—both of the living and the dead—those known to me and those unknown. There were more than could be counted—and they ran to and fro, from world to world, through the path provided by that column known to the adepts in the hidden science.

They were all in such a state of great rapture that the mouth would be worn out if it attempted to describe it, and the physical ear too indelicate to hear it. Many of the wicked had done *teshuvah* for their sins and were pardoned, for it was a time of much grace. In my eyes, too, it was a great marvel that the *teshuvah* was accepted of so many whom you know. They also enjoyed great rapture and ascended, as mentioned above. All of them entreated me to my embarrassment, saying: "The Lord has given your honor great understanding to grasp these matters. Ascend together with us, therefore, so as to help us and assist us." Their rapture was so great that I resolved to ascend together with them.

Then I saw in the vision that Samael [the Satan] went up to act the part of accuser because of the unprecedented rapture. He achieved what he had set out to do, namely, a decree of apostasy for many people who would be tortured to death. Then dread seized me and I took my life in my hands. I requested my teacher to come with me, since there is great danger in the ascent to the higher worlds, and since from that day I attained to maturity, I had never undertaken such high ascent.

I went higher, step by step, until I entered the palace of the Messiah wherein the Messiah studies the Torah together with all the *tannaim* and the saints and also with the Seven Shepherds. There I witnessed great rejoicing and could not fathom the reason for it, so I thought that, God forbid, the rejoicing was over my departure from this world. But I was afterwards informed that I was not yet to die, since they took great delight on high when, through their Torah, I perform [Kabbalistic] unifications here below.

To this day, I am unaware of the reason for that rejoicing. I asked the Messiah: "When will the Master come?" And he replied: "You will know of it in this way: it will be when your teaching becomes famous and revealed to the world, and when that which I have taught you and you have comprehended will spread abroad, so that others, too, will be capable of performing [Kabbalistic] unifications and having soul ascents as you do. Then will all the *kelippot* be consumed, and it will be a time of grace and salvation."

I was astonished to hear this, and greatly distressed that it would take such a long time, for when will such a thing be possible? Yet my mind was set at rest in that I learned three special charms and three holy names, and these are easy to grasp and to expound, so that I thought to myself: is it possible by this means for all my colleagues to attain to the stages and categories to which I have attained? That is to say: they, too, will be able to engage in ascents of the soul and learn to comprehend as I have done.

But no permission was given to me to reveal the secret for the rest of my life. I did request that I be allowed to teach it to you, but no permission at all was given to me, and I am duty bound on oath to keep the secret.

However, this I can tell you, and may God be your help. Let your ways be set before the Lord and never be moved [from them], especially in the Holy Land. Whenever you offer your prayers and whenever you study, have the intention of unifying a divine name in every word and with every utterance of your lips. For there are worlds, souls, and divinity in every letter. These ascend to become united, one with the other, and then the letters are combined in order to form a word, so that there is complete unification with the divine.

Allow your soul to be embraced by them at each of the above stages. Thus all worlds become united and they ascend so that immeasurable rapture and the greatest delight is experienced. You can understand this on the analogy of the raptures of bride and bridegroom in miniature in the physical world. How much more so at this most elevated level! God will undoubtedly be your help and wherever you turn you will be successful and prosper. Give to the wise and he will become even wiser. Also pray for me, with this intention in mind, that I should be worthy of being gathered into the inheritance of the Lord (the Holy Land), while still alive, and pray, too, on behalf of all the remnant still in the diaspora.

I also prayed there, asking why the Lord had done this and why this great wrath, to hand over so many Jewish souls to be slain by Samael, among them many souls who had aspostasized and had still been killed. Permission was granted for me to ask this of Samael himself. I asked Samael why he did this and what could have been his intention in having Jews become apostates and yet still be killed afterwards. He replied that his intention was for the sake of heaven. And afterwards, for our sins, so it happened, that in the holy community of Izyaslav there was a blood libel against many people, two of whom became apostates and yet they still killed them. But the others sanctified the name of heaven in great sanctity, dying by terrible torture. Afterwards, there were further blood libels in the holy communities of Shebitovka and Dunayevtsy. But none of them became apostates, having seen what happened in the aforementioned holy community of Izyaslav. They all resisted temptation, suffering martyrdom and sanctifying the name of heaven. By their merit, the Messiah will come to avenge us and to gain atonement for God's land and His people. . . .

It was my intention to write at greater length and discuss matters in detail, but I am unable to continue because of the tears which flow when I reflect on our parting. But I do beg to repeat the words of reproof I have said to you again and again. Have them always in your thoughts, meditate on them, and take note of them. You will undoubtedly find numerous sweet things in every word for that which I have told you is no empty matter. For God knows that I have not abandoned the hope of journeying to the Land of Israel, God willing, to be there together with you.

PART FOUR

Industrial Age Thinkers

ca. Eighteenth and Nineteenth Century

23

THE GAON OF VILNA

Elijah ben Solomon

IN POPULAR ACCOUNTS *today of Jewish history, Rabbi Elijah ben Solomon is typically cast as the archenemy of Hasidism, who fiercely—and ultimately unsuccessfully—battled its leadership in late-eighteenth-century Eastern Europe. Such is indeed true. But not at all accurate is the related description of the Vilna Gaon (Genius of Vilna as he was admiringly known) as a "rationalist" hostile to the Kabbalah so beloved among ardent Hasidic followers.*

For not only was Rabbi Elijah ben Solomon a prolific writer on Kabbalistic works including the Sefer Yetzirah *(Book of Creation) and especially the* Zohar, *but he also engaged in transcendental practices from an early age. Tradition has it that before his bar mitzvah, he tried to create a* golem *by consulting the Sefer Yetzirah— but then decided not to. According to legend, the Vilna Gaon regularly experienced* maggidic *visitations in his reclusive way of life, but preferred to solve Torah mysteries on his own rather than receive "spoon-fed" revelations from his celestial messenger. Though Rabbi Elijah ben Solomon never held an official position in any synagogue, yeshiva, or communal institution, he exerted tremendous Jewish influence as a scholar and legal thinker unparalleled in his*

era; among his most important disciples was Rabbi Chaim of Volo-
zhin, founder of what came to be a highly influential yeshiva for
nearly a century.

    This excerpt is from the Vilna Gaon's intriguing commentary
on the biblical book of Jonah. Stylistically far more accessible than
many of his other Kabbalistic writings, it remains well known
among Judaic readers today. Undoubtedly, its erudite author was
inspired by the Zohar's *classic dictum that the Jonah narrative is*
symbolic of each human soul's sojourn through myriad worlds.

In addition to its literal meaning, the story of Jonah can be understood on a deeper level as an analogy to the sojourn of the *neshamah*
(human soul) in this world. Jonah the Prophet represents man's
neshamah.

    God sent Jonah to rectify the moral condition of Nineveh, but
instead of fulfilling God's will, Jonah tried to escape his obligation by
boarding a ship bound for a different destination. Similarly, the *nesh-*
amah is sent to rectify the world through Torah study and *mitzvot,*
but instead of fulfilling its mission, it allows itself to be deceived by
the body's physical impulses. The body's ability to deceive the *nesh-*
amah in this manner is alluded by the name Jonah—in Hebrew, the
word *yoneh* is a verbal form related to the noun *hunaheh,* deception.
This etymological link forms the basis of the correlation between
Jonah the Prophet and the *neshamah.* The analogy has many facets.

    Just as Jonah initially failed to carry out his mission and conse-
quently endangered his life, so too, the *neshamah* initially fails in its
mission to rectify the world and consequently brings great harm
upon itself in the process. And although Jonah was granted a second chance to complete his mission, he was very distressed by
what he perceived as his bad fortune. The same is true of the *nesh-*
amah—when the *neshamah* fails in its mission—but like Jonah, it is
greatly disturbed by the necessity of reincarnation.

    It is these analogies which are elaborated upon in the commen-
tary. "And it came to pass that the word of Hashem came to Jonah."

The sages say that whenever the [Hebrew] term *vayehee*—"and it came to pass," appears in Scripture, it invariably conveys distress and hardship. This verse is not an exception, although at first glance it would seem to be announcing a most joyous event: the revelation of prophecy.

The note of distress in the verse stems from the fact that the *neshamah* is sent down to this world against its will. The *Zohar* teaches that when the time comes, God commands the *neshamah* to go to a particular place in the world and enter the body of a particular individual, within which it is to fulfill His will. The *neshamah* pleads with God not to banish it from its pristine heavenly environment and force it to descend to the corporeal world, where it will become subject to worldly desires and tainted by impurity and sin. However, God insists, saying, "Since the day you were created, it was for this that you were created—to be in that world." When the *neshamah* realizes this, it descends against its will and enters the person's body.

As a result of the *neshamah*'s great anguish over its descent to this world, it becomes disoriented and susceptible to the enticements of physical desires. It is entangled in sin just "like a gullible dove lacking understanding" (Hosea 7:11) and unwittingly steps into a trap (the Hebrew word for "dove" is the same as the prophet's name—*yonaw*).

There is another reason for the *neshamah*'s anguish over the prospect of descending to this world: It is aware that physical desire is not the only obstacle it must overcome in order to fulfill its mission—it must also face the antagonism of the nations.

In reference to this idea, the Talmud relates the incident of Elisha, who publicly donned *tefillin* in defiance of a Roman decree prohibiting the fulfillment of this *mitzvah*. He was discovered by a Roman guard, but Elisha proceeded to remove the *tefillin* and grasp them in his hand before he was apprehended. "What do you have in your hands?" the guard demanded, to which Elisha answered, "The wings of a dove (*yonaw*)." Elisha opened his hands, and miraculously, the *tefillin* he had been holding transformed into the wings of a dove.

The Talmud explains why the *tefillin* turned into the wings of a dove, and not some other object. "Because the Congregation of Israel is likened unto a dove . . . just as wings protect the dove, so too the *mitzvot* protect the Jewish people."

It is evident that the dove, which symbolizes the *neshamah,* also symbolizes the Jewish People's efforts to perform *mitzvot* in times of persecution. Since the *neshamah* foresees the obstacles it will face in this world, is it any wonder that it is filled with grief at the prospect of descending to this world?

Furthermore, in reference to the verse, "My dove is in the crevice of the rock, hidden by the cliff" (Song of Songs 2:14), the *Zohar* (vol. 3:61a) states, "'My dove'—this refers to the Congregation of Israel. Just as the dove never abandons its mate, so too, the Congregation of Israel never abandons the Holy One, Blessed is He. 'Hidden by the cliff'—this refers to Torah scholars, who are never at peace in this world," for they are constantly persecuted by their enemies. . . .

The dove is a fitting symbol for the Jewish people and the *neshamah,* since it is the only bird that does not struggle when it is about to be slaughtered. Like the dove, the Jewish People give up their lives without a struggle in order to sanctify the Name of God. The same can be said of the *neshamah*—it disregards its own needs and complies with God's command to descend into this corporeal world. This is the intention of the verse, "Because for Your sake we are killed all the time, we are considered as sheep for slaughter" (Deuteronomy 14:1).

In reference to this self-sacrifice, the *Midrash* states: "Those who love Me and observe My commandments" (Exodus 20:6)—this refers to the Jewish People, who . . . give up their lives for the *mitzvot.* For this reason, the *neshamah* is called "dove" in both the first and second incarnation, regardless of whether it performs good or evil deeds. In the first incarnation, it is "deceived" by the body's physical desires and is therefore called "a gullible dove lacking understanding" (Hosea 7:11). However, if it succeeds in fulfilling its mission during its second incarnation, it earns the appellation "My constant dove, My perfect one" (Song of Songs 6:9).

As mentioned [earlier in this work], this world is likened to a sea, while the World-to-Come is likened to a shore. The metaphor can be understood more clearly by pondering one of the ten questions that Alexander the Great asked the wise men of the Negev: "Where is it better to live? On the sea or on dry land?" The wise men of the Negev answered: "On dry land, for all those who embark on a sea voyage do not feel at ease until they have reached dry land."

There is a deeper dimension to Alexander's question than meets the eye. What he was really asking is whether spiritual existence in the World-to-Come is inherently superior to life in this world, or whether it is only superior in relation to the difficult living conditions experienced by the majority of humanity. Perhaps for a person in his situation—who ruled over the entire known world and to whom every physical desire was within easy reach—life in this world is in fact superior to life in the World-to-Come.

Alexander's question stems from his sharing the viewpoint of a certain non-Jew called Bar Sheishach, who, while up to his neck in a rose bath and wallowing in sensual pleasures, asked the sage Rava: "Is there anything like this in the World-to-Come?" Rava answered him, "Our [portion in the World-to-Come] is even better than this!" The non-Jew retorted, "Nothing can possibly be better than this!"

Rava said to him: "[Yes, it can]. You have the fear of the king upon you, whereas we [in the World-to-Come] will not have the fear of the king upon us."

The non-Jew answered: "Me? Why should I fear the king?" As they sat, an officer of the king approached and said to the man, "Get up! The king has summoned you!" As the man emerged [from his bath], he said to Rava, "May the eyes of all those who await to see the downfall of your people be gouged out!" to which Rava replied: "Amen!" At that exact moment, the man's eye was gouged out (*Avodah Zarah* 65a).

Rava answered that the World-to-Come is inherently superior to this world, and that its pleasures are of a sublime nature which cannot be perceived through human senses. For the joy to be experienced in the World-to-Come exceeds by far the most intense physical pleasure that the human body is able to feel in this world. This is the reason the World-to-Come is not mentioned in Scripture even once. As the sages say, "All the prophets only prophesied about the days of *Mashiach,* but regarding the World-to-Come, it is written, "O God, no eye has seen it but you" (*Berachos* 34b)....We now understand the deeper intention of the wise men of the Negev, who answered Alexander's question so eloquently by saying, "All those who embark on a sea voyage do not feel at ease until they have reached dry land." With these words, they conveyed the message that as long as the *neshamah* is afloat on the tempestuous "sea" that is this world, it cannot experience true serenity—and hence, absolute pleasure—until it comes upon its portion in the World-to-Come—"dry land." Clearly, then, the greatest worldly pleasure cannot even begin to be compared to the spiritual ecstasy of eternal, complete, and utter joy which awaits the *neshamah* in the World-to-Come.

24

THE ALTER REBBE

Schneur Zalman of Liadi

PERHAPS BECAUSE SOME *Hasidic leaders like the Baal Shem Tov wrote no books or treatises, they were accused by rabbinic opponents of not only popularizing Kabbalah to a potentially harmful degree, but also of trivializing and even vulgarizing it. Certainly, however, this accusation could not be effectively leveled against Rabbi Schneur Zalman of Liadi—founder of the Lubavitcher-Chabad Hasidic dynasty. Later known as the Alter Rebbe (Elder Rebbe) to his followers, he was born in mid-eighteenth-century Russia and achieved early renown as a Talmudic prodigy before studying with the Besht's chosen successor, Rabbi Dov Baer of Mezritch. The older teacher encouraged his young disciple—more than thirty-five years his junior—to develop a new code of Jewish Law that would update the work of Rabbi Joseph Karo.*

By this time, Rabbi Schneur Zalman became drawn to a more organized approach to Hasidism than that favored by many zad-dikim across the countryside. He was especially interested in explicitly relating Hasidic precepts to classic Kabbalistic ideas. Encouraged by his mentor, he published in 1797 the first part of his Tanya (It Has Been Taught). The meaning of the title derives from the book's opening word, Tanya, *as Hebrew books were frequently called after their opening phrase. Another name for the complex work is* Likkutei Amarim *(Collected Sayings), whose final parts were added in 1806 and 1814 respectively. Its author called his system Chabad—in abbreviation of the first letters of the two highest sefirot,* chochmah *and* binah, *and their synthesis,* da'at *(knowledge).*

The two excerpts presented here are from the authoritative English translation of the Tanya, *published and distributed by the contemporary Lubavitcher movement. These selections show how the Alter Rebbe viewed the human soul and its relation to the divine.*

In addition, every divine soul (*nefesh elokit*) possesses three garments: namely, thought, speech, and action [expressing themselves] in the 613 commandments of the Torah. For, when a person *actively* fulfills all the precepts which require physical action, and with his power of *speech* he occupies himself in expounding all the 613 commandments and their practical applications, and with his power of *thought* he comprehends all that is comprehensible to him in the *Padres* of the Torah—then the totality of the 613 "organs" of his soul are clothed in the 613 commandments of the Torah.

Specifically, the faculties of ChaBaD in his soul are clothed in the comprehension of the Torah, which he comprehends in *Pardes,* to the extent of his mental capacity and the supernal root of his soul. And the *middot*—namely, fear and love—together with their offshoots and ramifications, are clothed in the fulfillment of the commandments in deed and in Torah, namely, in the study of Torah which is "the equivalent of all the commandments" (*Mishnah, Peah* 1:1). For love is the root of all the 248 positive commands, all originating in it and having no true foundation without it, inasmuch as he fulfills them in truth, he truly loves the name of G-d and desires to cleave to Him in truth; for one cannot truly cleave to Him except through the fulfillment of the 248 commandments which are the 248 "Organs of the King" as it were, as is explained elsewhere; whilst fear is the root of the 365 prohibitive commands, fearing to rebel against the Supreme King of kings, the Holy One,

Blessed Be He; or a still deeper fear than this—when he feels *ashamed* in the presence of the Divine greatness to rebel against His glory and do what is evil in His eyes, namely, any of the abominable things hated by G-d—which are the *kelipot* and *sitra acha*—which draw their nurture from man below and have their hold in him through the 365 prohibitive commands [that he violates].

Now these three "garments," deriving from the Torah and its commandments, although they are called "garments" of the *nefesh, ruach,* and *neshamah,* their quality, nevertheless, is infinitely higher and greater than that of the *nefesh, ruach,* and *neshamah* themselves, as explained in the *Zohar,* because the Torah and the Holy One, blessed be He, are one. The meaning of this is that the Torah—which is the wisdom and will of the Holy One, blessed be He, and His glorious Essence are one, since He is both the Knower and the Knowledge, and so on, as explained above in the name of Maimonides. And although the Holy One, blessed be He, is called *Ein Sof* ("Infinite") and "His greatness can never be fathomed," and "No thought can apprehend Him at all," and so are also His will and His wisdom, as it is written: "There is no searching of His understanding" and "Canst thou by searching find G-d?" and again: "For My thoughts are not your thoughts"—nevertheless, it is in this connection that it has been said: "Where you find the greatness of the Holy one, blessed be He, there you also find His humility."

For the Holy One, blessed be He, has compressed His will and wisdom within the 613 commandments of the Torah, and in their laws, as well as within the combination of the letters of the Torah, the books of the Prophets and the Hagiographa, and in the exposition thereof which are to be found in the *agadot* and *midrashim* of our rabbis of blessed memory. All this in order that each *neshamah,* or *ruach* and *nefesh* in the human body should be able to comprehend them through its faculty of understanding, and to fulfill them, as far as they can be fulfilled, in act, speech, and thought—thereby clothing itself with all its ten faculties in these three garments.

Therefore has the Torah been compared to water, for just as water descends from a higher to a lower level, so has the Torah descended from its place of glory, which is His blessed will and wisdom; [for] the Torah has progressively descended through hidden stages, stage after stage, with the descent of the worlds, until it clothed itself in corporeal substances and in things of this world—comprising almost all of the commandments of the Torah, their laws, and in the combinations of material letters—written with ink in a book, namely the twenty-four volumes of the Torah, Prophets, and Hagiographa; all this in order that every thought should be able to apprehend them, and even the faculties of speech and action, which are on a lower level than thought, should be able to apprehend them and be clothed in them.

Thus, since the Torah and its commandments "clothe" all ten faculties of the soul with its 613 organs from head to foot, it [the soul] is altogether truly bound up in the Bundle of Life with G-d, and the very light of G-d envelops and clothes it from head to foot, as it is written, "G-d is my Rock, I will take refuge *in Him*," and it is also written, "With favor [*ratzon* = will] wilt Thou compass him as with a shield," that is to say, with His blessed will and wisdom which are clothed in his Torah and its commandments.

Hence it has been said: "Better is one hour of *teshuvah* and *mitzvot* in this world than the whole life of the World-to-Come." For, the World-to-Come is that state where one enjoys the effulgence of the Divine Presence, which is the pleasure of comprehension, yet no created being—even celestial—can comprehend more than some reflection of the Divine Light; that is why the reference is to "Effulgence of the Divine Presence" (*Ziv ha-Shekinah*). But as for the essence of the Holy One, blessed be He, no thought can apprehend Him at all, except when it apprehends, and is clothed in, the Torah and its *mitzvot*; only then does it truly apprehend, and is clothed in, the Holy One, blessed be He, inasmuch as the Torah and the Holy One, blessed be He, are one and the same.

For although the Torah has been clothed in lower material things, it is by way of illustration, like embracing the king. There is no difference in regard to the degree of closeness and attachment to the king, whether while embracing the king the latter is then wearing one robe or several robes, so long as the royal person is in them. Likewise, when the king, for his part, embraces one with his arm, even though it is dressed in his robes; as it is written, "And His right hand embraces me," which refers to the Torah which was given by G-d's right hand, which is the quality of *chesed* and water.

The real truth, however, is that there are two souls, waging war one against the other in the person's mind, each one wishing and desiring to rule over him exclusively. Thus all thoughts of Torah and the fear of Heaven come from the divine soul, while all mundane matters come from the animal soul, except that the divine soul is clothed in it. This is like the example of a person praying with devotion, while facing him there stands a wicked heathen who chats and speaks to him in order to confuse him. Surely the thing to do in such a case would not be to answer him good or evil, but rather to pretend to be deaf without hearing, and to comply with the verse, "Answer not a fool according to his folly, lest thou also be like onto him."

Similarly, he must answer nothing, nor engage in any argument and counterargument with the foreign thought, for he who wrestles with a filthy person is bound to become soiled himself. Rather, should he adopt an attitude as if he neither knows nor hears the thoughts that have befallen him; he must remove them from his mind and strengthen still more the power of his concentration. However, if he finds it hard to dismiss them from his mind, because they distract his mind with great intensity, then he should humble his spirit before G-d and supplicate Him in his thought to have compassion upon Him in His abundant mercies, as a father who takes pity on his children who stem from his brain; so may the Lord have pity on his soul which is derived from Him Who is blessed, and deliver it from the "turbulent waters"; for His sake He will do it, for verily "His people is a part of the Lord."

25

CHAIM VOLOZHIN

THE MOST IMPORTANT *disciple of the Vilna Gaon was Chaim ben Yitzchak of Volozhin, Belarus—known today as Chaim Volozhin, or the Volozhiner. Several years after becoming the city's rabbi at the remarkable age of twenty, he came to study with the famed "Genius of Vilna" in a close relationship that ended only with the latter's death in 1797. The Gaon exerted a tremendous influence on his eager young student, who later as founder of the Volozhin Yeshiva in 1802, put into practice many of his mentor's key notions about revitalizing higher Jewish education. The Volozhiner's goal was to create an institution that would provide the best rabbinic students of the country with comfortable housing, regular meals, and rigorous classes taught in a dignified, systematic, and orderly fashion. For nearly a century until its closing by the czar for alleged subversiveness, the Volozhin Yeshiva was the preeminent yeshiva academy in Belarus, and perhaps, in all Eastern Europe.*

Like his illustrious mentor, Rabbi Chaim Volozhin was committed to careful analysis of both Talmud and Kabbalah. In particular, he viewed the Zohar as an essential text—adding both insight and profundity to Jewish belief and observance. In this regard, the Volo-

zhiner's most important work is Nefesh HaChaim *(Spirit of Life), which probed topics such as prayer, contemplation, and Torah study from an esoteric perspective.*

Unlike his fiercely uncompromising mentor, Rabbi Chaim Volozhin espoused a conciliatory attitude toward Hasidism, which he viewed as far less threatening to Jewish religiosity in the modern era. These two selections are from Ruach Chaim, *the Volozhiner's influential commentary on* Pirkey Avot *(Ethics of the Fathers). They show his penchant for drawing upon Kabbalistic works, especially the* Zohar, *in presenting central principles of Judaism.*

> "Know what is above you: a seeing eye, a hearing ear, and all your deeds are recorded in a book."
>
> —PIRKEY AVOT 2:1

Even if you have acquired a good reputation in this world, realize that Hashem's opinion of you is what really matters. Strive to acquire a good reputation in the upper spheres.

This comment can be understood in a deeper sense. Hashem created myriad worlds, one beneath the other, culminating in our world. When He wills so, a flow of pure spirituality enters the uppermost world and filters down through the various worlds. As the flow descends, it gradually takes on a physical form until it reaches our world as the physical manifestation of the spiritual flow. Anything that affects one of these worlds will have a ripple effect on all the worlds below it, for each world acts as the source of stimuli and sustenance for the world beneath it. Although the individual resides in the lowest world, the root of his soul is in the highest worlds. Any action he takes, therefore, has a direct effect on the uppermost spheres, which have a ripple effect on the other worlds, whether for better or for worse.

Know what is above you. That is, know that what exists above results from your actions below. Every sight that you see, every sound that you hear, affects the uppermost worlds. All your deeds are automatically inscribed in a "book," as they manifest themselves in the upper worlds as either construction or destruction. Any improvements that you have wrought through your *mitzvot* will be your reward in the World-to-Come. Any damage that you have caused requires repair, either through *teshuvah* or personal suffering in this world or the next. Even a mindless or unintentional sin causes damage which needs to be repaired.

If a person commits a capital crime, the king can commute his sentence, but if he ingests poison, even unintentionally, the king cannot save him. The *Mishnah* warns us to be exceedingly careful, for sinning is like ingesting poison, and the only two antidotes available are *teshuvah* and personal suffering. It in this vein that Rav Chanina stated that anyone who says that Hashem forgoes punishing sin has forfeited his life (*Bava Kamma* 50a). In short, if one thinks that Hashem will allow any sin to go unrectified, he has forfeited his life, for the damage has been done and must be repaired. Interestingly, the Midrash quotes Rav Chanina as saying, "Anyone who says that Hashem forgoes punishing sin has forfeited his innards." This comment fits very nicely with the comparison of sin to poison. For if one does not do *teshuvah,* the poison of sin will destroy his innards. Hashem is not going to change the design of the world just to spare one person the effort of fixing the harm he has wrought.

"The world was created with ten utterances."

—PIRKEY AVOT 5:1

The *Zohar* explains that Hashem created myriad worlds. He caused to exist amongst them the power of evil—this power which recognizes Hashem and purposely rebels. When people perform the will of Hashem, they weaken this evil and can eventually destroy it. In the upper worlds, there is no hint of evil at all. Somewhat below, the evil becomes apparent, but it has no power at all. In the lower worlds, there is a slight inclination toward evil, and finally in our world, the power of evil becomes overwhelming. The individual can fight this power because he possesses a soul.

The soul is a repository of the highest worlds, even higher than the angels. It is this soul that is capable of fighting evil. Through the individual's good deeds, the power of evil will slowly diminish until it is totally eradicated. Thus, the entire purpose in the creation of evil is to give us the opportunity to destroy it. We will then be rewarded for our efforts.

King David alluded to this idea. "When the wicked flower like grass and all the doers of iniquity blossom, it is to destroy them forever. You raised my pride like a *re'eim*. The righteous will bloom like a date palm" (Psalms 92). Why does Hashem permit the existence of evil? The response is apparent. In order that we should destroy it and receive our reward.

One should not think that he is an independent entity whose righteousness or wickedness affects only himself. As a composite of all the worlds, the individual is analogous to the midpoint of a huge circle. If the midpoint is moved slightly, the circumference of the circle will change dramatically. Any good deed which a person does reduces the power of evil within him and exponentially reduces the power of evil in all the worlds. Any evil deed will have the opposite effect.

The Torah alludes to the individual's power with Hashem's declarations, "Let us make man" (*Bereshit* 1:26). Let us create a creature who is a blend of all our powers. "He blew into his nostrils a living soul, and man became a living soul" (ibid. 2:7). The expression "man became" seems inappropriate; "it became in man" would seem a better choice. The Torah is alluding here to the human individual's power. As a composite of all the upper worlds, he acts as the soul for all these powers. As the individual rises and ebbs, so do all the upper worlds.

If one would approach the basest of persons and suggest that his sins are worse than those of Titus and Nebuchadnezzar, the accused would be furious. Nevertheless, this accusation is true. Although Titus and Nebuchadnezzar destroyed the Temple of Jerusalem in this world, they had no impact on the upper spheres. They were capable only of destroying the earthly Temple after its parallel, celestial Temple was destroyed through the sins of the Jewish people. Asaf prayed, "May it be considered as if they brought axes in the thicket of trees Above" (Psalms 74:5). The psalmist requested that they be punished as if they had wielded their axes Above, although in fact they did not.

Man is a composite of all the worlds and contains the holiness of those worlds. Man's heart is the repository of his holiness, just as the Holy of Holies is the most sacred part of the Temple of Jerusalem. It is in this vein that the Talmud says that one should direct his heart toward the Holy of Holies while praying (*Berachos* 30a). . . . When one does *teshuvah,* he not only improves himself, but he improves the upper worlds as well.

"*Teshuvah* is so great that it reaches to the Throne of Glory."
—YOMA 86A

Hashem created the world with ten utterances. The first utterance resulted in a hint of the material, the second assumed a greater measure. This measure of physicality continued to grow until the last utterance, "I have given you . . . all green vegetables to eat" (*Bereshit* 1:29–30). This final utterance is totally physical. King David alluded to this notion with the ten expressions of praise in Psalms 150. The first expression is, "Praise Hashem in His holy place," in the highest spheres, the world of the angels. The last expression is, "Praise Him with blazing trumpets," which represents our physical world. The sound of the shofar is either a long, drawn-out sob or several short cries (*Rosh HaShanah* 33b). Both of these sounds are found in this world. King David, therefore, is instructing us to praise Hashem on all levels of creation, from spirituality to physicality.

26

ELIEZER PAPO OF SARAJEVO

HISTORICALLY, THE CITY *of Sarajevo, in Bosnia, was home for centuries to a dynamic Jewish community, and among its greatest figures was Rabbi Eliezer Papo. Few details have survived about his personal life, though scholars believe that his father was a pietistic rabbi who provided his son with a comprehensive Jewish education. He served congregations in Sarajevo and then Silistra, a small community in Bulgaria near the Romanian border.*

Influenced by the Jerusalem-born Rabbi Chaim Yosef David Azulai (known as the Chida), Eliezer Papo was likewise interested in applying the Kabbalah to the social dimensions of family, friendship, and community. Though he wrote several books comprising such topics as Torah commentary, Talmudic commentary, and Jewish law, Rabbi Papo's most influential work by far was Pele Yoetz (Wondrous Advisor), first published in 1824 Constantinople. Filled with allusions to the Zohar and other classic esoteric texts, its aim was to provide moral guidance and practical advice on subjects like gossip and quarreling, jealousy, and anger, with a constant loving eye toward harmonious marriage and parenting. With an

optimistic, encouraging style, Pele Yoetz from the outset proved
highly popular among Sephardic Jews—resonating well with their
cultural values of convivial family life, friendship, and joyful reli-
gious practice. These excerpts reveal Rabbi Papo's viewpoint on a
variety of daily issues facing individual Jews, ranging from Kabbal-
istic study and teshuvah *to strategies for inner growth.*

SACRED STUDY

The study of *Zohar* is very lofty, purifying, and sanctifying. Read it
regularly even if you do not understand the text. Our sages compare this to a baby who is learning to speak. His parents derive great
pleasure from his efforts even if he does not understand what he is
saying. God similarly derives pleasure when a Jew reads the holy
texts, even if he does not fully comprehend them.

Those who can grasp the *Zohar*'s profound teachings will find its
wise words sweeter than honey, drawing the heart closer to God.

Arrange a regular schedule daily to study such texts as the *Mishnah,* the Psalms, and the holy *Zohar* on the Torah portions of the
week. This will help to control the *yezer hara* and to avoid wasting
time. Study slowly. It is more beneficial to cover less ground with the
proper concentration than a lot of material in a distracted fashion.

While studying the *Zohar,* remember that there are hidden meanings in all matters, and that we are unable to comprehend it all.

SACRED IMAGES

It is very helpful to visualize certain images in your mind.

Rabbi Yitzhak Luria said that one should visualize the Name of
God spelled out in Hebrew letters, vocalized with the vowels of
the word *yirah* [fear]. This is a way of fulfilling the verse: "I will set
the Lord before me always" (Psalms 16:8).

The Talmud teaches that you should imagine yourself to be
standing before the Divine Presence while praying (*Sanhedrin* 22a).

Whenever you are tempted to commit an *avarah,* visualize yourself as being before God.

The Kabbalists write that constantly seeing the image of your rabbi is helpful for attaining wisdom. Those who engage in Kabbalah are well aware of the effectiveness of imagination, contemplation, and thought. The power of prophecy and spiritual perfection is dependent on the capacity to envision. The Talmud tells of four sages who entered the orchard (the world of mystical speculation). Their subsequent experiences were relative to the depth of their thought and their ability to create mental images (*Hagigah* 14b).

The state of your soul is directly dependent on where you focus your thoughts. Happy is the person who chooses to approach the inner sanctum! He who comports himself with sanctity in the physical world will be sanctified in the spiritual realm.

TESHUVAH (RETURNING TO THE SOURCE)

Teshuvah applies to each day of your life. The holy *Zohar* taught that before going to sleep each night, you should review your deeds of the day. If you realize that you committed an *avarah,* confess it, feel regret, and resolve to correct it. It is best to do *teshuvah* immediately. As an analogy, it is much easier to wipe off wet ink than to erase ink that has already dried. If you do not do *teshuvah* on the same day, then at least do so on the Friday of that week since Friday is also a time for *teshuvah.* Indeed, by accepting thoughts of *teshuvah* on Friday, you will recite the Kiddush with holiness and be able to receive the additional spirit of the Sabbath. The spirit of sanctity will carry over to the entire week. Before accepting Shabbat, recite words of *teshuvah* and supplication and immerse in a *mikva.*

The eve of *Rosh Hodesh* (New Month) is also a time to do *teshuvah* for *avairot* committed during the previous month. Many pious people fast on the eve of *Rosh Hodesh* and this day has therefore become known as "Little Yom Kippur."

If you have been spiritually asleep throughout the year, you have the chance to awaken yourself during the month of Elul and the Ten Days of Penitence. This is the time when God sits in judgment. Happy are the Jewish people! Most of them arise early to recite the penitential prayers and increase their Torah study.

STRATEGY FOR SPIRITUAL GROWTH

"For with strategy will you wage war" (Proverbs 24:6).

People devise numerous clever plans to increase their wealth and honor. They would be better off devising strategies to fight the *yezer hara*.

The *yezer hara* diligently attempts to prevent people from studying Torah. It is like a fire, and we are but flesh and blood. How can we overcome it?

My advice is to devise a military type of strategy against it. Give the enemy a false sense of security by making believe that you are not interested in fighting. When it is off guard, attack and destroy it. King David said each day, "I am going to such and such a place." He tricked the *yezer hara* into thinking that he was actually going there; and then he went to the House of Study.

As soon as you make a good resolution, act on it, or make a vow to fulfill it as soon as possible.

Our sages suggested an important strategy: engage in Torah study and in the performance of *mitzvot* even if not for their own sake, but for an ulterior motive. Ultimately, you will observe them for their own sake (*Peshahim* 50b).

The Torah is an antidote to the *yezer hara*. The *mitzvot* clarify one's vision. Devise your own strategies for defeating the *yezer hara*. God will help you to purify yourself.

THE POWER OF RESPECT

Do not treat anyone in this world with disdain. Everyone is a creation of God.

Conversely, do not be upset if others treat you disrespectfully. Remain silent rather than entering into an argument, and believe that your antagonist was sent by God. You should actually rejoice at the fact that God chose to correct you so lightly. A great honor was accorded to you by Heaven by cleansing you of your *avairot*.

Do not humiliate anyone who has benefited you in the slightest way. Our sages taught that food should not be treated with disrespect (*Berakhot* 50b), and that you should not throw a stone into a well from which you drew water (*Bava Kama* 92b). Moses did not bring the plagues from the river or from the earth, since both had once been helpful to him. You should clearly love anyone who has treated you kindly.

Control your temper and do not plan revenge even if someone hits you. Vengefulness is an *avarah* which will run against your interests, and your silence will be rewarded.

ANGER

Anger is a terrible, damaging sensation which must be controlled. Fine yourself each time you lose your temper and try to control what you say, speaking softly and calmly. Silence at times of anger is like water on fire.

Life is fleeting and few things warrant your anger.

THE SECRETS OF TORAH

The study of the secrets of the Torah is more profound than all other studies. The fortunate person whom God has blessed with the wisdom to fathom Kabbalah can fulfill the *mitzvot,* recite his prayers, and study Torah according to their mystical meanings. It is impossible to explain how wonderful that spiritual attainment is.

One who lacks this insight is unfortunate, but God, of course, does not expect a person to delve into studies that are beyond his understanding.

Every Torah scholar who has comprehensively studied the Talmud and Jewish law should turn to the study of Kabbalah and suffer any hardship to attain this wisdom.

Even if you are unable to delve deeply into Kabbalah, study the mystical works explaining the prayers, blessings, and *mitzvot*. Your heart will then burn with recognition of the profundity of these matters.

Even a cursory study of Kabbalistic works will give you a glimpse of God's greatness, the evil of an *avarah,* and the spiritual value of joyfully fulfilling *mitzvot.* It has been stated that one who has not tasted the wisdom of Kabbalah has not tasted the fear of *avairot* and cannot be a complete servant of God.

Nothing is outside the province of Kabbalah. It has lessons about the spiritual dimensions of the most mundane activities, such as eating, drinking, and sexual relations in marriage. Even if you do not understand those meanings, follow the practice of saintly people who do understand.

27

NACHMAN OF BRESLOV

AMONG THE BEST-KNOWN *Hasidic founders is Rabbi Nachman of Breslov. As the Baal Shem Tov's great-grandson, he was regarded as destined to be an important leader of the Hasidim. At an early age, Nachman became drawn to the beauty of nature as a divine manifestation, and spent long hours in solitary prayer and, rather unusual for European village Jews, in countryside meditations. While still in his teens, he began to experience visions and present talks on higher states of consciousness.*

Though steeped in the Kabbalah, Rabbi Nachman's ideas were bold and unorthodox, for he stressed heartfelt dialogue with God and daily meditation as the key to inner development. Late in life, he began telling stories to his followers. "People may be asleep all their lives," he observed, "but through tales told by a true zaddik *(holy one), they can be awakened." In the world of his stories, exiled kings and lost princesses, hidden treasures and stormy seas, undaunted heroes and saintly beggars, shipwrecked sailors and madmen all symbolize in some way our situation on earth. Most of the tales were recorded in an obviously garbled manner, for their author*

*did not write any of them down. But they continue to provide
inspiration to many.*

*With Rabbi Nachman's emphasis on the vast, creative depths of
the human soul, it is hardly surprising that he prized dreams as a
valuable source of guidance. In this regard, his viewpoint was consistent with the Zohar and subsequent Kabbalists like Solomon
Almoli, Moses Cordovero, and Chaim Vital. As most of Rabbi
Nachman's followers lacked training in Kabbalistic meditation,
he recommended the highly accessible realms of music and dreams
for attaining higher direction.*

*These selections are taken from Rabbi Nachman's dream diary,
for he gave careful attention to his own dreams.*

In my thirty-seventh year, on the first night of Chanukah, after the
lighting of the candle, I had this dream:

A stranger came and asked me, "How do you make your living?"
and I said, "My livelihood is not located in my home, it comes to me
from outside." He asked me, "What do you study?" and I told him,
and we began to speak of Torah. We began to speak like friends with
things that issue from the heart and I began to yearn and to muse,
"How does one reach any rung in holiness?" and my guest said, "I
will teach you." I began to think, perhaps he is not a human being.

So I sat and thought how he spoke to me like a human being
but then immediately my faith in him became strengthened, and I
called him, "Master, Rebbe," and I said to him, "Before I begin
anything else, I want to know how to honor you properly, so that
I will not not come to injure the proper honor due to you, for a
plain human being would not know what to do. Therefore, I want
you to teach me how to honor you properly." He said to me, "I
have no time now, I will come another time and teach you this."
So, I said to him, "Even this I must learn from you. How far must
I accompany you?" And he said to me, "Up to the door."

I thought in my mind, "I do not know him, and I do not know
who he is," so I said to him, "I am afraid to go with you." He said
to me, "Why are you afraid? Do I not sit and teach you? If I wanted

to harm you, who would have stopped me?" And so, I began to walk him to the door. Then he took hold of me and caused me to fly high and I felt cold. He gave me a garment and said to me, "Take this garment and you will feel good. You will have food and drink, and all will be good, and you will sit in your home."

Suddenly, I saw that I was at home. I did not believe it myself, and I looked around, and I saw that I was speaking to people. I was eating and drinking like any other human being, and then, suddenly, I see myself flying in the air as before.

I sat and saw again that I am at home, and so, back and forth between home and flying above in the air. Then he brought me down into a valley between two mountains. There I found a book. In that book, there were all kinds of connections of Hebrew letters, illustrations of vessels. And the vessels themselves were letters. Inside the vessels were more letters. With these letters that were inside the vessels, one could make such vessels.

I wanted to study this book. I began to see that I was again at home, so I returned and found myself once more again in the valley. I decided to go up on the mountain path, so that I would find some settled place.

As I ascended the mountain, I saw a golden tree with branches of gold. From the branches hung all sorts of vessels that were like those depicted in the book. Inside of these vessels were other vessels that were made out of these vessels and the letters in them. So I wanted to take the vessels from there and I couldn't, because the thicket did not permit me to get through.

Then I saw myself again in the house, and it was amazing to me that I was sometimes here and sometimes there. I wanted to tell of this amazing thing to the people, but how can you tell them such a thing, which is impossible to believe? I looked through the window, and I saw my guest. I importuned him to enter, and he said to me, "I have no time, for I am going to you." I said to him, "Even this is an amazing thing, for I am here. What does it mean that you are on your way to me?"

He said, "The hour when you decided to come with me and

accompany me to the door, I took your soul from you and gave her a garment from the lower garden of Eden. All that remained of you was *nefesh* (lower soul of the physical body) and *ruach* (spirit), while I had taken your *neshamah* (higher soul). Therefore, when you raise your thought up to there, that is why you are there, and you receive your illumination from there. When you return here, then you are here." And all this I saw, but I did not know from which world he was, but I decided that he truly was from the good world. And the story has not yet been completed, nor has it found its end.

In the winter of his 38th year, the Bratslaver recounted this dream to us: I am sitting in my house and no one enters. The thing so amazed me, I went into the two other rooms and there was no one there. So I went outside and I saw that people were standing in circles and whispering about me. This one is mocking me and this one winks knowingly in my direction, and this one laughs and this one shows arrogance against me, and so forth. Even among those who were my Hasidim there were some who were against me. Some of them looked at me with scorn and whispered against me.

I called one of my men and asked him, "What is this?" He answered me, "How could you have done such a thing, how could you have done such an awful sin?" I did not know at all what they were talking about, and why they were making fun of me, so I looked for that man that he should go and gather a group of my people. When he came back, I considered what to do. I decided to travel to a different country. I came there, and even there, there were people standing in circles and whispering about me. Even they had gotten to know the thing. So I went and sat down in some forest. Five of my Hasidim came with me. They sat with me, we sat there, and as we needed something to eat, we sent one of the men to buy it. So I asked him, did they already stop making all that noise against me? He said that the tumult was as great as it was before.

An old man came and said to me that he wanted to speak to me. I went with him and he said, "How could you do such a thing? Are you not ashamed before your ancestors, your grandfather Reb

Nachman, your grandfather the Baal Shem Tov? Why aren't you ashamed before the Torah of Moses and the holy forefathers, Abraham, Isaac, and Jacob? What do you think, you will continue to stay here? You can't stay here always, and finally, you will not have any more money and you are a weak man. What will you do? Do you think you can go to another country? Consider, either they know who you are, or they will have heard of your deed. If they don't know who you are, you will not be able to earn your keep."

So I said, "Well, if it is so, then what am I to do? Will I have a portion in the World-to-Come?" He said, "Do you think that they will still give you a portion in the World-to-Come? Even hell is not sufficient for you to hide there, for you have a caused a great desecration of the Name of God." I replied, "Go away, here I thought that you would console me and speak to my heart, and you bring me such pain, go away."

The old man went away. I feared that since I have been here for a long time, I might forget what I have learned, so I looked for the man whom I sent to buy provisions and also get a book for me. He went and could not bring me a book. It was impossible for him to get any book without telling me that it was I who needed the book. So I had great pains that I am not only in exile, but that I do not have a book, and that I am bound to forget all my studies.

The old man came and brought a book, and I asked him, "What have you got in your hand?" And he said, "A book," and I said to him, "Could you please lend me the book?" He gave it to me and I took it, and I did not even understand how to hold the book. I opened it and I couldn't even understand the meaning of the words, for it was to me like a strange language in a foreign script. The thing caused me great pain. I was afraid for my own people that if they were to recognize I cannot even read a book, they, too, would leave me.

So the old man called me to come so that he could speak to me again. And again he began to upbraid me for having committed such a grave sin without being ashamed and even in hell there would not be a place to hide, and I said to him: "If one of the souls from the higher world would have told me such a thing, I would believe him." He said to me, "I am from there," and he proved to me that he was from there. Then I remembered the story of the Baal Shem Tov, who, too, had thought at one point that he had lost his portion in the World-to-Come, and he had said:

"I love Him whose Name be blessed, even without reward in the World-to-Come."

And I cast my head backward with great bitterness, and as I cast my head backward, there gathered about me all the great people, and the old man said to me that I should be ashamed before them, before my grandfather and all the forefathers. And they said to me the sentence, "The fruit of the earth is for beauty and for pride." They said to me, "We are very proud of you." And they brought to me all my people and children. All of them consoled me greatly. With such great bitterness had I cast my head back, that even he who had transgressed the entire Torah would have been forgiven for it. And the rest of the good I don't tell you, though it truly was good.

One I saw in my dream that I woke up in a forest which is endless and I wanted to return. One came to me and said, "In this forest, one can never come to its end for it is so long that it is infinite and all the instruments and vessels of this world are made from this forest." He showed me a way to get out of the forest. This way brought me to a river. I wanted to come to the end of the river. A man came and said, "It is impossible to cross the river, for the river is boundless. All the people of this world drink from the source of this river." But then he showed me a way how to go out through the river.

Then I came into a mill which stood at the side of the river, and someone came and said to me, "Here is ground the food for all the people of the world." And I again entered into the forest where I saw a smith working, and entered the smithy, and they told me, "This smith makes vessels for the whole world."

It was Yom Kippur and I dreamed. It was very clear to me at that time that in Heaven every Yom Kippur they demand one person's life as a sacrifice. I volunteered. They said to me that I must put it in writing. So I wrote and signed. Then they wanted to offer me up as a sacrifice. I had regrets and wanted to hide. But I saw that a large group of people had gathered around to witness the sacrifice, and I could not hide. So I sought to go out of the city. But as I left the city, I noticed that I had just returned.

So I entered into the city and I wanted to hide among the non-Jews. I thought that if they were to come and search for me, they would surrender me to be sacrificed. But then there was another *zaddik* who agreed to be a sacrifice in my place. Nevertheless, I am still afraid for the future.

28

The Netziv

Naftali Tzvi Yehudah Berlin

As the nineteenth century *advanced with the appearance of such technological marvels as the steam engine and locomotive, Hasidism in Eastern Europe remained a bastion of the Kabbalah. Yet, following the staunch position of the venerated Vilna Gaon, the Mitnaggedim also continued to uphold the esoteric tradition as timelessly valid and relevant. They rejected Hasidim not for embracing works like the Zohar and its esteemed commentaries, but for two other main reasons: seemingly demeaning Talmudic study and deifying their rebbes in a manner echoing the disastrous messianic cult of Shabbatai Zevi.*

Among the most influential proponents of this position was Rabbi Naftali Tzvi Yehudah Berlin. Known as the Netziv in Hebrew acronym of his name, he served for forty years as head of the famous yeshiva in Volozhin, Belarus. Opened in 1803 by Rabbi Chaim Itzkowitz—the Vilna Gaon's greatest disciple—it became the "mother" of all Mitnagged yeshivot. Soon after marrying Rabbi Itzkowitz's granddaughter, the young Netziv enrolled in rabbinic study there, and in the mid-1850s became its charismatic director; reportedly, he often postponed his scheduled Talmudic lec-

tures by announcing, "My friends, I have nothing new to tell you. Upon reflection, everything that I prepared for today's lecture is in reality worthless!"

As head of the Volozhin Yeshiva, the Netziv received requests throughout the Jewish world to make halachic rulings, which came to be renowned for their clarity and precision. Many concerned essentially ordinary issues of inheritance, property ownership, or commerce. But in 1887, his rabbinic judgment was requested from the far-off Holy Land on the transcendental subject of the afterlife. His responsum, later published in a posthumous volume, presents in a new, scientific era, the classic, Kabbalistically influenced view.

Regarding a person who was known as a *zaddik* among his associates in the town of Tiberias, in the Holy Land: He sold half of his portion in the World-to-Come for a large sum of money—totaling 22,000 rubles—to a wealthy Jewish merchant who lived simply and wanted to buy the *zaddik's* reward in the World-to-Come for having fulfilled the holy commandments. The seller had already accepted half of the money. But before he was paid the second half, the wealthy merchant went to a local sage and discussed the purchase he had made.

Thereupon, the second man asked for guidance in a dream, and was told from above that the seller was not regarded so highly in the World-to-Come, but rather, was considered just an ordinary Jew. Once the wealthy merchant heard this information, he demanded that the seller cancel their agreement and return all the money he had already received. The seller immediately refused, and demanded the second half of his promised money.

And now the question has come to me: What is the *halacha,* and whether or not the very concept of such types of sales has any substance whatsoever. May God enlighten my eyes!

Firstly, the seller has already demonstrated that he is not a befitting person from the very fact that he sold his spiritual reward for mere money. This is like the characteristic of Esau who sold his birthright—for which the Bible denigrates him for his actions. As it says: "And Esau disparaged the birthright" (Genesis 25:34). Esau was not criticized because he sold [his birthright in exchange for lentils], for the Rashbam [a prominent medieval commentator] explained that Esau already received a worthy sum of money. Rather the lentils were only the specific object used to formalize the acquisition (while money also was given), and therefore the verse ascribes the term "and he denigrated."

One whose mind is lucid and truly comprehends will understand that there is no value placed on the spiritual that it can be sold even for great fortune in this world. . . . This is comparable to one whom the King honored with a medal and he sold it to someone else: such a man denigrates the honor of the King and is worthy of punishment. . . .

And now let's deal with the essence of the question: is there any substance to such a sale? First, it seems right to explain the difference between the reward for learning Torah and for performing the commandments. Afterward, I will return to the matter of which we were speaking. . . .

There are two types of reward. One type involves a particular service for the country which the King found praiseworthy: such a person will be rewarded with a medal. A second type involves one who works arduously in wars for the King—such a person will be exalted to a higher position in the army.

These two forms of reward are not equal. In the first case, anyone can accept the symbol of recognition, and there is not added effort necessary to accept it. However, for the reward in the second case, not any person is fit to accept it. For the King of the army is expected to be wise and knowledgable, offering relevant advice at the general's meetings before the King. And someone who, in truth, is really a simpleton, would not accept the promotion to general, for he would not risk sitting in silence during the meeting, which would result in more embarrassment than honor. . . .

Such, in a similar vein, is the difference between the reward for performing the commandments versus the reward for learning the Torah. The reward for peforming the commandments is comparable to the reward of a simple villager, and any Jew is able to accept such a reward—as opposed to the reward for learning Torah, where one sits in the heavenly yeshiva, and one who is unworthy for such a position will not be able to properly accept the spiritual enjoyment from such. . . .

And now we can return to our discussion. Even if one were to consider selling his reward in the World-to-Come for fulfilling the commandments, it is impossible to sell the reward accrued for learning Torah. . . . For is it possible to think that if the King were to honor someone by appointing him general and advisor during times of war, that such a person would go ahead and *sell* his position to someone else? The king does not desire the presence of the purchaser at all! And he does not desire one [who purchased such a position] to sit among the King's leaders.

Similarly, it is impossible in any instance for one to even contemplate selling his rewards for waging "the wars of Torah." And, therefore in our case, where he sold half of his reward, and the reward for learning the Torah, as mentioned, cannot be sold, it therefore must be that the sale is void.

After clarifying this, we must explain the ruling of the Ramah— Rabbi Moshe Isserles of Cracow in *Yoreh De'ah* (responsum #246)—who states that one is allowed to make a stipulation with his friend that he will learn Torah and the other will provide financial sustenance, and together, they will split the reward. This situation is allowed specifically in a case where the financer is the one who established the harmonious situation, so that his friend is able to be involved completely in learning Torah . . . but Torah *which has already been learned,* and the Torah which could have been learned without the added financial stability certainly cannot be included in such a stipulation. And an added point is that, based on the aforementioned points, the stipulation can only be applied to one who is involved in learning Torah and not just fulfilling the commandments.

For to make a stipulation regarding the reward for fulfilling the commandments is not even necessary, for we have already learned that one who helps a person fulfill a commandment—it is as he fulfilled it himself, as opposed to the study of Torah. For one who helps another learn Torah is not comparable to the actual person who learned it; therefore, specifically in regard to Torah study is such a stipulation necessary. And in truth, with such a stipulation, it diminishes a little the honor of one who is involved in learning Torah and it exalts the honor of he who facilitated the learning— until both of them sit together in the heavenly yeshiva, and rejoice in the presence of God.

29

THE BEN ISH CHAI

Yosef Chaim of Baghdad

THOUGH MANY *nineteenth-century European teachers of Kabbalah—especially Hasidim—remain prominent today, comparatively few Westerners are familiar with the life and work of Rabbi Yosef Chaim of Baghdad. Commonly known as the* Ben Ish Chai, *the title of his most famous work, he is revered as Sephardic Jewry's greatest religious figure of the past two centuries. Becoming Baghdad's chief rabbi at the incredible age of twenty-five following his father's death in 1859 while occupying this position, the* Ben Ish Chai *was an unparalleled* halachic *expert, whose decisions in Jewish law remain studied today, especially by Sephardim. He was also an impassioned Kabbalist, offering inspiring teachings through writings and* drashot *(Torah talks) for fifty years, until his sudden death in 1909 while visiting the Holy Land.*

According to his numerous followers, the Ben Ish Chai was not merely a brilliant scholar, but also possessed Ruach HaKodesh— *"the holy spirit" associated with true prophecy. He typically, however, downplayed such claims, offering this parable by way of explanation: One day a pious Arab sheikh was looking at a holy Hebraic work. When his gaze fell on the Name of God, he*

experienced such a level of reverence and awe that Ruach Ha-
Kodesh *swept over him. Rabbi Yosef Chaim explained this event
showed God's magnificent fairness: that neither age, nor gender, nor
even religion determines upon whom the* Shekinah *(Divine Presence) will rest; it depends only on one's behavior in God's eyes.*

*These selections reveal the Ben Ish Chai's literary style and
wide-ranging interests, such as the mysteries of the Hebrew alphabet, Torah observance and dreams, the human soul, and the afterlife.*

INTENTION IS EVERYTHING

There was once a Jew who was so ignorant that he did not know
a single verse of the Torah. Moreover, he did not even know the
meaning of a single Hebrew word. All he managed to absorb were
five words that he heard the other worshippers say in the synagogue daily as they recited the order of the sacrifices: *Eilu v'eilu nisrafin beveit hadeshen* ["These and those are burned in the chamber
of ashes."]

Every Friday night, after he made Kiddush, his children would
come and kiss his hand. He would then place his hands on the head
of each child in turn and bless him or her with the only words of
Torah that he knew, *Eilu v'eilu nisrafin beveit hadeshen.* He did not
know what the words meant, but he was sure that since they were
words of Torah, there was blessing in them.

And indeed, the "blessing seemed to work." His wife bore him
fifteen healthy children.

A Torah scholar once lodged in the home of this ignorant Jew
over Shabbat. Upon hearing how the man blessed his children, the
scholar was so shaken that his whole body trembled. "What are you
saying?" he said to his host. "These words are a curse, not a blessing.
You are telling your children that they will be burned in the chamber of ashes."

The host was sorely distressed. Thereafter, the Torah scholar was
told in a dream: "Why did you interfere with what your host was
doing? He said those words in all innocence because he knew they

are words of Torah. So what if, according to the straightforward meaning, they are a curse? Know that the Holy One, blessed be He, rearranged the letters to form a blessing. As a result, this simple man's children have been blessed."

SEEKING TREASURE IN THE WRONG PLACES

A magician bought five eggs from a vendor in the marketplace. On the spot, the magician broke open one of the eggs. In it there was a precious stone. He broke open the other eggs before the startled vendor's eyes. Lo and behold, the magician found a precious stone in each egg!

The vendor was upset that he had sold such valuable eggs for a pittance. "At least," he comforted himself, "I have another hundred eggs of the same type. I'll take the precious stones out of them all."

He broke open one of his eggs. "Why, there's nothing in here!" he exclaimed in amazement. "Surely, then, it must be in the next one."

One by one, the vendor broke open his eggs in search of precious stones. In the end, not only did the vendor find no precious stones, he was also left without a single egg to sell!

The person who spends years studying [secular] philosophy is like the egg vendor. He hopes that something good will come of it. All too late, he discovers that he has wasted his life on something worthless. He is left neither with knowledge nor time. For philosophy looks good at first, but after studying it, one recognizes its worthlessness. In contrast, the beauty, truth, and wholesomeness of Torah becomes more apparent the more one studies it. Therefore, the more a person toils in Torah, the more he will love it and the more he will crave to learn.

THE IMPORTANCE OF LIMITS

When God created heaven and earth, they continued to expand and expand until God told them, "Enough!" (*Hagigah* 12a). This limiting of their material expansion also established a paradigmatic law controlling their actions. For "God created the world to do" (Genesis 2:3). He created the world with the potential to function from then on, for the duration of its existence. For example, the sun must shine, plants must grow. However, by saying, "Enough!" God set limits on what nature could do: how much rain can fall, and how cold things can become. Each of these is beneficial for humanity, but only if they are within a certain measure. This very fundamental law of limits is therefore of crucial benefit.

Furthermore, the decree of "Enough!" is diametrically opposed to God's own attribute, for the Holy One is infinite. In addition, God's infinite majesty seemingly deserves to be honored by an infinite number of "attendants." Nevertheless, God issued the decree for the benefit of all that he created—especially the individual, so that one could study Torah and perform *mitzvot*. . . .

Man is a miniature world. His soul and body correspond respectively to heaven and earth. Just as the world cannot exist without limits, neither can man. Giving free reign to his body for wealth and physical pleasure can lead to his own destruction.

But even the desires of the soul must be in the right measure. The sage Ben Azzai was so enamored of Torah study that he did not marry. Thus he neglected the *mitzvah* to be fruitful and multiply, without which the world cannot continue. This is another instance in which Ben Azzai exceeded the limits, [for as in the Talmudic narrative] of the "four who entered the "orchard of Kabbalah study," Ben Azzai went beyond his limit . . . and died.

THIS WORLD AND THE NEXT

This world and the next are opposites. A person who chooses to pursue the pleasures of this world will not attain the World-to-Come, for he will undoubtedly forfeit many opportunities to do *mitzvot*. However, one who focuses on attaining the delights of the World-to-Come will find it impossible to attain the pleasures of this world.

But there is an individual who is able to enjoy the best of both worlds: that's the one in whose heart the Torah is firmly planted. Even if he attains the pleasures of this world, he will not sin at all. He will use all the pleasures for the sake of heaven, in a way that is permitted and pleasing before God. He will serve God with all his might, and the evil inclination will not be able to lead him astray. Indeed, there were a number of such *zaddikim* who enjoyed the best of both worlds. Perhaps most outstanding was King Solomon, who lacked nothing. God gave him peace with all the neighboring countries, tremendous wealth, and extensive sovereignty. Yet he remained absolutely righteous and God-fearing (see *Shabbat* 56b). . . .

As proof of the Torah's power to not only reconcile opposites, but also simultaneously afford blessing to them, one can consider the verse, "For they are life to he who finds them and healing to all his flesh" (Proverbs 4:22). Different parts of the body require different treatments. One part needs a cold compress, another a heating pad. The wrong treatment can aggravate a negative condition. However, the Torah can be "applied" to every part of the body, and each limb will receive exactly what it needs to cure it.

AN UPSETTING DREAM

A man had a dream in which he was reciting the Hebrew alphabet several times in succession. Each time, he skipped some letters and was unable to complete the entire alphabet correctly even once. He awoke feeling quite distressed, not knowing what his dream portended. Please give us the true interpretation of this dream.

The Ben Ish Chai replied: Our teacher, the holy Rabbi Isaac Luria, in his Gate of the Holy Spirit, which we have in manuscript, writes: "The twenty-two letters of the Hebrew alphabet are linked to the one hundred *brachot* [blessings] a Jew recites each day. If a person omits a particular *bracha,* the letter that is linked to it is missing. If he did say the *bracha* properly but did not concentrate on its meaning, then the letter linked to it is dim and murky."

Therefore, the interpretation of the dream is that this man is failing to recite some of the daily *brachot*. He must therefore strive his best to recite with concentration the full one hundred *brachot* each day. If he is careful to do that from now on, all will be well with him.

THE CHOFETZ CHAIM

Israel Meyer Kagan

AMONG THE MOST *celebrated European rabbinic thinkers of the mid-industrial age was Israel Meyer Kagan. A Polish-born yeshiva director and Jewish communal leader, he became revered in his lifetime as the Chofetz Chaim—which was also the title of his immensely popular book on speaking responsibly in daily life. Published in 1873, it was the first Judaic work ever to organize and codify the laws relating to idle talk and gossip. Over the course of Rabbi Kagan's long life, he produced twenty-one books on topics ranging from ethical speech and religious study to the future rebuilding of the Temple of Jerusalem. With a warm and down-to-earth literary style, his books became highly popular among Jews seeking Torah-based guidance for everyday living in an increasingly technological world. Asserting that science could aid in ascertaining divine wisdom, his writings effectively used epigrams, anecdotes, and gentle humor to make profound points.*

Rabbi Israel Kagan today is not typically viewed as a Kabbalist, but rather as an "applied ethicist" drawing upon traditional Jewish sources for personal direction and social harmony. Yet, similar to such influential rabbinic predecessors as Moses Cordovero and Moses

Chaim Luzzatto, the Chofetz Chaim drew extensively upon
esoteric sources—especially the Zohar—*to provide a foundation*
for understanding human existence in its totality. In this regard,
he clearly saw the Kabbalah's inspirational and visionary power.
This selection highlights the Chofetz Chaim's teachings about
the importance of kindness to others, in which he characteristically
draws on diverse Judaic sources including the Kabbalah.

STRIVE TO FULFILL THIS *MITZVAH* EVERY DAY

We have [previously] explained the great significance of the virtue
of *chesed* [kindness]. It is effective in prolonging a person's life, in
atoning for his sins. It protects him from all manner of plagues. One
thereby comes to shelter under the "shadow" of God Himself, may
He be blessed, and not under the shadow of cherubim. He enjoys
the fruit of his actions in this world, while the stock remains for
him in the world to come. He succeeds in raising wealthy and wise
[children]. . . . He is worthy of vindication in the final judgment and
he obtains other exalted benefits as well. How intensely should one
strive to embody this holy trait in himself and to love it immensely,
as Scripture lays down (Micah 6:1): "What does God want of you
but to do justice, to love *chesed,*" for this *mitzvah* stands by man until
the end of all generations.

One should be especially careful not to neglect practicing *chesed*
even for a single day of his life, in the same way that one takes care
to set fixed times for daily Torah study. I have found in *Sefer Ha-*
Kedushah [Book of Holiness] of [Kabbalist] Rabbi Chaim Vital
that, every day, one should bemoan: "Woe is me! Another day has
passed without Torah and *gemiluth chesed* [acts of kindness]!" The
tenor of the statement is that the power of holiness in the world is
brought to the full by the three chief preoccupations: Torah study,
service in the Holy Temple of Jerusalem, and *gemiluth chesed.* The
second activity—service in the Holy Temple—has been denied
to us as a result of the multitude of our sins, since the day of its

destruction. Because only two activities now remain, we must reinforce them all the more. Then our iniquities will be forgiven, as the biblical verse (Proverbs 16:6) expressed it: "By *chesed* and truth, iniquity is atoned for."

The reason for all this is, as the *Zohar* explains, is that a person's days on this world have a permanence. From each day a spiritual creation comes forth into existence. And in the future, when the time arrives for one to leave this world, all his days appear before the Lord of all things to give evidence concerning him. Hence the individual must take care to keep all his days completely holy. From the daily study of Torah, he attains to the love of God. . . . One should also strive to cling to the divine attributes, which are goodness and kindness alone. Then one will be worthy to have God cause the light of His countenance to shine upon him, as Scripture expresses it (Isaiah 58:10): "And if you draw out your soul to the hungry, and satisfy the afflicted soul, then shall your light rise in darkness . . . and satisfy your soul in drought."

We have dwelt at length on this subject to remove the erroneous idea entrenched in certain minds that after a person has once practiced *gemiluth chesed* toward another, he has discharged his obligation for several weeks to come, even though he still is capable of doing good to others. On the contrary, every day of his life, whenever the need presents itself to him, he is obliged to fulfill the mitzvah, as long as he has the means, even if he is called upon several times on a single day. So we have recorded in our "Laws Governing Loans" in this volume. . . .

Now if a person were to scrutinize in this light the days of his life that have already passed, he would find most of them devoid of this holy trait, and some of them empty even of Torah and the fear of God. He should therefore strive to sanctify the remaining days of his life, not to allow another day to pass without Torah study and *chesed*. One should not wonder how it would be possible to perform acts of *chesed* on the Sabbath, for this virtue includes a variety of activities besides free loans, as we have [already] explained.

See how great is the reward for Torah and *chesed*! The Talmud [ibid.] expounds the significance of all the letters of the alphabet in sequence, and continues with *Zayin Chet Tet Yod Kaf Lamed:* "If you do thus, the Holy One, blessed be He, will sustain *(Zan)* you, and be gracious *(Chen)* onto you, show goodness *(me-Tiv)* to you, give you a heritage *(Yerushah)* (this is what is stated in the Talmud [*Bava Kamma* 17a]): "Whoever is occupied with Torah study and *gemiluth chesed* is worthy of inheriting the understanding of Issachar [one of the twelve tribes, associated in tradition with religious study] and binding a crown (Keter) on you in the World-to-Come."

The meaning of this passage is that one should not fear through extending charity and making loans that his capital and food will be diminished, or that through occupying himself with Torah he has to worry where his bread will come from. The passage answers the argument by saying, "The Holy One, Blessed be He, will feed you." Contrary to what you think, your performance of these acts will bring increase to your possessions. (As our sages of blessed memory have declared in *Sifrei* Deuteronomy 14:22): "Give a tithe [*aser*], so that you will become wealthy [*titasher*]"—and the same applies to *chesed*). . . . Similarly, in regard to Torah, when a person studies constantly, he consequently will not suffer, God forbid, financial loss. Our sages of blessed memory have indicated that for this purpose, God commanded the placing of the jar of manna "before *Hashem*" (Exodus 16:33) as a lesson for the generations to come.

The Prophet Jeremiah thereby demonstrated to the people of Israel that without natural causes, the Holy One, blessed be He, would be able to provide the sustenance of the entire population, as in the days of old (See Rashi). And the Talmud (Shabbat 104b) quoted above expressed it precisely by saying: "The Holy One, blessed be He, sustains you"—meaning that your food will come to you by supernatural means. "He will put a crown upon you, just as a father himself crowns his beloved son." Here is what Scripture says (1 Samuel 2:30): "For them that honor Me, I will honor (that is, God Himself will bestow the honor—not through any agent). And they that despise Me shall be lightly esteemed (indirectly; God will not directly humiliate them but will hide His Presence from them and, in the natural course of events, they will be put to shame)." For the measure of good exceeds the measure of punishment.

PART FIVE

Twentieth-Century Thinkers

31

REB ARELE

Aharon Roth

BORN IN HUNGARY *at the cusp of the twentieth century, Aharon Roth was a Hasidic master who achieved widest influence after immigrating to Jerusalem in the 1930s. Known to devoted followers as Reb Arele, he effected a break with Hasidic tradition by choosing to become an "independent" rebbe, unaffiliated with any particular dynasty. In part, he was driven to this position by the fierce intergroup rivalries dominant among Hungarian Hasidism of his era. Ironically, after Reb Arele's death in 1944, his own loyalists fell prey to decades of similar feuds and schisms.*

Not surprisingly, little of Rabbi Roth's work has yet appeared in English translation, for he wrote exclusively for the small but intense community of Hasidim that he founded and that continues through the present day. For those seeking God in the modern world, he regarded the modern world as a dangerous place, founded on materialism and filled with baseness and innumerable distractions. Two motives essentially shaped his writing and talks: to help observant Jews strengthen their awareness and mindfulness while performing religious acts, and to fortify their faith in God through individual and communal means.

These two selections, focusing on personal development, are from a new volume of Reb Arele's writings, produced by Hasidic Rabbi Zalman M. Schachter-Shalomi and his Jewish Renewal colleagues. The first presents Reb Arele's view of Torah study as a transcendental activity, and the second, on his concept of bittul hayesh, a fundamental meditational teaching in Hasidism attributable to the Baal Shem Tov.

OPEN YOUR HEART TO THE PERFECT TORAH

And so, my brother, my beloved, see that according to the teachings of the holy Zohar, whoever studies the holy Torah with complete faith, the person has the deepest possible insight that is conceivable and whose soul will in the future merit the soul of the soul of the Torah. The holy Baal Shem Tov explained the verse, *"God's Torah is a perfect Torah"* that the Torah today is still a perfect Torah, for everything which is in existence today is nothing compared to the greatness and depth of the Torah.

And all of the prophets, the teachers of the Mishnah and the Gemara, and all the great, holy righteous ones from ancient times until today, have added understanding and insight as they ascended from one world to the next—for our holy Torah has no boundary or limit. For the truest understanding of Torah can be opened only at the time of the coming of the messiah, soon in our day—when the fifty gates of understanding will be opened and the highest gate of wisdom, as will the thirty-two pathways of wisdom that themselves have no limit or end. And they will understand much more than did the prophets, and they will make manifest the meaning of the verse, "And I will pour my spirit on every person and upon your sons and daughter" (Joel 3:1). And their understanding of Torah will exceed even that of the angels.

Therefore, if you study Torah with this intention, you will know that in every single letter of our holy Torah there are deep, hidden mysteries, and in the words of those who make legal and rabbinic rulings, which they have received from above. These descend from above, from their highest source and from the highest of all worlds in the holy Torah. And if you carefully explore the letters and words, and if you speak them with *kavana* [intention] and with life-giving force, through all this within the supernal worlds, your soul will be greatly moved and transformed in accordance with the core qualities of your soul, and the extent to which you can hold onto your holy connection to God.

The activity of *bittul hayesh* (self-effacement) is work enough for one's life: doing it over and over again, finding new ways to do it, for everything is contained in that act. It begins with *bittul hayesh* and moves with purpose toward *bittul bimitzuit* [negation of self-substantialness], total and complete annihilation. This was a goal set by the greatest of the *zaddikim,* and blessed are those who merited its achievement, for it allowed them to see their real world during their life here on earth. The work of *bittul* begins with zeal, moving about with speed. Our sages have said that zeal brings one to purity, one step after another, until one comes to real humility. From this we see that all begins with zeal and leads to humility, which is *bittul hayesh.*

What does zeal mean? It means to be light on one's feet, to go and seek God, search after search, to seek, to find God in the actual observance of *mitzvah*. It means to run and step and search and seek, to be inventive trying to find new ways to cause delight before Him, blessed be He. It means not to be lazy, not to be closed off in solitude, but to run to do a kind deed, to serve to invigorate human beings, to rise early in the morning with zeal in the service of our Creator. . . .

It is clearly indicated in the Holy Torah that the root of all [spirituality] is *bittul*. We see how Korah and his people were all great and tremendous, but because they could not manage to obliterate themselves, to accept the discipline of Moses and Aaron, they caused what they caused. We find the same thing with Ahitophel, who was a very great man—almost in the category of Moses our Teacher. But because he did not want to be subject to David our King, peace be upon him, you are aware what happened to him.

And if Zedekiah had gone to Nebuchadnezzar and made himself subject to him, all of Israel would have been spared the exile.

Now let us look and see what this feeling of selfness is. It is the feeling that I am a somebody, I am this, I am that, I am thus, I am such, I deserve, I need. And what is *bittul hayesh*? That is the full recognition that other than He, nothing exists, that everything is God and besides Him there is no "self" and no "personal power." The purpose of *bittul hayesh* is to come through it to *bittul bimitzuit,* which is the attainment of great persons, who are totally lost in their Root, becoming *nihil* and nothingness. All this is true *bittul.* But the mere reflection of this pertains to us when we subject ourselves to the glory of the Lord. . . . "God is the Lord and He gives us light." The smallest of all the Hebrew letters, the *yud,* points to humility and selflessness: this is all of humanity, all of the totality of the Jew, the Yid. For a Jew to be as naught and subject to the Creator of all the world: this is *bittul hayesh.*

To this, one comes via zeal, for one must not worry about the heaviness of the body, but must annihilate oneself before one's friend, especially one that is greater. One must subdue and chop down the passions of the body—the flesh cadaver—so that he will cease to experience physical passion. As long as man is caught up in passions, as long as he still wants a good pot of coffee with sugar, he is unable to arrive at true *bittul hayesh.* As is pointed out in the *Ma'or VaShamesh:* "One who can have a physical passion even once during a year, shows that he still is on the outside."

Ah, those *zaddikim* who subdue their minds with meditation on *bittul;* they are already holy and pure. They already despise physical passions. They have already taught their body mortification, effort, and self-sacrifice before the Lord. Therefore you should, with ease and zeal, annihilate yourself totally before everyone, and even if darkness has fallen, and one has become [blind], one should be able to bend with ease. . . .

Today I felt before prayer that I had no strength at all to stand up to pray, so what could I do? I felt it was impossible to expend any effort, so I girded myself with *bittul* and brokenheartedness, and got help through this means. You have seen the counsel of the holy books which point out that at times of eclipse, one must draw upon himself the category of nothingness. Then one prays in the category of the Oneness of God. O how deep this is, how much we could go on talking about it.

Do not think this is such a simple thing for people like us. O how much we must beg of God! And when it happens that it seems to be impossible, that one is weak and without the strength for such effort, then He whose name is blessed, helps us to draw down through *bittul* and brokenheartedness. This what we said earlier—the Lord is E'L/strength and power to us, giving us our light. He then helps and manifests grace. Let Him please, please give us the light under the category of the broken heart.

Sweet children, what do we have to fear? The body is merely skin and glue. We must take care of every single moment in this world, and do something for the Most High.

The great Tosaphists—the night before they were taken to be burned at the stake—knowing full well that this was their last night, at that time, wrote the most difficult comments on the Talmud, such as *Babar Kama,* because they thought each moment they still had in this world was precious.

See how one needs to strengthen oneself? Consider, what does it mean to be afraid? So one dies? Was I created for myself? Did not the Lord our God create us for his glory, to praise Him, to glorify Him, to tell of His greatness? So, therefore, it is our obligation, as long as we live, to achieve the work for which we were created in this world.

32

YEHUDAH ASHLAG

AMONG THE MOST *intriguing and influential Kabbalists of modern times was Rabbi Yehudah Ashlag. Born in 1885 Warsaw, he became drawn to Hasidism but did not affiliate with a particular dynasty; throughout his life, he maintained an undeniable maverick streak like his Hungarian contemporary Reb Arele Roth.*

Upon achieving early prominence as a Talmudic scholar and halachic *adjudicator, Rabbi Ashlag turned intensely to Kabbalah. Precisely how he mastered the Jewish esoteric tradition remains unclear. In his own account, beginning in 1919, he studied privately with a mysterious businessmen who died the day after imparting his final lesson. With a strong idealistic bent, Rabbi Ashlag also absorbed the writings of Western philosophers including Hegel, Marx, Nietzsche, and Schopenhauer during Europe's tumultuous years following World War I. Unusual for a religious Jew of the time, he joined socialist and communist Warsaw street demonstrations clamoring for revolutionary economic change.*

In 1921 Rabbi Ashlag made the sudden decision to settle in the Holy Land. He seemingly felt that his life purpose was over in Poland, and that only in the Land of Israel could his soul find

challenge to grow. He went straight to Jerusalem's famous Beit El
Yeshiva for inspiration, but experienced bitter disappointment in
seeing how this once renowned academy of Kabbalah had fallen in
rigor. Rabbi Ashlag then underwent an epiphany: he would devote
the rest of his life in the Holy Land to revealing the magnificence
of the Zohar *and Rabbi Isaac Luria's teachings. Also an iconoclast,*
Rabbi Ashlag saw a tremendous need to promulgate the esoteric
tradition to all contemporary Jews—not just a tiny elite.

Over the next three decades, he produced several highly influen-
tial works, including the first translation of the Zohar *into modern*
Hebrew, a major treatise on the ten sefirot, *and his magnum opus*
entitled HaSulam *(The Ladder), comprising a twenty-one-volume*
commentary on the Zohar. *Drawn from the introductions to these*
two works, these selections reveal his ability to explain abstruse
metaphysical concepts about Torah, God, and human existence
with admirable clarity.

FUNDAMENTAL QUESTIONS

In this Introduction, I would like to clarify some seemingly simple
matters. These are issues with which everyone is, to some extent,
involved and much ink has been spilt in the effort to clarify them.
Despite this, we have not arrived at a sufficiently clear understanding of them.

The first question we would like to ask is, "What is our essence?"

Our second question is, "What is our role as part of the long
chain of reality of which we are such little links?"

The third question concerns the paradox that when we look at
ourselves, we feel that we are defective or fallen to the extent that
there can be none as despicable as ourselves. But when we look at
the Creator who made us, then we find that we must really be
creations of such high degree that there are none more praiseworthy than ourselves, since it has to be the case that from a perfect
Creator only perfect works can issue. Our fourth question is, "According to our intellect, God must be Good and do good, there

being no higher good than that which He does. How, then, could He create so many creatures who, right from the start, suffer and feel pain throughout all the days of their lives? Surely it is in the nature of the Good to do good or, at any rate, not to do so much harm!" Our fifth question is, "How is it possible that an eternal Being, without a beginning or an end, could bring into existence creatures which are finite, die and have an end?"

REVEALED AND HIDDEN TORAH

The wisdom of Kabbalah and that of the revealed Torah are actually one. However when a person is in the state of consciousness of concealment of God's face, then he or she finds that God is similarly concealed by the Torah. Under these circumstances, when a person studies the revealed Torah, he or she cannot receive the light of Torah which pertains to *Yetzirah* and, one need not add, certainly not that which pertains to a higher level. Only when a person attains the consciousness of revelation of God's face, do the garments of the revealed Torah start to become more transparent and does the revealed Torah become one with the Torah of *Yetzirah* [Formation, the third-lowest of the four worlds of creation] which is the wisdom of Kabbalah.

As for one who attains the level of the Torah of *Atzilut* [Emanation, the highest world], the letters of the Torah are in no way changed. It is just that these very same garments of the revealed Torah in this world have become transparent to the person and no longer conceal God. As it is written, "And your Teacher will no longer be covered by wings and your eyes will see your Teacher." Thus, that which is written in the *Zohar*, "He, His life force, and his vessels are One," is fulfilled.

OUR TRUE NATURE

So common sense dictates that we understand the opposite of what appears, superficially, to be the case. We are actually good and supremely high beings, to the extent that there is no limit to our importance. We are entirely fitting creatures for the Craftsman who made us. Any lack that you might like to raise concerning our bodies, after all the excuses one might make, must fall squarely on the Creator who created us. He created us together with all our tendencies. It is clear that He made us and we did not make ourselves. He also knows all the processes that are consequent on our nature and on the evil tendencies He planted within us.

But, as we have said, we must look to the end of the process of creation and then we will be able to understand it all. There is a proverb that says, "Don't show your work to a fool while you are still in the middle of it."

Our sages have taught us that God's only purpose in creating the world was in order to give pleasure to His creatures. It is here that we need to put our eyes and focus our thoughts because it is the ultimate aim and purpose of the creation of the world. We need to consider that since the purpose of creation was in order to give His creatures pleasure, it was therefore necessary for God to create within the souls an exceedingly large desire to receive all that He planned to give them. After all, the measure of any joy or of any pleasure is commensurate with the measure of our will to receive it, to the extent that as the will to receive grows larger, in like measure the pleasure received is the greater. Similarly, if the will to receive pleasure is lessened, then, in like measure, the pleasure in its receiving is correspondingly reduced.

The very purpose of creation itself necessitates the creation within the souls of a *will to receive* that is of the most prodigious measure, compatible with the great amount of joy with which God intends to give delight; for great pleasure and a great will to receive it go together.

PHYSICAL HEALING

The worlds unfold until we arrive at the reality of this physical world where body and soul exist, and likewise a time of spoiling and a time of healing. Our body, which is formed from the will to receive for itself alone, comes forth from its root within the purpose of Creation. But it passes via the framework of the worlds of uncleanness, as Scripture says, "A man is born like a wild ass" (Job 1:12). It remains subject to this framework until a person reaches thirteen years of age. This period is designated as "the time of spoiling."

Then, from the age of thirteen onwards, through performing *mitzvot* which he or she does in order to give benefit to others and pleasure to the Creator, the person begins to purify the will to receive for oneself which is inherent within them. The person gradually transforms the will to receive for oneself alone into a will to give benefit. By this means, a person progressively attracts to themselves a holy soul from its root within the purpose of Creation. This soul passes through the framework of the worlds of holiness and enclothes itself within the body, and this is the time of healing. . . .

Through the practice of Torah and *mitzvot,* the will to receive is eventually transformed into the will to give. Then the souls are able to receive all the Good that is implicit in the thought of Creation. With this, they merit to a wondrous unity with God, since they have earned affinity of form with their Creator through their work in Torah and *mitzvot*. This state is designated as the end of the healing process.

RECEIVING DIVINE LIGHT

That which the souls attain of God's light comes directly from His Being, from His essence. So from the perspective of God's light which the souls receive within their vessel—the vessel being the *will to receive*—no separation exists between the essence of God and between themselves, as the light which they receive is a direct emanation of His Being. The only difference that exists between the souls and God's essence lies in the way that the souls form a portion of His essence. In other words, the measure of light that the souls receive within the vessel which is their will to receive, already constitutes a part which has separated from God. . . . There is no difference between God and the souls except that one constitutes a whole and the other constitutes a part, just as in the case of a stone quarried from a mountain. Understand this well, as there is nothing more to be said in this very high place!

33

ABRAHAM ISAAC KOOK

BORN IN 1865 LATVIA, *Abraham Isaac Kook was an early Talmudic prodigy and studied as a youth with the Netziv, head of the famous Volozhin Yeshiva. Under his wing, young Rabbi Kook intensively studied Kabbalah before eventually immigrating to the Holy Land in 1904. As a rabbinic leader in Jaffa, he began espousing a unique religious message blending esoteric thought with economic-political practicalities—centering on reclaiming the Land of Israel for renewed Jewish identity and religious fervor. More than any other modern Judaic thinker, especially for one with a Kabbalistic perspective, he viewed this reclamation in grand historic—and essentially messianic—terms. To the enduring outrage of conservative rabbinic colleagues, he consistently praised antireligious Zionists for helping to fulfill the divine plan.*

Rav Kook, as he was popularly known, held two influential positions during his tenure in the Holy Land: initially, Chief Rabbi of Jerusalem in 1921, and eight years later, Chief Ashkenazi Rabbi for the entire country, then under British mandate. While occupying both posts, he idealistically strove to promote unity between the religious and nonreligious Jewish communities. Rav Kook wrote prolif-

ically on such themes as the nature of human history and spiritual growth, but few of his books were published in his lifetime due to their difficult, hyperflowery style. Unquestionably, his most popular work is Orot HaTeshuva *(The Lights of Penitence), first published in 1925. Drawn from this evocative book, these two selections present Rav Kook's thought on two diverse topics long the focus of Kabbalists—the purpose of God's commandments to the Jewish people and the sanctification of the world through seemingly ordinary daily activity, such as eating.*

LEARNING FROM MAIMONIDES

When we enter the vast domain of probing the reasons for the commandments, we cannot help being astonished at the meager attention paid to this important branch of literature, which, in the light of its subject matter, should have been of wider concern than any other branch of Torah study. In our generation, we are more conscious of the lack of research into this important field of inquiry. The concern with strengthening Judaism, on the ideological and the practical levels, occupies the attention of our most talented sprits, who all are firmly committed to Judaism and ready to sacrifice their lives for it. On the face of it, it should be clear to us that Judaism's revival and revitalization, even its remaining firm in its present position, must be based on an inner light, on knowledge and feeling, which distill love and give firmness to the actions that derive from them. Toward this end, the most important task is a popularization of the study of the reasons for the commandments in depth and originality.

The first one to illumine our horizon by probing the reasons for the commandments was Maimonides in his *Guide for the Perplexed*. But how surprising it will be for us to assess the impression all his thoughts concerning the reasons for the commandments registered on the people generally and on individuals who investigate religious themes, from his own time to the latest generation! Less than any other conceptual theme in his writings did this subject, the reasons for the commandments, evoke any reaction. We know

of almost no resultant stimulation and apparently no resultant em-
ulation in response to his work. The facts indicate clearly that we
have here a certain deficiency that needs to be mended, so that this
beloved subject be pervaded by a new vitality and creativeness.

The connecting thread that links all the explanations for the
commandments by Maimonides is: the uprooting of idolatry. We
have here a noble cultural force of the past, which continues to
release an idealistic spirit, the pride of our people in having been
an important participant in building the spiritual and cultural
world, but by its nature this is bound to weaken, since its brightest
epoch is the *past*. In truth, however, the basic principle immanent
in the reasons for the commandments points to the *future*. The past
by itself, though it is very important, can, by itself, only bring to us
values of archaeological information that have no substantial contribution to ongoing life. The present alone surely will not suffice
to radiate a light of idealism that can elevate the spirit with poetry
and with an influence of holiness. It is only when the past flows on
toward the great and progressively unfolding future that this branch
of scientific knowledge can meet the conditions of life, both in
establishing the worth of this noble branch of knowledge and in
contributing to the revitalization of Judaism. . . .

When Judaism had to defend itself as the champion of the basic
idea of the divine, and then encountered the Greek conception of
the eternity of the universe, Maimonides was very successful, not
only in demonstrating a way of maintaining the divine idea on the
basis of the belief in creation, but also by utilizing the ideology of
the adversary. He spoke confidently about the conception of God,
even on the basis of the theory of the eternalists. Then the results
reached offered ample light on the well-trodden path of the belief
in creation, with double vigor abounding in courage and life.

RAISING UP HOLY SPARKS WHILE EATING

As there are holy sparks in the food we eat, so are there in all human
activities, and similarly so in everything we hear and read. At times

worldly pursuits from the most remote order of being become associated with the profound principles of the Torah; and everything serves a divine purpose, in the perspective of the body.

One need not be unduly concerned with having eaten to excess. Retroactively, all the holy sparks will be raised to great holiness. But initially, one must be very careful to be in the category of the righteous person who eats only to satisfy his hunger.

The holy sparks imbedded in the food we eat rise together with the holy sparks that ascend from all movements, all speech, all actions, and acquisitions. To the extent that there is good and uprightness in all expressions of life is there an ascent of the holy sparks in food and drink and in all things that yield keenly felt pleasures. What is naturally experienced in the soul in its relationship with all existence becomes the basis for perceiving the most profound wisdom concerning the nature of things, and serves as a free-flowing fountain and as a river that never ends its movement.

Impressions registered from the outside are raised toward the heights during sleep, and this is their perfection. The spiritual elevation that takes place through a transfer from involvements with the pursuits of the outer senses and the limitations imposed by the environment is manifested on the whole world, with great mercy. Many moral attributes, opinions, actions, and dispositions are ennobled; the chain of life is lengthened, and a dimension of kindness is extended in the world.

When the dislocations of travel effect a spiritual impoverishment, it is necessary to make redress with firmness and courage, and not with timidity and sadness. The impoverishment that results from various encounters stems not only from negative causes. It arises also because new impressions seek hurriedly to force their way into the soul, displacing the old impressions as a result of the narrow zones in which they find themselves. On restoring the old to their place, one must be careful not to distort the character of the new impressions. This can be effected only through high-level *teshuvah,* free of all lowliness. Then everything is strengthened, the perceptive vessels are broadened and the new impressions are accommodated with the old.

Eating in proper measure and in a holy disposition sanctifies the person and the world, and lends joy to life. Sadness induces over-eating, and the act of eating takes on heaviness, and it expresses anger and despair. The holy sparks fall to a depth more dark than where they were before, and the soul is aggrieved. But a person can, in the end, turn everything to joy, and through the noble thoughts in the inwardness of his heart all forces that have any bearing on his life are elevated, and there is an enhancement of light. However, it is necessary to add to the dimension of the holy in the future, to eat in order to satisfy his hunger, and with ordered joy, without any timidity or sadness, thus raising the holy sparks directly, rather than in a roundabout way.

Excessive eating and drinking certainly induces pride, and like-wise so if these take place without any holy intention. The extent to which proper intention is needed depends on the level of the person involved. The holy sparks in food and drink, by their nature, seek to ascend. When one eats with the proper motivation one paves a way for them to ascend in holiness. The evil admixture in them descends, while the good rises for enduring benefit and holy and noble delight. In the soul of the eater there is automatically stirred an elevation of the good and a lowering of the evil. In the absence of proper motivation, there is no prepared path for the holy sparks and they reach to ascend without ordered selection. They take evil along with them in their ascent, thereby also stirring in the person who has eaten an elevation of evil attributes, which is the basis of all pride.

In the light of this, eating before prayer is very difficult, for it is difficult to gain the spiritual disposition needed to differentiate and select the good before enhancing one's spiritual state to evaluate life through prayer. Therefore all eating and drinking before prayer is in the category of pride. Concerning such a person does the verse say, "You have turned your back on Me" (I Kings 14:9). After he ate and drank and became proud, he took on himself the disci-pline of the kingdom of God!

Only when this is done for medicinal reason is the concern about pride inapplicable, for the commandment to heal is associated with holiness. The Holy One, praised be He, sustains the sick person, and the divine presence is with him. The basis of holiness is humility, the sick person is needy and depressed because of his illness, and his eyes are turned in prayer toward the mercies of God. The beneficial aspect of the holy sparks of the medicine always ascend on the path of holiness. It rises ever upward on a straight and readied path.

34

Kalonymus Shapira

Rabbi Kalonymus Shapira *was the last great Hasidic educa-
tor of pre-Holocaust Poland. Aiming to overcome the threats of secularism and materialism, he produced innovative pedagogical works
gaining renewed interest today. Born in 1889, Kalonymus was descended on both parental sides from illustrious Hasidic rebbes including the Seer of Lublin. At the age of twenty, following the death
of his father-in-law, Kalonymus became the rebbe of Piaseczneh,
later becoming the town's chief rabbi as well. After the First World
War, he moved to Warsaw, yet he loyally maintained his position at
Piaseczneh, once commenting that "any rebbe not willing to descend
into hell to save his hasid from there is not a rebbe at all."*

*As a yeshiva head in Warsaw, Reb Kalonymus, as he was popu-
larly known, emphasized the importance of creativity and innova-
tion in education. He recommended experiential techniques such as
guided imagery to develop higher consciousness and, ultimately, to
achieve a constant awareness of God's presence in one's everyday
life and closeness to the divine realm. In this respect, Rabbi Shapira
shared the view of Maimonides, Rabbi Chaim Vital, and other*

Jewish visionaries that the imaginative faculty is a key force for inner development.

In the winter of 1942–1943, when the Warsaw Ghetto was doomed, Reb Kalonymus carefully buried whole manuscripts that were found after the war ended, for he correctly intuited his death in a Nazi concentration camp. Subsequently published in Israel, these works focused on such topics as methods for fostering individual spiritual service and building spiritual community. In this regard, among the rebbe's most widely read posthumous books is Bnai Mahashavah Tovah *(Children of Heightened Consciousness). Fortunate for posterity, he also kept a journal during the Nazi occupation, in which he recorded his wide-ranging thoughts on inner development. These selections are taken from this inspiring work, entitled* To Heal the Soul.

THE NEED FOR STIMULATION

The human soul relishes sensation, not only if it is pleasant feeling but for the very experience of stimulation. Sooner sadness or some deep pain rather than the boredom of nonstimulation. People will watch distressing scenes and listen to heartrending stories just to get stimulation. Such is human nature and a need of the soul, just like all other needs and natures. So he who is clever will fulfill this need with passionate prayer and Torah learning.

But the soul whose divine service is without emotion will have to find its stimulation elsewhere. It will either be driven to cheap, even forbidden, sensation or will become emotionally ill from lack of stimulation.

BECOMING WHO YOU REALLY ARE

People are always bemoaning what seems to them to be their lack of freedom of choice. They feel so compelled by earthly desires that they feel they cannot control themselves. But know that for every choice that must emerge from an individual chooser himself, there must be an individuated self to choose. There must be a person who can stand by himself, who can decide what he wants for himself. But if there is no person, just one of the crowd, there can be no free choice or personal will. Because who will choose if, besides the herd mentality, there is no one there at all?

So look deep inside to see if you have individuated your real self. Are you a person who can stand by himself or are you just a member of the human species? Are you like a plant or an animal whose individual essence is just one of the kind? What is in the species is in the specimen, which is why they have no free will. Their instincts are not under their individual control but under that of the collective laws of the species. Their willfulness does not rise out of individual need but out of collective need of the species.

But how is a person individuated from mankind—by differentials in intelligence or willfulness? No, this cannot be—animals also have differentials of this kind. At its prime, an animal has greater strength, willfulness, and perhaps even intelligence than when aged. Nevertheless, the basic nature encompasses them all, without the ability of individual choice.

So a person must individuate himself with the essence of who he really is: not only must he not remain imprisoned by social rules, cultural customs, or accepted thought without the ability to see beyond them, but he must also have a mind of his own. Without this, not only is he not a Jew but he is also not even a person.

This means bringing out that which is unique within you, that which depicts your very self. Your Torah learning or divine service should be not just an expression of your intelligence, but of your very essence as well. The way you approach Torah learning or prayer should represent you. When someone hears a Torah thought or a specific spiritual practice, let him be able to identify it as typically one of yours.

Take for instance the Rambam's [Maimonides] works—they can be identified by their style and distinct wisdom. The same is true of the Ramban's [Nachmanides]. This is so because each of them expressed his unique and essential self through the vehicle of Torah wisdom.

And this is not some privilege observed only for the great luminaries. Rather, each and every little one of us has not only the right but the obligation to express his unique and individual self. And to the degree that you are able to live in this world from the very center of your unique self, to that degree will you be able to exercise your individual free will.

Raise yourself up above the crowd; bring out what makes you unique. Become a person who can choose for himself—the prerequisite for reaching God.

THE DYNAMICS OF PASSIONATE EMOTIONS

When a person has not prepared himself for the spiritual afterlife, when he departs he will be exposed to the naked experience of a wasted life. These are called "naked souls," who, spiritually homeless, must enter the spiritual netherworlds.

But even in this life, when a person sins and channels his passions in the wrong direction, parts of his soul already enter into the spiritual netherworlds. And even if he doesn't sin—just does not channel his passions into spiritual service with no outlet of holiness in which to go, his passions will fall toward the netherworlds. These parts of his soul, his potential passion for God, are transformed into baser passions.

The greater the soul, the greater the danger if he does not channel his passions Godward. His greater soul with its greater passions remain naked, and his passions will go somewhere else.

So as sitting back and refraining from sin is tantamount to doing a *mitzvah* (*Kiddushin* 39b), sitting back and not serving God with passion is sometimes tantamount to a transgression.

ENVISIONING YOUR IDEAL SPIRITUAL SELF

If you have already tried everything without success, if you have tried to rouse your soul with all your means but it has not been aroused to lead the conscious life that it should and to yearn for the spiritual life that behooves it, this is what you should do:

Envision yourself as already the ideal spiritual person you really are. Just imagine the greatness of your soul . . . see how your soul shines in God's garden, in Eden, as He comes to enjoy your company with His holy entourage. . . .

Meditate deeply on these pictures. . . . Hold these images in your mind's eye. . . . Inevitably, you will be roused to a higher awareness. . . . You do not want to sully your soul. . . . Savor the bliss of embrace by the great Creator as you yearn to actualize this from the depths of your soul.

PASSING OPPORTUNITIES FOR GROWTH

When your conceit is at wane, when your boldness is low, when you ego defenses are down—do not yet think you have "made it." Rather, move fast to go deep inside, grab the chance to work on yourself. Plow through your hardened inner blocks, heal the wounds of your soul. With honest soul searching, without self-deception, clean out all the poison from your soul.

But quickly! Because even though now you feel a surrender to God, you may only be responding to an unfulfilled wish. Maybe it's sadness over an unreceived honor, or some other frustrated wish turns you to God, although you yourself are unaware of it. You cannot be sure that the minute your wish is fulfilled your broken heart will not reosiffy. An iron curtain will close off the temporary breach, your heart itself will feel like stone. Sealed and boarded up at every possible entrance, you remain locked outside yourself. You now may long to heal the wounds of your soul, but alas, how can you care when you are outside?

35

YOSEF YITZCHAK
SCHNEERSOHN

FEW JEWS IN THE WORLD *today are unfamiliar with the Hasidic movement known as Chabad-Lubavitch. Originating with Rabbi Schneur Zalman of Liadi in the late eighteenth century, it seemed doomed to near-extinction with the triumph of Communism in Russia, followed by World War II and the Holocaust. Yet, to Rabbi Yosef Yitzchak Schneersohn such calamitous events were ultimately a spur for more intense and vigorous Jewish religious activity. Rescued from Nazi-controlled Warsaw in 1939 by high-level U.S. diplomatic intervention, he quickly established a new Hasidic base in New York City with a small staff, including his son-in-law, Rabbi Menachem Mendel Schneerson, and assertively launched a historically unprecedented set of Jewish educational, communal, and outreach ventures whose influence is still being felt today.*

The sixth Lubavitcher Rebbe strongly emphasized inner growth through Hasidic prayer, study, and meditation. Thus, at the time of his death in 1950 at age seventy, leading Chabad-Lubavitch teachers were still actively imparting specific methods for achieving higher consciousness, reflecting his view that soul development was paramount for every Jew.

These selections are drawn from Rabbi Schneersohn's final treatise, known as Basi LeGani *(My House in the Garden), cherished by Lubavitchers as among his most important work. It comprises a four-part series of Hasidic discourses based on the biblical verse Song of Songs 5:1, "I have come into my garden, my sister, my bride." Its first part was released in advance, with the intention that it be studied on the yahrzeit of his beloved grandmother's passing; as it transpired, this was also to be the date of his own passing. Focusing on the nature of earthly life,* Basi LeGani *expresses the sixth Lubavitcher Rebbe's view that "all the effort of man for which his soul toiled during his lifetime . . . becomes revealed at the time of his passing."*

Two very different levels of God's infinite light are represented in the particular teaching of *Tikkunei Zohar:* "God's infinite light extends without bounds and downward without end."

The light that "extends upward without bounds" is a hidden and sealed light that transcends—and will never enter—the realm of descent into worldly revelation. This is the light referred to in the classic statement, "You are exalted above all the exalted ones, hidden from all the hidden ones." This light is by nature sealed.

The kind of light that "extends downward without end" can come within the realm of revelation and is related to the worlds. In general terms, it is a light that is revealed to God Himself (to his *Atzmus*): within His Essence it is revealed to Himself, so to speak. In this it differs from the former kind of light, which is not revealed even within His Essence, but remains sealed.

These two kinds of light represent two kinds of God's transcendent light [or *makkif;* literally, "encompassing light"]: the transcendent spiritual influence known as *or yashar* [literally, "direct light"] and the transcendent spiritual influence known as *or chozer* [literally, "reflected light"]. [The term "transcendent" or "encompassing" described a light too intense to be internalized within a limited recipient; "direct light" signifies light enclothed within creation; "reflected light" signifies light that cannot be enclothed and hence is "reflected" back to its source.]

The *makkif* of "direct light" is known as the "near *makkif*," inasmuch as it can become revealed; the *makkif* of "reflected light" is known as the "distant *makkif*," because it cannot be revealed.

An analogy from intellectual influence: When a teacher communicates an idea to his student, those [limited] aspects of the idea and their underlying rationale that the student can receive and soundly integrate may be called *or pnimi,* an internalized light. The profundity that now remains beyond his reach may be described as a light that "encompasses" his mind, impinging upon it in subtle and unseen ways. Nevertheless, this profundity is close to him: there will come a time when it will become accessible. In the words of our sages, "No one understands his Rebbe's teachings in all their depth until the passage of forty years." His time will come.

Another analogy for this kind of potential closeness: If a person sees or senses that a profound idea lies hidden, still quite unknown, in the subject of his study, then despite his temporary ignorance that idea may be said to be close to him. His wisdom, too, will ripen one day.

These analogies describe the encompassing light of *or yashar:* though it encompasses [the limitations of its recipients] it still is close to their inner selves [because it is ultimately accessible]. For a glimmer of it is already perceptible, and that which is hidden will eventually be revealed.

However, there are also concepts that are so profound that they are by definition hidden: no glimmer of them is revealed. King Solomon, for example, was granted a sublime understanding that utterly surpasses the grasp of created beings. As it is written, "And God gave wisdom to Solomon as He had promised him." No aspect of this wisdom was ever revealed or will ever be revealed.

Wisdom of this order is presented by means of garments that hide it, such as parables and riddles whose apparent superficiality is deceptive. This is true of the parables of King Solomon, the depth of which can be gauged in limited measure through the study of the *Midrash,* that is, only insofar as it was revealed to our sages through *Ruach HaKodesh* [the holy spirit], divine inspiration. In the parables themselves, however, one does not detect the light of intellect.

Similarly, the narratives of the Torah embody secrets and sublime mysteries to a higher degree than do the Torah's laws. However, they are not at all recognizable, for the essence of their light is a sealed secret, and is revealed only (as with parables) by means of concealment. Since by nature this light stands apart, even when revealed it remains separate and obscure, something closed off and hidden even from its *mashpia,* its [intellectual or spiritual] fountain-head. As a rule, intellectual exertion elicits an increase in the revelation of light. But when, in the case of this kind of light, its *mashpia* applies his intellect to it, though he will in fact experience an enhanced illumination, it will become hidden in his inner essence.

By contrast, in the case of intellectual light which is appropriate to a recipient, even when its *mashpia* delves deeply into it [without considering how to communicate it], it may be said to be close to the recipient. Though he will catch only a glimpse of the fresh insights that this teacher has unlocked (and even that glimpse will be attenuated to his measure), light of this kind is by definition close and accessible; it can be drawn downward. Since it is characterized by a thrust toward descent and revelation, the more that is revealed to the *mashpia,* no matter how deep his independent thinking may be, the more will be drawn down and revealed.

By contrast, the natural thrust of the deeper concepts that are innately sealed from any relation to a recipient, is toward self-concealment. In the case of such concepts, even when the *mashpia* applies his intellect to them and masters them, their light remains separate, and becomes hidden in his inner essence. . . .

The soul does not descend into the body for its own sake: as for itself, it is in no need of correction. The entire purpose of its descent is to correct, refine, and elevate the body and the natural soul. Before its descent into the body and the natural soul it was in the ultimate state of *devekut,* truly and constantly cleaving to its source in the living God without any separation whatsoever. As it is written, "The sublime image of each and every soul used to stand before the Holy King." At that level, the soul has one wish: for God alone and none other.

It descended from that state to enclothe itself in the body and natural soul in order to refine and elevate them, and in order to bring light into its environment, its portion of the world. This is the entire intent of the soul's descent below. To this end, "days were formed." Every individual has been allocated a certain number of days to carry out his divine service through the refinement and restitution of the body and natural soul, and to bring light into his portion of the world through the light of the Torah and the light of prayer.

The real place for this labor is here below. For when the soul is in the spiritual worlds, as we have said, it enjoys the ultimate state of *devekut*. However, it descends into a body that is filled with alien wishes and physical and material desires that prevent it from expressing itself in Godly service. This challenge eventually calls for strenuous exertion in a most formidable battle, which can be won only by a determined desire for victory.

This determination allows a person to stand firm and fortify his involvement in Torah and in his service of God. For the animal soul seeks to overwhelm him, to cause him to sin, and to vex him, heaven forbid, with alien thoughts and all kinds of concerns, and to confuse him with the yoke of earning a livelihood and the bothers of business, or with other matters that disturb him until he is robbed of his peace of mind....

Ultimately, when a person conquers his own animal soul, he causes the forces of holiness on high to vanquish the forces of evil. Moreover, he causes the sublime treasures of the spiritual realms to be drawn down to this world below: he brings about the revelation of the innermost essence of God's infinity.

36

Abraham Joshua Heschel

"Just to be is a blessing. *Just to live is holy*," *declared Abraham Heschel, among the most widely read Jewish theologians of the past half-century. Celebrated for his inspirational writings extolling the Bible's prophetic, visionary tradition—and its contemporary relevance—he achieved philosophical renown far beyond the confines of his early Hasidic upbringing in pre–World War I Warsaw. Especially in the United States, where Rabbi Heschel lived for the last half of his life upon escaping Nazism, his influence on both popular and academic religious thought has been immense. Yet, only recently is the Kabbalistic foundation of his work gaining true recognition— for more than his famous contemporaries Martin Buber and Gershom Scholem, Heschel drew upon works like the* Zohar *to promulgate a new spiritual ethos for people of diverse faiths today.*

Heschel was born in 1907 Warsaw, and descended from a distinguished Hasidic lineage. After completing yeshiva training, he certainly could have followed closely in his family's rabbinic tradition. But strongly drawn to Western philosophy and history, he went a different path: earning a doctorate at the University of Berlin, and then teaching Judaism from a modern intellectual perspective.

Several years after immigrating to the United States in 1940,
he was appointed to the faculty of New York's Jewish Theological
Seminary, a post he held until his death more than twenty-five
years later. During those years, his books, such as The Sabbath:
Its Meaning for Modern Man, God in Search of Man, *and* The
Insecurity of Freedom *spurred many Jews and non-Jews alike*
to find personal meaning and direction in biblical and post-biblical
Judaism.

In this beautiful essay on awe and wonderment, Rabbi Heschel
relied partly on the Zohar, Joseph Albo, and the biblical book of
Psalms.

The message that the Bible conveys is not that of despair or agnos-
ticism. Job does not simply say, "We do not know," but rather that
God knows, that "God understands the way to it," He knows where
wisdom is. What is unknown and concealed from us is known and
open to God. This, then, is the specific meaning of mystery in one
sense. It is not a *synonym for the unknown,* but rather a name for a
meaning which stands in relation to God.

Ultimate meaning and ultimate wisdom are not found within
the world but in God, and the only way to wisdom is through our
relationship to God. That relationship is awe. Awe, in this sense, is
more than an act of emotion; it is a way of understanding. Awe is
itself an act of insight into a meaning greater than ourselves.

The question, therefore, *where shall wisdom be found?* is answered
by the Psalmist: *the awe of God is the beginning of wisdom.* The Bible
does not preach awe as a form of intellectual resignation; it does
not say, awe is the end of wisdom. Its intention seems to be that
awe is a way to wisdom.

The beginning of awe is wonder, and the beginning of wonder is awe.

Awe is a way of being in rapport with the mystery of all reality.
The awe that we sense or ought to sense when standing in the
presence of a human being is a moment of intuition for the like-
ness of God which is concealed in his essence. Not only man; even
inanimate things stand in a relation to the Creator. The secret of

every being is the divine care and concern that are invested in it. Something sacred is at stake in every event.

Awe is an intuition for the creaturely dignity of all things and their preciousness to God; a realization that things are not only what they are but also stand, however remotely, for the reference everywhere to Him who is beyond all things. It is an insight better conveyed in attitudes than words. The more eager we are to express it, the less remains of it.

The meaning of awe is to realize that life takes place under wide horizons, horizons that range beyond the span of an individual life or even the life of a nation, a generation, an era. Awe enables us to perceive in the world intimations of the divine, to sense in small things the beginnings of infinite significance, to sense the ultimate in the common and the simple; to feel in the rush of the passing the stillness of the eternal.

In analyzing or evaluating an object, we think and judge from a particular point of view. The psychologist, economist, and chemist pay attention to different aspects of the same object. Such is the limitation of the mind that it can never see three sides of a building at the same time. The danger begins when, completely caught in one perspective, we attempt to consider a part as the whole. In the twilight of such perspectivism, even the sight of the part is distorted. What we cannot comprehend by analysis, we become aware of in awe. When we "stand still and consider," we face and witness what is immune to analysis.

Knowledge is fostered by curiosity; wisdom is fostered by awe. True wisdom is participation in the wisdom of God. Some people may regard as wisdom "an uncommon degree of common sense." To us, wisdom is the ability to look at all things from the point of view of God, sympathy with the divine pathos, the identification of the will with the will of God. "Thus says the Lord: Let not the wise man glory in his wisdom, let not the mighty man glory in his might, let not the rich man glory in his riches; but let him who glories in this, that he understands and knows Me, that I am the Lord who practices kindness, justice, and righteousness on the earth; for in these things I delight, says the Lord" (Jeremiah 9:22–23).

There are, of course, moments of higher or lower intensity of awe. When a person becomes alive to the fact that God "is the great ruler, the rock and foundation of all worlds, before Whom all existing things are as nought, as it has been said, all the inhabitants of the earth are as nought" (Daniel 4:32), he will be overwhelmed by a sense of the holiness of God. Such awe is reflected in the exhortation of the prophets: "Enter into the rock, hide thee in the dust, from before the terror of the Lord, from the splendor of His majesty" (Isaiah 2:10). . . .

Fear is the anticipation and expectation of evil or pain, as contrasted with hope, which is the anticipation of good. Awe, on the other hand, is the sense of wonder and humility inspired by the sublime or felt in the presence of mystery. Fear is a "surrender of the succors which reason offers;" awe is the acquisition of insights which the world holds in store for us. Awe, unlike fear, does not make us shrink from the awe-inspiring object, but, on the contrary, draws us near to it. That is why awe is compatible with both love and joy.

In a sense, awe is the antithesis of fear. To feel "The Lord is my light and salvation" is to feel "Whom shall I fear?" (Psalms 27:1). "God is my refuge and my strength. A very present help in trouble. Therefore will we not fear, though the earth do change, and though the mountains be moved into the heart of the seas" (Psalms 46:2–3).

Awe precedes faith; it is at the root of faith. We must grow in awe in order to reach faith. We must be guided by awe in order to be worthy of faith. Awe rather than faith is the [primary] attribute of the religious Jew. It is "the beginning and gateway of faith, the first precept of all, and upon it the whole world is established." In Judaism, *yirat hashem,* the awe of God, or *yirat shamayim,* the "awe of heaven," is almost equivalent to the word "religion." In biblical language, the religious [person] is not called "believer," as he is for example in Islam (*mu'min*), but *yere hashem.*

There is thus only one way to wisdom: awe. Forfeit your sense of awe, let your conceit diminish your ability to revere, and the universe becomes a marketplace for you. The loss of awe is the great block to insight. A return to reverence is the first prerequisite for a revival of wisdom, for the discovery of the world as an allusion to God. Wisdom comes from awe rather than from shrewdness. It is evoked not in moments of calculation, but in moments of being in rapport with the mystery of reality. The greatest insights happen to us in moments of awe.

A moment of awe is a moment of self-consecration. They who sense the wonder share in the wonder. They who keep holy the things that are holy shall themselves become holy. . . .

Reverence is one of [humanity's] answers to the presence of mystery. We do not sense the mystery because we feel a need for it, just as we do not notice the ocean or the sky because we have a desire to see them. The sense of mystery is not a product of our will. It may be suppressed by the will, but it is not generated by it. The mystery is not the product of a need, it is a fact.

The sweep of mystery is not a thought in our mind, but a most powerful presence beyond the mind. In asserting that the ineffable is spiritually real, independent of our perception, we do not endow a mere idea with existence, just as I do not do so in asserting, "This is an ocean," when I am carried away by its waves. The ineffable is there before we form an idea of it.

37

BABA SALI

Yisrael Abuchatzeira

TO MOST NORTH AMERICAN *and European Jews today, the name Baba Sali is unfamiliar—and most likely, suggestive of a Hindu holy man. Even those conversant about Kabbalah and Hasidism are likely to report ignorance. Yet, this name, which means "our praying father" in Arabic, was the laudatory designation bestowed upon Rabbi Yisrael Abuchatzeira by contemporary Sephardic Jewry. Born in 1890 Morocco into a renowned family of rabbinic leaders steeped in Kabbalah, he became in his own lifetime the subject of countless legends about his piety and miracle-working capability.*

Though charismatic figures often vanish to obscurity soon after their deaths, such has definitely not been the case with Baba Sali— who settled in Israel only during the last twenty years of his life. For each year at his grave site in the southern town of Netivot more than one hundred thousand followers come to celebrate his yahrzeit *in an exuberant daylong event known as* hillulla. *In a land replete with holy sanctuaries and age-old pilgrimage traditions, this celebration has incredibly become Israel's second-most-popular religious*

*gathering—eclipsed only by ancient Rabbi Simeon bar Yochai's
yahrzeit in Meron each Lag B'Omer.*

*How is this possible? Is it all due to Israel's changing demo-
graphics, particularly the rising role of Moroccan Jewry, with its
traditional Kabbalistic embrace? Or does it reflect some deeper
spiritual process at work in the Jewish world? To be sure, Rabbi
Abuchatzeira was a respected scholar from a family long admired
for its deep involvement in public affairs. Following his father's
death, he also became head of the Tafilalt yeshiva in Morocco, and
was widely admired for his lectures on halacha and esoteric works
like the Zohar. But even more important, it seems, in his elevation
as a sage was his reputation as a practicing Kabbalist—and a daily
life marked by strict reclusiveness, asceticism, and exacting religious
observance.*

*Baba Sali wrote no books, though anthologies of his discourses
have been posthumously published in Israel. More widely circulated
among his admirers are works concerning his inspirational and
seemingly paranormal deeds, often involving prayer, trance, or
dreams. These selections draw upon such books, except for the final
selection, which was provided through a personal interview conducted by an Israeli rabbi specially for this chapter.*

KNOWLEDGE OF KABBALAH

Once during one of the many *hillullahs* held in Rav Yisrael's home,
the assembly sang the song "Bar Yochai." When they came to the
word *b'ketoreth,* one of the guests asked the Rav to explain it
according to the Kabbalah. Baba Sali refused, stating, "It's forbidden
to reveal everything—let's continue the song."

A few moments later, the guest again repeated his request, asking if the Rav could reveal the meaning of the word through hints
and suggestions. Rav Yisrael put a quick end to the discussion by
saying, "If I were to spend three months explaining the meaning
of this word, I would not be finished. Please let us continue with
the song."

AN INDELIBLE MIND

Rav Yisrael had a phenomenal memory. Perhaps this ability of total recall came through his knowledge of hidden things. Everything that he learned literally lived "in his mouth." He could summon information immediately, whether it dealt with matters pertaining to Jewish law, Talmud, Kabbalah, or anything else.

He once said, "My grandfather, the holy Rabbi Yaakov Abu-Chatzeirah, had a gift regarding the *Zohar HaKadosh.* Every page he studied, he knew by heart. I am blessed in that every page that I learn from the Talmud, I need only learn once and I never forget!"

READING THE HOLY BOOKS

"Every Jew is required to complete the Book of Psalms at least once a month," he would say. He added that there is a special significance and power in the words of the Psalmist, David HaMelech (King David). "They can, indeed, work wonders...."

Every *Shabbat,* Baba Sali was called to the Torah for the sixth *aliya,* in accordance with his wishes. The reason for this is that all the *aliyot* correspond to certain Kabbalistic tenets, the sixth one being "yesod," which is "foundation."

When he was called up to the Torah, Baba Sali read his own portion. Throughout the year, he went up on the sixth *aliya,* with the exception of the reading of the Ten Commandments.

When he was called to read the Ten Commandments, he wept and the reading took more than an hour. When he reached the second half of the commandments, the "Thou Shalt Not(s) ..." he would cry bitterly.

Whenever Rav Yisrael went to Jerusalem he studied the *Zohar HaKadosh.* Often he would ask to be taken there for a few hours just to study the book. "It is worth going there to learn only one chapter of the *Zohar,*" he would say. "One chapter there is like ten chapters in another city!"

A PROGRAM OF EXCHANGE

Through his love for his fellow Jews, Baba Sali brought people closer to Torah. On occasion, he would give a *bracha* [blessing] in "exchange" for the better observance of a *mitzvah,* or the effort to change a bad habit.

"If you will give me your word that you will change your ways, then I will pray for you," he would say. In this way, people would initially change, and many would become *Baalei Teshuvah,* and his blessings changed their lives.

COUNTING THE OMER

The performance of *mitzvot* was a priority for Baba Sali and he took great joy in doing them. Typical of his manner in doing *mitzvot* was the way he performed the *mitzvah* of the counting of the Omer. Every day was a new *avodah* [spiritual service]. For hours he would prepare himself so that he could perform it properly.

His *gabbai* [rabbinic aide] said that more than an hour before the time of *maariv,* after which it was customary to perform the *mitzvah,* the Rav would be impatient. "Nu, when can we *daven* and complete the *mitzvah* of the counting of the Omer?" he would ask. After *davening,* when everyone had already finished counting the Omer and were in the midst of reciting various chants and hymns, Baba Sali would just begin to say the blessing! He concentrated on the meaning of every letter of every word according to Kabbalah. Each day had another order and a different designation; each thought he examined carefully. His gabbai recalled that time after time, he would review the number of the day with a *minyan.* What's more, in the middle of the night, Baba Sali awoke members of his family to ask them if they recalled whether he had counted that day in accordance with *halacha.*

Once, regretting that he had disturbed them so incessantly about the *mitzvah* of counting the Omer, he said to them, "Do you think that *Hashem* [God] needs our counting? *Hashem* favors us with the merit of observing various *mitzvot* every day, and so we have to be careful to do them diligently. The better we do each *mitzvah,* the more merit we receive!"

"THROUGH DREAMS, I SHALL SPEAK!"

One day, a frantic man burst into Rav Yisroel's waiting room. He tearfully begged everyone to allow him to go with his sick relative who lay on a stretcher before them to the Rav. Moments later, the sick man was brought weeping before Rav Yisrael. The doctors had given up hope in him. Now, as a last resort, he had come to appeal to Baba Sali for a *bracha.*

Rav Yisrael listened and, in a broken voice, blessed the sick man with a complete and speedy recovery. The Rav also told him to drink from a certain bottle of water every night before he went to sleep. After a few weeks, the man returned to the Rav and was walking normally. With shining eyes, the man told the following story:

Several days after I came to the Baba Sali, I had a dream. Baba Sali came to me and showed me a photo of a man. "This man," he said, "is Dr. Rafael Carso. He lives on a certain street in Tel Aviv. Go and ask him to treat you. He can help you."

The next morning, I remembered my strange dream. I quickly telephoned my daughter, who lives in Tel Aviv, and asked her to find out who this doctor was. She knew exactly who he was.

"But how do you know who he is?" she asked in aston- ishment. I described how he looked from the photo that the Rav had shown me in the dream. My daughter could not understand how I could so accurately describe someone I had never seen before. I told her about my dream. Imme- diately she went to the home of the doctor to arrange an appointment.

On the appointed day, I went to see the doctor. He examined me, and then told me to disregard all that I had been told by my previous doctors. From his diagnosis, I understood that I was not as sick as I had been led to believe. He prescribed new medication and today I am a well man.

The man completed his story and asked to be allowed to visit the Rav to tell and thank him personally. When his turn came, he was ushered in by the gabbai. The Rav's face lit up as soon as he saw the man. Before he could utter a word, Rav Yisrael smiled and said, "Through dreams I shall speak!"

Two years passed. One day a man from Tel Aviv telephoned the home of Rav Yisrael. The man asked if the Rav could give him a *bracha* over the phone for a speedy recovery. The caller was asked to identify himself and reveal his profession. "I am a doctor, and my name is Dr. Rafael Carso," he replied. When the gabbai heard this, he recalled the man who had visited on a stretcher some two years earlier. "Tell me," the gabbai asked, "Do you live in Tel Aviv?"

"Yes," said the man, astonished. The gabbai surprised him even further by proceeding to describe his appearance. "From where do you know me?" the doctor asked. He had never been to the Rav's home, and neither had he treated anyone from the Rav's home.

"Should you decide to come here, I will tell you," replied the gabbai, wanting the doctor to visit the Rav soon. He wanted to be present when the Rav and the doctor met. They were two people who had never met before, yet the doctor's picture had been in the hands of Rav Yisrael in a dream. Only a few hours later, the doctor and his family arrived at Baba Sali's home. The doctor was eager to meet this mysterious rabbi who had appeared with his photo in one of his patient's dreams.

When the doctor entered the room, the gabbai introduced him to the Rav and explained that this was the doctor whose photo Rav Yisrael had displayed in the sick man's dream. When Baba Sali heard this, his face lit up and he said, "Through dreams, I will speak." Immediately he requested a table be set lavishly with food and drink. He then blessed the doctor with a speedy recovery, and many more years.

THE TUMOR

The year was 1964, and Yaakov was the fourteen-year-old son of one of Morocco's most prominent Jewish émigrés to Israel. Back in Marrakesh, his father Laviv had been a wealthy businessman and philanthropist, and a close supporter of Baba Sali, who had recently immigrated to the historic town of Yavneh. Laviv believed that he had been blessed with a large family, thanks in part to Rabbi Abuchatzeira's holy prayers.

Though Yaakov had enjoyed good health, he suddenly developed a rapidly growing tumor on his right ear. Laviv promptly consulted medical specialists, who advised immediate surgery, lest Yaakov lose the ear entirely. The operation was duly scheduled, but Yaakov seemed frightened about it. This seemed odd to Laviv, as his oldest son rarely showed worry about anything. Yet, as the surgery day approached, Yaakov became more and more frightened about the impending operation and begged that it be canceled. With less than a week to go, Laviv decided to take Yaakov to Baba Sali for advice.

Without even phoning for an appointment, Laviv drove with Yaakov to Baba Sali's home in Yavneh. The gabbai knew Laviv well from their educational fund-raising together in Morocco, and warmly greeted him. The gabbai immediately conferred in an inner room with Baba Sali, who soon ushered him into his presence. Laviv explained the seemingly urgent medical situation and Babi Sali then turned to Yaakov.

"Do you put on *tefillin* and *daven* every day? he asked.

"Of course," answered Yaakov decisively, "I'm religious."

Baba Sali nodded and then silently gazed at him for what must have been several minutes. He then stepped into an adjoining room and fetched a bottle of water. After pronouncing a blessing over it, he handed it to Laviv and said: "Cancel the operation immediately.

Make sure that every day your son drinks some of this holy water and also puts some on his ear. Don't let the bottle go empty. When the water is almost gone, you may add additional water at your home." Baba Sali then asked his gabbai to serve lunch to his guests, and they all ate together.

Later that day, the doctors called and asked to confirm the surgery for the upcoming Monday. Laviv explained that he had just been to Rabbi Yisrael Abuchatzeira in Yavneh and had decided to cancel the operation. The doctors emphatically advised against this decision, and the conversation abruptly ended. Over the next few weeks, Laviv and Yaakov did as Baba Sali had advised, and Yaakov's tumor began to shrink each day until it was gone. The doctors phoned at this time to ask about Yaakov's medical condition, and Laviv informed them that the tumor was gone—which they regarded as medically impossible!

38

MENACHEM MENDEL SCHNEERSON

UNDOUBTEDLY, THE MOST *influential Hasidic leader in the world during the past half-century was Rabbi Menachem Mendel Schneerson—known simply as the Rebbe to Chabad-Lubavitchers and numerous admirers. Born in 1902 Russia, he gained a reputation as a brilliant Talmudic scholar interested in modern science and technology, and worked closely as an administrator with his father-in-law—the sixth Lubavitcher Rebbe—in Eastern and Baltic Europe before reaching the United States through diplomatic intervention in early 1940. Exactly one year after the latter's death in New York City in 1950, Rabbi Menachem Mendel Schneerson became the Lubavitchers' charismatic leader, greatly expanding existing programs in Hasidic education, communal service, and Jewish outreach around the globe for the rest of his life.*

To those familiar with both figures, the last Lubavitcher Rebbe downplayed advanced Hasidic meditation in rabbinic training, as well as Kabbalistic practices in general. He was temperamentally more interested in encouraging external religious activity—such as good deeds and mitzvot—*than in promulgating methods for achieving exalted inner states through prayer or meditation, in*

*comparison to his father-in-law. Nevertheless, throughout Rabbi
Schneerson's many public talks, voluminous correspondence, and
many private sessions with Hasidim and other individuals, he
clearly applied concepts from the Lurianic Kabbalah to bless and
guide individuals seeking greater purpose and meaning in life.*

*Particularly vital in the seventh Lubavitcher Rebbe's approach to
spiritual counseling was his emphasis that everyone must find their
God-given mission to reach their full potential on earth; and that
this mission usually involved recognizing and then actualizing one's
skills and talents in helpful ways, always seeking to make our world
a better and holier place. These selections present his perspective on
the purpose of human existence, and the more specific issue of true
leadership.*

WHY DO WE EXIST?

Once we recognize G-d as the absolute reality, we must question
human existence. We know now that we exist (because G-d told
us so), but we also know that there is nothing to say we *must* exist.
G-d's universe would hardly cease to be if any one us had not been
born. Indeed, G-d's absolute reality would not be affected in any
way if our entire existence had never occurred.

Our creation, therefore, is G-d's way of *choosing* each of us to
exist. None of us is here by accident; we are here because G-d
wants us to exist. But why? G-d created the universe and life as we
know it in order to fulfill His vision as a divine architect. "G-d
desired to have an abode in the lower worlds." He created the
earth, the resources that rest within it, and the human beings who
dwell upon it. It is our duty to tap those resources in order to refine
and perfect the material world and make it a home for G-d. That
is the purpose of human life.

In order for us to achieve this purpose, G-d created this "lowest"
world, our world. It is a world in which G-d's reality is initially obscured, where we see human reality as primary. Why did G-d choose
to obscure His "authorship"? Because in order for man to truly

exist, to make choices in life, we are allowed to experience ourselves as an independent reality. If we had no independence, our existence would be meaningless; we would be like mere puppets on a string.

Instead, G–d created an "agnostic" world, where His reality is not visible. He obscured His presence from us so effectively that we actually perceive *ourselves* as the *only* reality. We may understand that G–d is reality, but we experience G–d's existence as something outside ourselves, as a superimposed reality, whereas in truth, it is G–d who is real, while our existence is "on the outside."

There are layers and layers of comprehension dividing our sensory reality from the absolute reality of G–dly energy. Is this a game that G–d is playing, hiding Himself from human eyes? On the contrary, it is actually a gift, an opportunity for us to grow accustomed to the landscape. Before a child can write, he or she must first learn the alphabet. And before we can understand the brilliant light of G–d's reality, we must first let our eyes grow accustomed to the light that surrounds us. Then we can use our light to peer inside the many layers of a deeper reality.

But if our entire existence is based on the principle that G–d is obscuring his presence, how do we know that we actually exist in *His* eyes? How do we know that we are actually accomplishing anything by perfecting our material world? In the Bible, G–d tells us that He wants us to know Him, but how can we know a G–d that is totally beyond us? And does G–d really care about what we do?

The answer to these questions lies in understanding the mysterious and complex process by which G–d created human existence. G–d, who is Himself undefinable and indescribable, chose to create man and place him in a physical world that is both definable and describable. He also chose to manifest Himself in this world through the laws of logic that He created, through the awesome design of nature and of each human being, and through divine providence. We are allowed to experience these divine attributes so that we can begin to comprehend G–d and have a personal relationship with Him. Then we learn to abstract Him, ultimately realizing that G–d is even beyond anything that we can abstract.

Yes, we do actually exist from G-d's perspective, and G-d does care what we do—not because we *need* to exist or because G-d *needs* to care, but because He *chooses* it to be that way. So His care for us is absolute, nonarbitrary, and noncompromising.

The fact that G-d obscured his presence from us so that we feel that we are an existence onto ourselves does not mean that we do not exist from G-d's perspective. G-d's concealing His presence is not an absence of light; rather it is like a "container" that hides from our eyes that which is within the container. And what is inside the container is G-d's pure light and energy.

On our own, though, we do not exist, for "there is nothing else besides Him." But "with Him," we exist. What is *not* real is our perception that our existence is all there is. It is not within the scope of human intellect to comprehend how G-d can conceal His presence while allowing us to carry out an independent existence. But this mystery does not limit our relationship to G-d; it actually enhances it, further demonstrating how far removed G-d is from our existence, thus inducing our further awe of Him, and our longing to draw closer to Him and integrate His reality into our lives.

In order to unite with G-d, we must combine both perspectives, G-d's and ours. We must first fully use our minds and hearts to discover and understand G-d as much as we are capable; then we must accept that the human mind is not everything; that some things simply cannot be understood with our limited perception. This acknowledgment allows us to better relate to the very mystery of G-d's existence. We recognize the paradox that G-d is *beyond* reality as we know it, while at the same time *encompassing* reality. That G-d is able to create both the finite and the infinite, the physical and the transcendent—because He is beyond both; He is neither defined nor undefined. By contemplating this mystery, we raise ourselves to an entirely new plane; above all, we come to relate to G-d on *His* terms.

Since G-d does want us to unite with Him, He created an elaborate and elegant process by which we can do so. We begin by probing and asking questions, then emotionally grappling with our existential pain through our search for meaning. We slowly scale the vast mountain of reality, step by step, answering some questions, and discovering new ones, continually finding deeper answers until we finally begin relating to and uniting with G-d. We come to realize that we cannot define G-d; we accept that He is beyond all definitions, including the term "beyond all definitions." This is the ultimate unity. In a world of definitions and paradoxes, we recognize G-d, who is beyond all definitions and paradoxes.

Everything in this universe consists of two dimensions, an outer dimension and an inner dimension. Over time, we come to understand this dichotomy within ourselves. We recognize that although the physical body is our more visible, outer dimension, it is our inner dimension—our emotions, our desires and aspirations, our souls—that is far more important.

We must train ourselves to look at the universe in the same way. It is a matter of changing our perspective from "outside-in" to "inside-out." Instead of looking first at the outer layer, then traveling inward, we must learn to see the inner layer as our primary force. And we must cultivate the experience of this layer to the point where we can use it to inform the outer layer.

This is not a simple task, for we spend our entire lives looking at the universe from the outside in. At first, it may seem impossible to get to know a G-d who is so different from us. But G-d gave us the ability to talk about Him, and told us that we must do so. We can find G-d within ourselves, and we can even find the G-d that is well beyond us.

It is our duty, and our greatest challenge, to recognize the difference between human reality and G-dly reality, and to accept the opportunities he has provided to transport ourselves from one realm to the next.

HOW CAN EACH OF US BECOME A LEADER?

It is true that not everyone can become a leader like Moses. But every person, no matter how uneducated or poor, has something to teach the wisest and richest among us. No one is incapable of being a leader in some way, and no one is exempt from the responsibility.

You may think that you were not a "born leader." But why, then, were you created? Each of us has been given unique strengths and abilities; we have the choice to use them selfishly or to share them with others.

Every generation places particular demands on its leaders, and the leadership of every generation is linked to its predecessors. We have just as much to learn from Moses as from the leaders of the twentieth century; although the future may be vast, we can see a great distance when we stand on the shoulders of giants.

Our current generation is so hungry for meaning and direction, for spiritual nourishment, that each of us must serve as a leader. Whatever you have learned, whatever you have been touched by, you must share it with others. You cannot waste time wondering if you are truly equipped to help your fellow man. When someone is drowning, you don't take a life-saving course—you jump in the water and save a life!

So examine the areas in your life where people look to you as a leader—within your family, in your class at school, at work or at play. Ask yourself: Are you doing everything you can to influence them positively? Are you using all your abilities to inspire them intellectually, emotionally, and spiritually? Are you helping them live up to their true potential, so they can become leaders in their own right?

One leader creates another and another, ad infinitum, just as one candle's flame lights another and another, until the once-impenetrable darkness has turned to brilliant light.

PART SIX

Contemporary Thinkers

39

Zalman M. Schachter-Shalomi

REB ZALMAN, *as he prefers to be known, is founder of the Jewish Renewal movement. He was born in 1924 Poland and raised mainly in Vienna. Among the first Chabad rabbis to serve in Jewish outreach throughout the United States, Reb Zalman spent several years at yeshiva and synagogue posts in New England. He later begun his "second career" as a professor of Jewish Studies—initially at the University of Manitoba and later at Temple University—with influential writings focusing on such issues as innovative Jewish ritual and practice with an ecumenical outlook.*

It was in 1970s Philadelphia that Reb Zalman created the organization Bnai Or (Sons of Light), later renamed Pnai Or (Faces of Light). Rooted in what came to be called neo-Hasidism, its influence on American-Jewish religious activity for decades far exceeded its tiny staff and budget. After retiring from active academic life in 2004, he has continued to write, lecture, and mentor rabbinic students, cantors, and Jewish educators around the world.

In the first selection, Reb Zalman addresses a theme that has inspired Jewish mystics for millennia: the Messiah. To many drawn

to the Kabbalah today, the notion of the messianic age seems anach-
ronistic—stemming from a sense of historical or individual power-
lessness. After all, didn't the revered Rabbi Akiva in the second
century foolishly proclaim the soldier Bar-Koziba the Messiah
(renaming him Bar-Kochba or Son of the Star) after a few early
victories against Rome? Yet, Maimonides had much to say about
the messianic age, and the concept never really disappeared from
traditional Jewish belief. In this provocative excerpt adapted from a
discourse titled "The Kabbalah of Tikkun Olam," Reb Zalman of-
fers a fresh, spiritually empowering perspective. The second selection
reveals his thought on an important Kabbalistic theme: strengthen-
ing our devotion to God. It appears in his book Paradigm Shift.

THE TREE OF LIFE IS AWAKENING

Jewish Renewal speaks of paradigm shifts and "reformatting" our
tradition. We who are rooted in Hasidism and Kabbalah are seeking
to consciously reinterpret our relationship to that tradition. Even
at its inception, Hasidism was not well understood by most Jewish
leaders and instead erroneously labeled as another manifestation of
the terribly destructive messianic movement spearheaded by Shabbatai Zevi in seventeenth-century Turkey. I wish to compare and
contrast the theological, psychological, and cosmological foundations of our current self-understanding about Judaism concerning
the Tree of Life and the Tree of Knowledge.

I want us all to be partners in the work of "reformatting" Jewish
theology, so that the word of Jewish Renewal can spread. It is vital
that the reformatting of Jewish theology does not remain in the
hands of those who cannot handle the tension of what it takes to
be involved in the necessary paradigm shift. I ask you to be partners
with me in true renewal, not merely in the restoration of what
Judaism was like before the Holocaust. . . .

There have been strong voices recently calling for "Moshiach
[the Messiah] now!" This is not a completely new phenomenon. I
lived through such an apocalyptic time in the year 1943. There

have been seven Lubavitcher Rebbes since the Hasidic sect was founded in the late eighteenth century, and the sixth was my spiritual mentor, Rabbi Joseph Isaac Schneersohn. In that year, he published four broadsides in which he was saying that the Moshiach is coming now. He wrote that the walls of the Galut [the Great Diaspora] are burning down. Oy! It was 1943, after the Warsaw Ghetto uprising against the Nazis and with all the destruction that was occurring. In one sense, his statement was true.

Years later, I asked myself: what would Judaism have been like without its belief in the Moshiach? How would we have managed if, in the first two historical paradigms of Judaism, belief in the Moshiach had not been an option for us? Historically, as Jews, we were not put into a position of surplus powerlessness because we believed so fervently that a redemptive future was drawing us. We were being energized not only from the past at Mount Sinai, but also intensely energized by our future. For it was always the vision of Moshiach and world redemption that catalyzed us.

Think about that word *moshiach,* literally meaning "anointed with oil." What is so interesting is that the word also has something to do with what we might call "greasing the wheels." Figure that term: it involves a reduction in friction. Can you imagine a people full of friction, and then you take some oil and reduce the friction around them? So, from this perspective, what would Moshiach work be like? It would be for those wonderful healers who do aura cleaning and the like, and who could take friction from individuals: that which sets one individual against the other.

As Jews, we have had that element, that lubricant, that thing that gets us through tough birthing spaces, that greases the way. Every child who is born comes anointed with vernix, that white stuff on the skin. What a wonderful sliding, gliding material that substance is! Every child born is anointed in this way, a Moshiach. We wipe it off, but every newborn child has it. It is amazing.

I am convinced that the vision of Moshiach is one of the essential amino-blocks in the composition of being Jewish. It is a necessary and vital psychospiritual ingredient—the creedal affirmation

"I believe in the coming of the Messiah"—absolutely necessary for having a vital Jewish thrust in the world. . . .

In the Land of Israel early in the twentieth century, Rabbi Abraham Isaac Kook was imbued with the notion of *teshuvah* (returning inwardly to the divine source) because to him the notion of the Moshiach flows from that special grace of God which he poetically called "the light of *teshuvah.*" This is the light that brings about a great "turning" or transformation on psychological, spiritual, and societal levels. Rav Kook believed that the transformative principle is going to take hold of us all and change us to what we need to become—and that we could not even imagine what this process would be like. That conception of Rav Kook seems to be very relevant to us today. The degree of transformation happening at present is so accelerated that its speed appears incredible. Our entire perception of that which is "subject-object oriented"—in other words, when one person does something to another in a Newtonian or billiard-ball fashion—simply is no longer applicable. There seems to be a lot of transformation occurring, and also a huge amount of *fear* about transformation. . . . We must understand that there is so much birthing going on, so much shifting and transforming. By and large, people today lack a meaningful belief system to accommodate this amount of transformation. It is beyond anything that we have ever previously experienced.

That is the reason why, if we understand the Moshiach as a transformative principle, then we begin to understand that, in a way, the Moshiach is coming right now. We are in the midst of the coming of the Moshiach. In other words, I do not want to get rid of that "building block" that I need for my Jewish "amino acid" and inner well-being, but I wish to understand its function and process within my psyche. That is the key issue here.

Historically, every level of societal development had its technology. At one time, humanity's way of connecting to God was by offering animal and vegetable sacrifices: giving in kind. Then the preferred method became giving to God through language and words. Now we are moving into the realm of consciousness and energy. These seem to be the three paradigm shifts. I have devoted a lot of thought to this notion, and it has given me an understanding that we are experiencing today a periodic crisis of *geulah,* redemption from spiritual exile. In a positive sense, we are being redeemed from one hard set of being-in-the-world that no longer works, that is falling apart. And from underneath that brittle surface that is disintegrating comes something that lacks shape and form, yet which we can nonetheless recognize: the Moshiach principle. And we need to become Jewish spokespersons for that energy, shape, and form. . . .

Remember the biblical vision of the "peaceable kingdom?" How the sheep and wolf shall live together peacefully, and how the little child shall lead them? What is this all about? The Bible says that a day will come when the peaceable kingdom will exist on earth. Certainly, it gives us a sense of nostalgia for the Garden of Eden's harmony, and it projects our nostalgia into the future. It is an undeniably powerful image, and it resonates.

Now, when did you last experience that vision personally? What did it feel like for you? Can you describe it fully?

That experience is the source of theology. Theology is what happens when you have a transformative experience. You think about it, talk to yourself about it, discuss it with other people, and you end up with a new way to talk about God: a theology thus becomes created. Theology is the afterthought of the believer. It is not what gets you to believe. First you have the experience. Then you seek to understand it. So I also want you to remember the very first time you had this vision of the peaceable kingdom. That was your Moshiach seed.

When the medieval rabbis declared that "in the messianic age, people will understand the language of birds and trees," that was their way of description. But what is your own primary feeling about the peaceable kingdom? That is the key starting point. The imaginal wardrobe for the Moshiach always comes afterward.

THE BUILDING OF DEVOTION

The heart needs to love, to emulate an adored model. If God as a person were to face us in a tangible and sensory way, we would not need to work on making ourselves present to Him/Her. In the past, we looked for the highest in the models of our society and came up with parent, king, and judge. These models became the root metaphors into which we entered via emotional emulations. They took us to polarized extremes most easily available in the feudal systems. They also produced action directives most often urging our submission to God's providence. Traditional prayer was often a form of "apple-polishing" and "soft-soaping" of the exalted authority figure.

When people signed letters with, "Your most obedient and humble servant," it fit to use such expressions. However, the feudal, traditional models no longer are available to us in real beings. Presidents are not kings, parents are much more fallible to post-Freudians; judges are seen often as autocratic and worse, corrupt.

As a result, the devotional vocabulary is today very anemic. Without generating and nurturing a grateful attitude toward the Source of Life, prayer becomes barren. The masculine imagery connected with God is also a source of much pain and difficulty, and to this day, it is being used to deny access to women who wish to serve in sacerdotal capacities.

Somehow, chanting the words of the classical prayerbooks in one of the melodic modes of the tradition makes them more connotational, and thus, transparent to one's heart rather than reciting them as speech. Paradoxically, at times, significance and emotional focus is heightened by using the sacred language instead of the vernacular. This helps in group worship as well as in solo prayer. Another way utilized by some is the "arrow prayer"—short exclamations, like sighs addressed to God in one or another of His/Her Names or Attributes. This helps in directing our focus of affect, to better experience divine attributes.

Let's say that I am in need for guidance and sigh, "Oh Guide, Oh Light, Oh Helper!" The attributes invoked ad lib in free experience or according to a traditional pattern: Oh Goodness, Oh Power, Oh Heart, or Harmony, Oh Life, and Oh Majesty help in the arousal of affect. The Book of Psalms is still a very effective help when it is not merely recited. Each psalm is someone's experience with God. By placing oneself in the position of David upon being set free by Abimelekh after having feigned idiocy, it is easier to recite "I sought YHVH and He answered me, saving me from all my adversaries" (Psalms 34). . . .

Dawn and dusk are the natural times in which we would join not only the choirs of angels and archangels, but also of insects, amphibians, birds, and mammals. The sanctus is a law revealed by nature, echoed in the Bible, where in Leviticus we are bidden to offer a lamb at dawn and one at dusk. Services that begin at eleven o'clock in the morning cannot offer the same natural lift that a vigil for the dawn supplies.

Thus prayer, meditation, spritual practice at these times are more potent. The social compulsions of industrial time are set aside, and organic time is in force. This has great healing power and realigns the person to his/her God. Once rhythms of body and soul, of person and group, of male and female within the same person and in relationships are part of one's primary experience, the teachings of the calendar, the flow of the liturgical year, begin to make a natural sense. "Teach us to number our days that we may get us a heart of wisdom" (Psalms 90:12).

Cycles of the year and in life's stages are sure guides to the growth of the soul.

40

DAVID HANANIAH PINTO

AMONG THE LEADING *teachers of Kabbalah in the Sephardic Jewish world today is Rabbi David Hananiah Pinto. Like the Abuchatzeira family to which he is distantly linked by marriage, Rav Pinto, as he is often known, comes from a distinguished Moroccan rabbinic lineage. Born in Mogador (Essaouira), as a young man he studied Talmud,* halacha, *and Kabbalah at British yeshivot. When the Israeli Six-Day War involving Egypt, Jordan, and Syria erupted in 1967, David's parents left Morocco to settle in Israel, but advised him to remain in Europe. "My father told me, 'You're the foreign minister of your grandfather, the* zaddik *Rabbi Chaim Pinto. There are enough Torah centers and yeshivot in the Land of Israel. You have to spread Torah in the Diaspora. When the time comes, you'll live in Israel.'"*

Young Rav Pinto followed his father's advice, and at the age of only twenty-nine, opened his first Jewish study center in Manchester, England. Eventually, he became a rabbinic leader in Paris, which for more than thirty years has remained the base of his global network, today comprising Judaic educational, communal, and charitable organizations. Following well the Sephardic path set by his-

torical figures like the Chida and the Ben Ish Chai, Rabbi Pinto
typically integrates Kabbalah—particularly the rabbinic teachings of
Isaac Luria, Moses Cordovero, and Moses Chaim Luzzatto—with
biblical, Talmudic, ethical, and halachic sources in his numerous
public lectures and writings aimed at a broad audience.

These selections come from Rav Pinto's most influential work, a
five-volume commentary on the Pentateuch. They present his
thought on two Kabbalistic topics: the flow of divine energy through
the four realms of existence and the step-by-step process of individ-
ual growth, symbolized by the age-old biblical symbol of Jacob's
ladder.

THE GREATNESS OF MAN
AND HIS REASON FOR BEING

"Life propagates itself in all the worlds via the emanation from on high, and the propagation of this plenitude is only possible thanks to the connections that exist between them. To give a concrete example, if the pipes are not watertight, the water will flow outside, through the cracks, and it will be inevitably lost—but when the hosepipes are perfectly, hermetically sealed, the water reaches its destination, wherever it is necessary. The connection between all the worlds can only be realized by man, for it is to realize the union of all the worlds that he had been created, and it is through him that the abundance of blessings and of success diffuses in all the worlds," writes the author of *H'essed LéAvraham,* who continues: "The vitality of man derives from the world of the *Assiyah,* his spirit from the world of the *Yetzira,* and his soul from the world of the *Bryia.* He bears the name of Adam, which derives from all the worlds, and it is through him that the abundance of good deeds fills all the worlds." Such are his holy words.

On account of the fact that man carries within himself a part of all the worlds, he alone can work the connection between the worlds *Atzilut, Bryia, Yetzira, Assiyah,* through the intervention of which the abundance diffuses through all the worlds. We see that the responsibility to reconnect these worlds among one another falls essentially to man, for he derives from each of them. If he suppressed, for only an instant, one of the ties that reconnect them, all the creation would suffer on account of that.

Let us try to understand. It is written (*Bereshit* 2:3): "On this day G-d took a rest from the work of the creation that he had created in order to make it perfect." G-d had accomplished the work of the creation on the sixth day, just before the start of the Shabbat—while one day ends, the other begins—and man, whom he preferred, had been created last, in order to be responsible for the whole creation. This resembles the history of the king who constructs a splendid palace down to the smallest details, who calls in a male servant and commands him to watch over the cleanness of the place, telling him: "This house is mine and it must always stay in a perfect state, just as radiant as it is at the present!"

And yet, at the end of the verse, it is said: "to perfect it," signifying that something still remains to be accomplished. According to what we saw above, it is clear that man, in this world, has as task to watch over the creation as he received it and to add beauty to it. The Sages said (*Sanhedrin* 38a): "Man was created on the eve of Shabbat . . . in order to present himself immediately at the feast; as a king who builds a palace down to the smallest accommodations prepares a great feast and, once all is ready, introduces his guests to it, as it is said (*Mishley* 9:1–3): Wisdom built herself a house, she sculpted the seven columns, she prepared the animals for the meat, she mixed the wines, she set the table, and she sent her female servants to send out the invitations from the high points of the city. . . . "To preserve the creation in its entirety, man must first of all care about not breaking the connection between all the worlds, in order that the abundance of the eternal light that emanates from G-d may diffuse everywhere.

We know that the first man was created in such a way that he understood in himself to be a part of all the worlds (in the terms of the Kabbalah, this refers to the ten *sefirot*), it is thus he who orders them and reconnects them among one another, and it is in this way that the light and the fullness of G-d can pour themselves out in all the corners of the creation, for these worlds are connected to one another.

How can man reconnect the worlds *Atzilut, Bryia, Yetzira, Assiyah,* and the ten *sefirot,* to their source, to G-d? Uniquely thanks to the Torah, as it is said: "The upper knot of the *tefillin* is a commandment from the Torah" (*Mehah'ot* 39a). The Torah is the light (*Mishley* 6:23) that clarifies all the worlds. The intention of G-d is that man fulfill his task in a holy way, that he subsists by the sweat of his brow, without being dependent on charity. As long as he lives in holiness and purity, he receives from G-d compensation proportionate to his good deeds, according to divine promise.

MOVING FORWARD STEP-BY-STEP IN THE SERVICE OF G-D

"He had a dream: there, a ladder erected on the Earth and its summit reached Heaven" (*Bereshit* 28:12).

The commentators say on this subject that the ladder symbolizes man who is placed on the Earth, standing on his two legs but who, by the forces that he acquires, can expect to attain the heights of Heaven.

Let us clarify this idea. If the Torah wants to make us feel that man, although attached to the Earth by his physical and terrestrial nature, is capable of achieving a spiritual level comparable to that of the angels, why does it render this idea through an image, that of the ladder? Why is it not shown to Yaakov that he himself will reach Heaven?

It is necessary to point out that a ladder is made out of rungs that make it possible to climb—or to descend—that which would be impossible without those steps. This signifies that to reach summits, man is obliged to put himself in danger and to make an effort, for the service of G-d is a progressive elevation. He who climbs the rungs grows tired, gets out of breath, and complains, as much due to his continually greater efforts, as due to the time it takes to reach the goal—that which is the opposite of the descent, which only requires a little bit of effort and time. Along the same lines, he who wants to move forward and to arrive at his spiritual ends must advance through his own force, in steps.

Several times in the Talmud we find the following teaching (*Chekalim* 6a; *Avoda Zara* 20b; *Yeroushalmi Shabbat* 1:3): "Rabbi Pin'has ben Yaïr says: The Torah leads to prudence, prudence leads to attention, attention leads to propriety, propriety leads to asceticism, asceticism leads to purity, purity leads to piety, piety leads to humility, humility leads to fear of error, fear of error leads to holiness, holiness leads to divine inspiration, divine inspiration leads to resurrection, and piety is the greatest of all the qualities." In the books of ethics, this teaching is called "the ladder of Rabbi Pinchas ben Yaïr" and it serves as the basis for the book of Rabbi Moshe Hayim Luzzatto, *Messilat Yecharim* (The Gaon of Vilna said about this book that he did not find in it one word too many).

The word *soulam* (ladder) has the numerical value of a hundred and thirty, indicating the hundred and thirty years during which Adam separated himself from his wife Hava (*Yirouvin* 18b), after having eaten the fruit from the tree of life. Adam wanted to distance himself from material things, so mortified he was to have caused death in the world, and that separation merited him to be called "pious" (*Yirouvin* 18b; *Zohar* III:76b). This teaches us that to reach the step of piety, which is at the summit of the ladder—since piety is the greatest of the qualities of the ladder of Rabbi Pinchas ben Yaïr—man must distance himself as much as possible from the futilities of this world, and it is in doing so that he will be able to raise himself higher and higher in the steps of sanctification. After having successfully climbed all the steps that lead to piety, he will arrive at the height of perfection.

Ya'akov's ladder—and his secret—represents the forward march, the step by step climb, that makes it possible to expect to attain the heights, to the point of arriving at the virtue of piety and the resurrection of the dead.

We must add that the verse: "And there, the angels of G-d climbed and descended the ladder" (*Bereshit* 28:12) teaches us that to abandon the attractions and temptations of this world is so difficult that despite himself, man "climbs and descends," he moves forward and he falls. But man does not have to become terrified or discouraged, for it is said immediately after: "The Eternal holds himself upright at the summit." If man understands that G-d holds himself above him, that He is there to support him despite his climbs and descents due to the fact that he is "on the Earth," attached to material and terrestrial things, he will always rise higher—and will reach Heaven.

Nevertheless, he risks getting discouraged and telling himself: how is it possible that a being such as myself, of flesh and blood, of dust of the Earth, anchored in materiality, attains the level of a celestial angel? But this thought must not disturb him. He must know that G-d loves him and does not abandon him, but that he demands of him to always make more of an effort. This is not any easy thing, because the bad tendency keeps watch and "seeks daily to kill virtuous man" (*Kidoushin* 30b) and to make him fall as low as possible.

We see in effect that Ya'akov elevated himself progressively, even above the angels, such as in his struggle against Essav's guardian angel (*H'oulin* 91a), whom he vanquished and to whom he said: "I will only let you leave if you have blessed me" (*Bereshit* 32:27). But the angel cannot leave without the permission of Ya'akov (*Bereshit Rabba* 78:2). "He tells him: Let me leave, now he who sends back is superior to he who is sent back," and (*Bereshit Rabba* 78:6): "You have struggled with the celestial powers and you have vanquished them." The celestial powers make reference to Essav's angel.

41

JONATHAN SACKS

BORN IN 1948 *London, Jonathan Sacks is only the sixth person to serve as Chief Rabbi of the United Hebrew Congregations of Great Britain and the Commonwealth since the position was created in 1845. He received philosophy degrees from Cambridge and then Oxford before gaining rabbinic ordination from Jews' College—where he later became principal—and London's Yeshiva Etz Chaim. At his installation as Chief Rabbi in 1991, Dr. Sacks presented his vision of a reinvigorated Anglo-Jewry and launched it with a Decade of Jewish Renewal, followed by a series of innovative projects. These included Jewish Continuity (a national foundation established to encourage education and outreach), the Jewish Association for Business Ethics, the Chief Rabbinate Awards for Excellence, and Community Development, designed to enhance Jewish community life. In recognition of his commitment to interfaith dialogue, Rabbi Sacks was knighted in 2005.*

In such works as Crisis and Covenant, To Heal a Fractured World, *and* A Letter in the Scroll, *Rabbi Sacks has emphasized the importance of sustaining and expanding Jewish study in an increasingly secular era. Thus, he declares in the latter book, "I am a*

Jew because I cherish the Torah, knowing that God is to be
found not in natural forces but in moral meanings, in words, texts,
teachings and commands." For spiritual insight and inspiration
today, he has often turned to Maimonides, Hasidic masters, and
Jewish mystics.

    This selection is drawn from Rabbi Sacks's provocative essay
"Implications of Infinity," which appears in the anthology To
Touch the Divine. *It not only importantly presents the Kabbalah*
from a grand historical perspective, but also highlights the seminal
contribution of Rabbi Simeon bar Yochai—beloved second-century
thinker and resistance leader.

What is mysticism? The word conjures up connotations of lofty abstraction, other-worldly meditation, abstruse speculations into the meaning of existence—a world apart from, perhaps even opposed to, the mundane and prosaic questions that make up the texture of daily life. If that is so, what does mystical have to do with Judaism? It is, after all, the defining feature of Judaism, which some praise, others criticize, that its concern is with the small details of conduct....

It is one of the strange facts of the history of the Jewish mind that the great mystics have also been the great *halachists.* Their concern with infinity took them into some very finite areas indeed. To mention only the most familiar names: Joseph Karo, author of the *Shulchan Aruch* [Code of Jewish Law], was a member of the great mystical circle in Safed. Rabbi Schneur Zalman of Liadi, the first Rebbe of Lubavitch, is as well known for his code of law, the *Shulchan Aruch HaRav,* as for his mystical writings. Perhaps the greatest of all the early rabbinic teachers, Rabbi Akiva, whose methods shaped the whole development of the *Halacha,* was a profound mystic whose views sometimes perplexed, sometimes scandalized his contemporaries.

This mysticism/*Halacha* connection (for which a whole string of names can be adduced) is all the more striking compared with the other approach for resolving the fundamental questions of religion: philosophy. Of the great Jewish philosophers who were distinguished as *halachists,* only the name of Moses Maimonides stands out, with perhaps the lesser-known figure of Rav Saadia Gaon.

The reason lies deep. But for a single-sentence summary it would perhaps be fair to say that while the philosopher attaches great significance to great truths, the mystic attaches it to small ones as well. Since every fragment of the infinite is also infinite, perhaps it could also be said that while the philosopher thinks his way toward G-d, the mystic experiences and lives his way. For the mystic, every detail of the *mitzvah* is important. And hence his concern with detail—the essence of the *Halacha.*

But did all this make a practical difference?

In some ways, its impact was obvious. In the area of *minhag,* a great many Jewish customs are based upon considerations that are Kabbalistic: the way we hold the *kiddush* cup or the double loaves of bread on Shabbat, for example; or the retention of *mayim acharonim* [the handwashing at the conclusion of a meal] after the original reason ceased to apply. Perhaps the most dramatic incursion of a Kabbalistic practice into the normal routines of Judaism is the *Kabbalat Shabbat* service on Friday evenings. The *Lecha Dodi* song and the turning at the end to meet the Sabbath Bride coming from the direction of the setting sun—all originate from the sixteenth-century mystics in Safed.

Also, the mystics attached great significance to what is known as *hiddur mitzvah*—performing a precept in the most beautiful manner possible. This is an age-old concept:

"This is my G-d and I will beautify Him (Exodus 15:2)—beauty your fulfillment of His commandments. Make a beautiful succah, a beautiful lulav, a beautiful shofar, beautiful tzitzit and a beautiful Torah scroll—write it with fine ink, a fine pen, a skilled scribe, and wrap it in beautiful silks" (Talmud, *Shabbat* 133b).

Nonetheless, it received a prominence among the mystics, certainly among Hasidim, that it had not hitherto.

But both custom and beautification, intensity and adornment, are themselves dimensions of depth within the basic framework of the *Halacha*. Given then that the mystics had a profound motivation to be interested in the details of Jewish law, and that they added to it refinements which went beyond the essential requirements, do we have instances where the mystical vision affected the Halacha itself, in the sense that, in response to certain practical issues, the answers which emerged did so because of a certain fundamental orientation toward the infinite dimension in existence?

RABBI SIMEON BAR YOCHAI
AND RABBI JUDAH BAR ILAI

The figure whom Jewish tradition invests with the honor of being the grandfather of mysticism—not the first but the most influential—is Rabbi Simeon bar Yochai. Rabbi Simeon was one of the greatest of the rabbis of the late Mishnaic period, and he is a dominating presence in the early rabbinic literature, in both *Halacha* and *Aggadah*. Mysticism as such does not figure largely in the statements attributed to him in the Talmud: that belongs to the more esoteric literature of the *Zohar*. Nonetheless, a graphic picture of his personality emerges. He was a man of extremes, always uncompromising, always radical, a man for whom the study of the Torah transcended all else, and a man who cared nothing for the clichés of conventional wisdom.

The Talmud relates that, because of his opposition to the Roman government then in power in Israel, Rabbi Simeon was forced to escape for his life and to take refuge in a cave, where he and his son lived for twelve years, oblivious to the hardship, and only concerned not to waste a moment of time that could be spent in studying Torah:

> So they went and hid in a cave. A miracle occurred and a carob-tree and a well of water were created for them. They would take off their garments and sit up to their necks in sand. The whole day they studied. When it was time for

prayer, they robed, covered themselves, prayed and then took off their garments again so that they should not wear out. (Talmud, *Shabbat* 33b)

What is of interest to us here is: what occurred that Rabbi Simeon had to escape from the Romans? The account given by the Talmud is intriguing:

> Rabbi Judah [bar Iliai], Rabbi Yossei, and Rabbi Simeon were sitting, and Judah ben Gerim was sitting near them. Rabbi Judah began the discussion by saying: How fine are the works of this people [the Romans]. They have made streets, they have built bridges, they have constructed baths. Rabbi Yossi was silent. Rabbi Simeon bar Yochai answered and said: All that they have made, they have done for themselves. They built marketplaces to put harlots there; they made baths to rejuvenate themselves; they made bridges to levy tolls. (Talmud, *Shabbat* 33b)

Judah ben Gerim, who had overhead the conversation, reported it to the authorities. Rabbi Judah, who was silent, was sent into exile. Rabbi Simeon, who had so castigated the achievements of the Romans, was sentenced to death. It is fascinating, apart from the historical significance of the account, to overhear the two great rabbis, Rabbi Judah and Rabbi Simeon, who so often disagreed on matters of *Halacha,* this time debating a question of political and moral values.

In the broadest sense, the opinions they expressed were consistent with all we know about these two personalities. But what, specifically, was the argument between them on this occasion? Rabbi Judah was a politically sensitive individual, and there can be no doubt that he was fully aware of Rabbi Simeon's truth, that behind the remarkable technological achievements of the Romans—feats of construction that are no less awe-inspiring today—

lay moral bankruptcy. And Rabbi Simeon, in turn, knew that what Rabbi Judah said was true. What then divided them?

There are many possible ways of putting it. Amongst them, we will pursue just one line of thought. Namely, that Rabbi Judah looked at the facts, and Rabbi Simeon looked at the intentions that lay behind them. For Rabbi Judah, a fact, an achievement, could be impressive in its own right. For Rabbi Simeon, the question was always, "To what end was this intended?" If it is a corrupt or self-centered one, then I refuse to be impressed. Because no evaluation of human creations can be made without a consideration of the purpose for which they were meant.

It is an argument which in other forms can be heard today. There are those who argue, for example, that something can be considered a great work of art even if it is morally objectionable, because it should be considered in itself and without reference to any wider context. And there are others who say, to the contrary, that the moral context must be considered before we can pronounce any judgment at all.

But does the argument between Rabbi Judah and Rabbi Simeon have anything to do with mysticism? In a superficial sense, we could say that Rabbi Judah looked at the concrete, physical facts, while Rabbi Simeon looked instead at the realm of thought and intention. To this extent, Rabbi Simeon is interested in the intangible while Rabbi Judah focuses on the reality that is grasped by the senses.

But we must go deeper. What in general is the mystical vision? Is it that reality lies deeper than the appearances presented to our senses? To express it in a way that is at least roughly true of the Jewish mystical tradition: the physical world conceals more than it reveals. Beneath all appearances lies the reality of the Infinite, the Ein Sof, that can neither be perceived nor described....

And so it happens that a deeply esoteric view of the nature of G-d and the universe may carry with it quite simple implications for the way we interpret human behavior. While Rabbi Judah is

content to look upon the glittering surface of Roman achievements, Rabbi Simeon's restlessly searching mind takes him beyond,
to the less than impressive intentions and qualities of the soul which
set the civilization on its course. The mystic became a political
radical.

42

ADIN STEINSALTZ

BORN IN 1937 *Jerusalem, Rabbi Adin Steinsaltz was the only child of secular, socialist parents. But when he reached early adolescence, his father unexpectedly provided a Talmud teacher and declared, "I don't care if my son is a heretic, but he's not going to be an ignoramus." His early Judaic learning was supplemented by studies in physics, mathematics, and chemistry, and at the age of twenty-four, Rabbi Steinsaltz became the youngest high school principal in Israel. About the same time, he began offering inspirational talks on the Torah.*

In 1967, with the encouragement of then Israeli President Zalman Shazar—who was one of Rabbi Steinsaltz's students—he published the first of his multivolume, monumental project of translating and interpreting the entire Babylonian Talmud. Internationally, he is probably best known for this erudite work and related sponsorship of Talmudic study throughout the Jewish world. Beginning in the early 1990s, he turned his scholarly attention to Kabbalah and Hasidism with such books as The Thirteen Petalled Rose, In The Beginning, *and* The Strife of the Spirit.

*This selection is drawn from his commentary "Hidden Aspects
of Shabbat," based on teachings in the Liquetei Torah of Rabbi
Schneur Zalman of Liadi. For the nineteenth-century founder of
Chabad Hasidism closely followed the long Kabbalistic tradition of
venerating the Sabbath as no mere "day of rest," but a foretaste of
celestial bliss. In Rabbi Steinsaltz's view, many such classic works
of Hasidism are highly relevant to contemporary life. As he explains
in this essay, full Sabbath enjoyment involves dimensions of pleasure truly comprehensible only from a mystical perspective.*

Pleasure ranges from the highest to the lowest elements in the human soul. And there is perhaps no other force so all-encompassing,
so all-inclusive. But the totality of the many versions of pleasure
may be seen as having been derived from the Shattering of the
Vessels, which is also the origin of everything else that we consider
reality in this world. Those many pleasures are also fragments of
the higher substance that, together with the higher lights, fell at
the Shattering of the Vessels. They may thus be viewed as "waste"
or superfluous matter in so far as concerns the highest joy at its
supreme level, when the Godhead was undivided, prior to the
creation of heaven and earth and the "separateness" of higher and
lower worlds. Creation made the firmament to serve as a barrier
between above and below. As a result, the lower waters weep with
longing for the King; what is below suffers from the separation, the
great distance.

Therefore, all the pleasures of this world, no matter how great or
lasting, are relatively worthless in comparison to an hour in the
Garden of Eden, when the souls enjoy the radiance of the *Shekhinah.* As the Sages say: "One hour of contentment in the next world
is more wonderful than all the living in this world" (*Pirkey Avot*
4:17). And this because the nature of the joys of the next world are
of another order, infinitely superior to the pleasures of this world.
Whatever we experience below is limited by the physical body and
by the human mind. Even the mind of man is a biologically based
function, very much restricted to life and the brain. The soul, un-

restricted by the body, is free to receive far more, to experience exquisite joys, indescribable in our terms.

In other words, there is no way of comparing the pleasures of this world—for all their sweetness, intensity, and variety—with the pleasure of the next world. We have no common denominator. Just as we cannot compare a color, such as blue, with a number. We can have more blueness or less, a larger number or a smaller one; we cannot compare them. All we can say about the joys of the next world is that they are so superior to the joys of this world, that it is worth going through the torments of hell in order to attain them. As it is said, there is a river of fire between the Eden below and the Eden above and the souls have to immerse themselves in this river, called *Dinur,* to forget the pleasures of the lower before reaching the upper Paradise, and to avoid confusion when they get there.

The point of the matter is when a person has to pass from one level of existence to another, one of the rites of passage is the forgetting of what he knows of the past. If he does not do so, he is liable to get mixed up and his appreciation of the new experience will be weakened, if not distorted, especially if there is some relation between the two levels. As in learning a new language, the old has to be functionally forgotten or discarded; otherwise, there would be a tendency to mix them up. Every experience leaves an impression that has to be wiped out, more or less, in order to proceed to the next experience. Like professional wine testers who have somehow to obliterate the taste of the previous sip in order to evaluate the next and have developed ingenious ways to do so.

So, too, as said, the passage of the soul to the next world involve the crisis of forgetting. There is usually a transition period to enable a development of higher awareness to take place, just as people who move to foreign countries need time because they continue to see things with the eyes of their own past culture. All of which, incidentally, is one of the reasons for the saying that there are several things that can be obtained only by suffering, among them being the Land of Israel (also Torah and the next world). Because these things are of the nature of another realm of being, a better world, that require a certain process of eliminating the previous world. This may also be the meaning of the endless struggle of *tzadikim,* who move up from one stage to another and have to keep discarding familiar sources of satisfaction and of joy in order to achieve ever-higher levels of experience.

This points to an endless elevation of values and levels of happiness. But our capacity to experience them is limited. We are confined to a certain limited scale of response. Beyond a particular extreme, we cannot appreciate what is happening; just as our vision reacts only to certain wavelengths of light, so that we cannot see the infrared, the ultraviolet, or the X-rays, thus, too, for the most part, we do not enjoy the radiance of the *Shekhinah,* the source of all delight. In order to do so, we have to reach an equal, or similar, quality of light in ourselves, going through a process of soul purification both in this world and in the next. Herein in the secret of education in general and of the holy name of God in particular. The highest delight, the joy without a cause, comes from life itself, and the source of life is "with" God. "For with You is the source of life" (Psalms 36:10); it is not "You yourself." "With You" implies His Holy Name. The source of life and supernal happiness is thus next to the Divine, that which comes directly from God as His Holy Name. His Being and Existence give rise to the ten *sefirot,* of course, and these contain their own version of life and joy. But what we experience as joy comes from this other aspect of existence, it comes from being "with" Him.

All of which is intended to explain what is meant by *"Oneg Shabbat,"* the joy of the Sabbath. For obviously this joy is not that of gefilte fish or any other delicacy of the table. It is the particular essence of that which the Sabbath is, and it is somehow connected to "will," known in Hebrew as *"Ratzon,"* as well as to delight, which is *"Oneg."* The *mitzvot* are simply God's Will. He wishes it. And in performing the *mitzvot,* one is acting in obedience to His Will, even if only in its most exterior aspect. For it is not given to us to see His face. And the Divine face is the Divine inwardness. All we know is the heavenly exterior, that which is outside, visible, or graspable. Concerning inwardness, or the "face" of man, for instance, it may be viewed as that part of him in which is to be found his greatest achievement, his essential being.

Indeed, everything has its inner essence and its exterior. The revealed aspect comes forth from the inner significance. The external aspects of the *mitzvot* are that they are commandments. It is God's will that something should be done in a certain way. Thus, their inner aspect and their real meaning lies in the delight of the Supreme One, Blessed be He, which delight in the inwardness of will. Joy is thus the inwardness of will.

We may digress here a little to wonder at the incomprehensible partnership of body and soul. For the most part, it is a woeful association. If we were granted only one of the two to live with, life would be much easier. The combination is endlessly problematic; the body is continually struggling with its own needs, its failures to get what it wants, and its troublesome relationship with the soul, while the soul never seems to be thoroughly at ease with the body, and both of them fret at the difficulty of achieving any fruitful interaction or cooperation. If only the body were left alone, without the complications of the soul, how free and unencumbered it could be to enjoy the simple life of its creatureliness. Nevertheless, it cannot be refuted that the very superiority of man over other creatures of the earth is derived precisely from this additional dimension of soul. The advantage is inestimably greater than he can guess, but meanwhile, man is left struggling with the problems—the anguish of his two-sidedness—at least until the Messianic era of the resurrection.

One may intervene here with a note of compassion for man. Why wait? Why this long interval of pain and suffering before the release of the soul into the Infinite Light? Do we have to go through this terrible bother with death and resurrection? The answer, according to the Sages, seems to be that no man has to be prepared. Just as answer has no meaning without the question. No matter how profound or wise the reply may be, it remains devoid of all meaning without the question to which it supplies the answer. It's a matter of stages in a progression: without first clearly posing a problem, a challenging interrogation, or a contentious doubt, the truth has no possibility of appearing as a statement of any kind, much less as an answer, because there can be no answer to a nonexistent question. The whole structure of this world may thus be seen as a framework for man's response to God. First, man has to learn to listen, then to ask the right question, and finally hear the answer. Only then will the world have meaning.

In order for the Divine to be completely revealed to man, the instrument for receiving such salvation has to be slowly fashioned by time. Just as any radio broadcasting device needs a proper apparatus for its reception. The Torah fills the task of preparing man for this final redemption when the human soul, in its combined totality of matter and spirit, body and soul substance, will unite with the Godhead.

GLOSSARY

agadot (sing., agada): The nonlegal material in the Talmud, primarily of a legendary character.

bittul hayesh: Hasidic term for ego-annihilation, in order to experience higher states of consciousness.

Chabad: The metaphysical system developed by Rabbi Schneur Zalman of Liadi. The basis for Lubavitcher Hasidic thought, this term derives from the abbreviation of the first letters of the highest two *sefirot*—*chochmah* (wisdom) and *binah* (understanding), and an intermediary known as *daath* (knowledge).

chesed: Kindness. *Chesed* is also the name of one of the ten *sefirot*.

daven: Eastern Yiddish verb meaning to pray.

devekut: The inward state of cleaving to the divine.

Ein Sof: The "Infinite," from which all forms in the universe are created. This concept is similar to the Eastern notion of the "shining void."

halacha: Literally "the way to walk." The legal system of Orthodox Judaism today. Historically, *halacha* has been viewed by Kabbalists as reflecting many levels of hidden meaning.

Hasidism: The popular, charismatic movement that arose among East European Jewry in the late eighteenth century. *Hasid* means "pious" in Hebrew. In twelfth-century Germany, an unrelated group was likewise known as the *Hasidim*.

Kabbalah: From the Hebrew root word "to receive." Often used as a generic term for Jewish mysticism per se, it more precisely refers to esoteric thought from the late twelfth century onward.

kavana: The classic rabbinic term for mental concentration. Among the Hasidim, *kavana* came to be associated with the type of "one-pointedness" of intent necessary for higher states of awareness.

Kavanot: The technical name for the meditative exercises developed by Kabbalists in sixteenth-century Safed. These methods involve a complex visualization format related to the ten *sefirot*.

kelipot: Literally "husks" or "shells." A term in Lurianic Kabbalah referring to the encasements that surround the divine sparks lodged in all things.

Ma'aseh Bereshit: "The Act of Creation." The mystical, conceptual teachings concerning the secrets of Creation.

Ma'aseh Merkabah: "The Act of the Divine Chariot." The mystical experiential teachings associated with the biblical vision of Ezekiel.

maggid: A supposed spiritual entity that communicates through the adept when in a trance state; *maggid* also refers to a spiritually advanced human.

Maskilim: "Enlightened Ones," referring to the first assimilationists among Western European Jews in the late eighteenth and early nineteenth centuries. The *Maskilim* were highly contemptuous of Kabbalistic and Hasidic elements of Judaism.

middot: Character traits, such as generosity or courage.

Midrash: The legendary tradition of Judaism. A *midrash* (lowercased, with the plural *midrashim*) is a specific Midrashic legend.

Mishnah: The earliest postbiblical text of Jewish law and belief. It comprises six orders, each divided into tractates. It is believed to have been completed in the early third century C.E.

Mitnaggedim: Orthodox Jews who were "opponents" of the Hasidic movement. The Mitnaggedim went to great lengths to attempt to suppress the spread of Hasidism among East European Jewry.

musar: Literally, "ethics." The *musar* movement arose among the non-Hasidic Orthodox Jews of Lithuania in the mid-nineteenth century, and stressed character improvement.

nefesh: The lower human soul, linked to the physical body.

neshamah: The higher, transcendent aspect of the human soul.

Oral Law: The legalistic tradition of Judaism based on the Pentateuch. After flourishing orally for centuries, it was first presented in writing in the Mishnah and later the Talmud.

Pardes: The term for the four levels of understanding the Hebrew Bible, ranging from the literal to the esoteric.

rabbi: Literally, "my teacher." Originally a title for addressing a sage or a scholar, it now refers to an individual ordained according to Jewish law.

rebbe: Hasidic term for spiritual teacher.

ruach: In Kabbalah, this is the intermediate aspect of the human soul, linked to breath and ultimately tied to the physical body.

Ruach HaKodesh: Literally "the Holy Spirit." It refers to the quality felt to illumine the inner life of a holy person.

sefirot: The ten energy-essences that are said to be in constant interplay and underlie all of the cosmos. The *sefirot* have historically been portrayed in various configurations, the most important being the Tree of Life.

Shekinah: The female aspect to the deity. The *Shekinah* is described as dwelling among holy persons but as being in exile from its own Source.

sitra acha: Literally, "the other side." A Kabbalistic term for the realm of impurity and associated with evil.

Talmud: The summary of the Judaic oral tradition, compiled in writings by sages in the two centers of world Judaism at the time—Israel and Babylonia. Completed about 500 C.E., it exists today in two editions, one for Israel and one for Babylonia. The Babylonian edition is by far the more comprehensive and authoritative version. The Talmud comprises the Mishnah and the Gemara (the commentary about it).

tannaim: Literally "teachers." The early sages who are mentioned in the *Mishnah*.

tefillin: Phylacteries, traditionally worn daily by Jewish men during prayer.

teshuvah: "Repentance," or more broadly, return and ascent to one's source of divine origin. In Judaism, the process is accomplished by prayer, sacred study, or the performance of religious commandments or good deeds in general.

tikkun (pl. tikkunim): The divine rectification or redemption of the universe. Every human act, word, and even thought is believed to aid or impede this process.

Torah: In a narrow sense, the Pentateuch (Five Books of Moses). More generally, Torah is understood to comprise the twenty-four books of the Hebrew Bible, plus the Talmud.

Tree of Life: The central metaphor for the universe and every aspect of it. The ten *sefirot* are most typically arranged in a pattern known as the Tree of Life; all animate and inanimate forms are said to mirror this structure.

zaddik: "Pious one." In Hasidism, the *zaddik* is the spiritual leader of the community and is regarded as intermediary between it and the divine world.

CONTRIBUTORS

Yisrael Abuchatzeira (1890–1984). A Moroccan-born sage and Kabbalist of venerable lineage, he immigrated to the State of Israel soon after its founding. Rabbi Abuchatzeira was known as Baba Sali ("our praying father" in Arabic) to his many adherents, especially Moroccan Jews, who revered him as a holy man.

Abraham Abulafia (1240–after 1291). Born in Saragossa, Spain, he gained followers throughout the Mediterranean region for his prophetic writings and meditative manuals. Abulafia remains influential for his system of meditation based on the letters of the Hebrew alphabet.

Joseph Albo (ca. 1380–1444). Born in Aragon, Spain, he was a prominent rabbinic preacher and among the last great Jewish medieval philosophers. His most renowned work is *Sefer Ha-Ikkarim* (Book of Principles), lucidly presenting the key tenets of Jewish theology.

Solomon Almoli (ca. 1485–1542). A rabbi-physician who lived in sixteenth-century Turkey, he wrote several books, including a Kabbalistic treatise on the human soul. Rabbi Almoli's most famous work was on dreams, *Pitron Halomot*.

Tzvi Ashkenazi (1658–1718). Known admiringly as Chacham Tzvi ("Sage Tzvi"), he was born in Moravia—now the Czech Republic—and served as chief rabbi of Amsterdam. His collection of *halachic* responsa remains his most enduring theological contribution.

Yehudah Ashlag (1884–1954). Born in Warsaw, he immigrated as a rabbi in 1922 to Jerusalem, where he became a major authority on Kabbalah. Rabbi Ashlag was admiringly known as Baal Ha-Sulam ("Master of the Ladder") for his immense *Sulam* commentary on the *Zohar*. In popularized form, Rabbi Ashlag's writings are widely disseminated today.

Yair Chaim Bachrach (1639–1702). Born in Worms, Germany, he was descended from Rabbi Judah Loew ben Bezalel. Rabbi Bachrach was a prodigious writer whose works include a forty-six-volume encyclopedia. Rabbi Bachrach's book of *halachic* responsa entitled *Havvot Yair* ("Villages of Yair") is his most influential work.

Bahir. The *Sefer HaBahir* (Book of the Clear Light) first appeared in Provence, southern France, around the year 1175; its author is anonymous. The *Bahir* is among the first Jewish texts to present the notions of reincarnation and a life-energy flow throughout the human body.

Naftali Tzvi Yehudah Berlin (1817–1893). Known as the Netziv by acronym, he served for nearly forty years as head of the Volozhin Yeshiva in Belarus until it was closed by the Russian government in 1892. His son, Chaim Berlin, likewise became a renowned rabbinic leader.

Judah Loew ben Bezalel (1525–1609). Inextricably linked in popular Western culture with the legendary Golem of Prague, Judah Loew was an acclaimed rabbinic scholar and communal leader during his lifetime. Known by acronym as the Maharal, he has been regarded as an intellectual forerunner of both Hasidic and Mitnagged Kabbalah.

Yosef Chaim of Baghdad (1834–1909). Known as Chacham ("The Sage") Yosef Chaim or the Ben Ish Chai, in acronym, he became the chief rabbi of Baghdad at the age of twenty-five, succeeding his father upon his death that year. Celebrated as a Sephardic leader of his era, he composed religious poetry and wrote on Talmudic and Kabbalistic topics.

Moses Cordovero (1522–1570). Born in Safed, he ranks with his contemporary Rabbi Isaac Luria as among the most influential Kabbalists in Jewish history. Rabbi Cordovero's theosophical writings were highly abstruse; his most well-known work is *The Palm Tree of Deborah,* presenting ethical improvement from a mystical perspective.

Simeon ben Zemah Duran (1361–1444). A native of Majorca, he later settled in Saragossa, Spain, where he authored many tomes, including an influential book of *halachic* responsa. As a physician and scholar, Rabbi Duran became celebrated during his lifetime as a miracle worker.

Israel ben Eliezer (ca. 1698–1760). Commonly known as the Baal Shem Tov ("Bearer of the Good Name") or Besht in acronym, he was the charismatic founder of Hasidism in mid-eighteenth-century Eastern Europe. Born in the obscure village of Okup in the Carpathian Mountains, he taught abstruse Kabbalistic ideas through parables and folktales, and emphasized joy as a vital path to serving God.

Meir ibn Gabbai (1480–after 1540). A Spanish-born Kabbalist, he wrote his first book at the age of twenty-seven. Authoring eso-teric works on topics such as prayer and the Sabbath, he influenced such later thinkers as Rabbi Moses Cordovero and Rabbi Isaac Luria.

Abraham Joshua Heschel (1907–1972). Among the most ac-claimed Jewish theologians of our time, he was born into a lead-ing Hasidic family in Warsaw. After completing rabbinic study, and then a doctorate at the University of Berlin, he immigrated to the United States just before World War II. As a professor at the Jewish Theological Seminary, Heschel became best known for such books as *The Sabbath* and *God in Search of Man.*

Israel Meyer Kagan (1838–1933). A Polish native, he was revered throughout the Jewish world as the Chofetz Chaim, the name of his most influential work, on guarding and sanctifying one's daily speech. Besides writing many popular Judaic books, Rabbi

Kagan was an energetic speaker and fundraiser for European *yeshivot* during the interwar period.

Joseph Karo (1488–1575). Born in Spain, he immigrated to Turkey after the 1492 Great Expulsion and later joined the Safed mystics in the Holy Land. Both a celebrated legalist and Kabbalist, Rabbi Karo produced the enduring codification of Jewish Law entitled *Shulkah Aruk* (The Prepared Table).

Abraham Isaac Kook (1865–1935). Born in Latvia to a Hasidic mother and Mitnagged father, he immigrated to the Holy Land in 1901 to become rabbi of Jaffa; and in 1921, he was appointed Chief Rabbi for the British Mandate of Palestine. A mystical and fervent Zionist, Rav Kook, as he was popularly known, wrote many works, including *The Lights of Penitence*.

Moses Chaim Luzzatto (1707–1747). Born into an illustrious Italian family, he gained both early fame and rabbinic enmity for disseminating Kabbalah while still an unmarried youth. Later settling in Amsterdam, and then the Holy Land, Rabbi Luzzatto became revered posthumously for such inspiring works as *Derech HaShem* (The Way of God). His ethical writings are still avidly studied.

Moses Maimonides (1138–1204). Celebrated as the greatest Jewish philosopher of medieval times, Moses ben Maimon was born in Cordoba, Spain. Forced to wander with his family due to a dominating Muslim sect, he eventually settled in Fostat, near Cairo. There he practiced medicine and wrote prolifically on Judaic, philosophic, and medical topics. Maimonides' most influential works include the *Mishneh Torah* (a monumental codification of the Talmud) and *The Guide for the Perplexed*.

Solomon Molko (1500–1532). Born to Portuguese *conversos,* Molko converted to Judaism as a youth, and traveling widely, gained a devoted following as a brilliant Kabbalist and impassioned messianist. Executed by the Inquisition in Italy, Molko posthumously became revered as a sainted martyr among later Kabbalists, including his associate Joseph Karo.

Nachman of Breslov (1772–1810). A great-grandson of the Baal Shem Tov—the founder of Hasidism—Rabbi Nachman likewise lived in the Ukraine and was an ardent Kabbalist. Late in his career, he created alluring stories to teach esoteric concepts more effectively, and today remains best known for these tales.

Nachmanides (1194–1270). Moses ben Nachman (known as Nachmanides in acronym) was born in Gerona, Spain, and died in the Land of Israel. Like Maimonides, he was a physician, philosopher, and revered rabbinic leader. However, Nachmanides presented a more transcendent approach to Judaism—for example, emphasizing the dazzling spiritual rewards of the afterlife.

Eliezer Papo (1785–1826). Born in Sarajevo (Bosnia), he came to serve as a leading rabbi in Bulgaria. His most famous work is *Pele Yoetz* (Wondrous Advisor), a widely circulated ethical guide—drawing often upon the Kabbalah—for insights and advice on daily life.

David Hananiah Pinto (b. 1947). Born into a distinguished family in Morocco, Rabbi Pinto now leads a congregation in France, and with his brother Rabbi Yoshiyao Pinto, he travels widely on behalf of Sephardic religious, educational, and charitable institutions. He has written books of Torah commentary and Kabbalah.

Aharon Roth (1894–1947). Born in Satmar, Hungary, Rabbi Aharon (Arele, to his admirers) Roth served as a rabbinic leader in central Europe until immigrating late in his life to Jerusalem. There he was the founder of what became several Hasidic dynasties. His writings, emphasizing acts of daily piety, include *Shomer Emunim*.

Jonathan Sacks (b. 1948). London-born Jonathan Sacks became Chief Rabbi of the United Kingdom and the British Commonwealth in 1991. He is a prolific writer whose books, including *To Heal a Fractured World,* apply classic Jewish thought to contemporary issues. Rabbi Sacks also serves as senior rabbi at Western Marble Arch Synagogue in London.

Zalman M. Schachter-Shalomi (b. 1922). Founder of today's Jewish Renewal movement, Reb Zalman, as he prefers to be known, was born in Poland and raised in Vienna before immigrating to the United States in 1940. Ordained as a Lubavitcher Hasidic rabbi, he has taught at various universities and authored many books, including *Wrapped in a Holy Flame.*

Yosef Yitzchak Schneersohn (1880–1950). The sixth rebbe and next-to-last Rebbe (Grand Rabbi) of the Lubavitcher Hasidim. Born in Czarist Russia, he came as a refugee to the United States in 1940. There he effectively initiated Lubavitcher Hasidim's unprecedented global expansion—involving educational, religious, and Jewish outreach institutions.

Menachem Mendel Schneerson (1902–1994). The last Lubavitcher Rebbe was born in Russia and worked closely with his father-in-law—the sixth Lubavitcher Rebbe—both in Europe and the United States, until his death in 1950. One year later, Rabbi Menachem Mendel Schneerson became Lubavitcher Rebbe; many volumes of his letters, as well as Torah talks known as *sichot,* have been published.

Sefer HaYashar (Book of Righteousness). An anonymous Judaic work whose title is shared by several others, written in the thirteenth century and first published in 1544 Venice. Lucidly synthesizing ethics and mysticism, it may have been written by a Kabbalist wishing to conceal his identity.

Sefer Yetzirah (Book of Creation). Appearing anonymously in the third to fifth century C.E., it is regarded as the most influential work of early Jewish mysticism. It presents the notion of the ten *sefirot* and the twenty-two Hebrew letters as secret paths to the divine.

Kalonymus Shapira (1889–1943). Born in Grodzisk, Poland, he was an influential Hasidic rabbi who helped lead the Warsaw Ghetto Uprising in 1943 and died in the Holocaust. He wrote many books on such topics as Jewish education, communal life, and personal development.

Shalom Sharabi (1715–1772). A Yemenite Kabbalist who helped promulgate the teachings of Rabbi Isaac Luria and his exponents. Immigrating to Jerusalem, he became head of the prominent Beit El Yeshiva—and, like Rabbi Luria—revered as a miracle worker for his piety.

Elijah ben Solomon (1720–1797). Celebrated in Jewish history as the Gaon ("Genius") of Vilna, he was among the greatest Torah scholars of his epoch. Though an ardent and prolific Kabbalist, he spearheaded East European opposition to Hasidism during his lifetime.

Adin Steinsaltz (b. 1937). Born into a secular Jerusalem family, he became famous as a young rabbinic scholar and teacher. Rabbi Steinsaltz has written many books, including *The Thirteen Petalled Rose* and *The Longer Shorter Way* on Hasidism, and has produced numerous volumes on the Talmud. He teaches at the Mayanot Institute of Jewish Studies in Jerusalem.

Joseph Taitazak (ca. 1487–1545). Born in Spain, he immigrated to Salonica, Greece, after the Spanish Expulsion. There Rabbi Taitazak became one of his era's most influential Kabbalists whose devoted protégés included Joseph Karo and Solomon Molko.

Chaim Vital (1543–1620). Sometimes known historically as Rabbi Chaim Vital Calebrese—as his family was from Calabria, Italy—he became a leading figure in the Safed Kabbalist community. After Rabbi Isaac Luria's death, Rabbi Vital succeeded in establishing himself as his mentor's chief scribe and exponent.

Chaim Volozhin, or Chaim Volozhiner (1749–1821). Born in Volozhin, he became the most prominent disciple of Elijah, the Gaon of Vilna—and in 1803, founded the Volozhin Yeshiva, the "mother" of all Lithuanian-style yeshivot. His most famous work is *Nefesh HaChaim* (Spirit of Life).

Schneur Zalman of Liadi (1745–1812). Founder of the Lubavitch-Chabad Hasidic dynasty, he was born in the White Russian town of Liozna. Among the leading Hasidic thinkers of his era, he is undoubtedly best known for his influential philosophic tome entitled the *Tanya* (It Has Been Taught).

Zohar. The *Sefer HaZohar* (Book of Splendor) first appeared in late-thirteenth-century Spain and became the most influential and revered work of Jewish mysticism. Attributed by traditionalists to

Rabbi Simeon bar Yochai of the second century C.E., today most scholars view the thirteenth-century Kabbalist Rabbi Moses de Leon as its author.

REFERENCES

Alfasi, Eliyahu, and Yechiel Torgeman. *Baba Sali: Our Holy Teacher: His Life, Piety, Teachings, and Miracles: Rav Yisrael Abuchatzeirah*. Written and edited by C. T. Bari. Translated by Leah Dolinger. New York: Judaica Press, 1986.

Almoli, Shelomo. *Dream Interpretation from Classic Jewish Sources*. Translated and annotated by Yaakov Elman. Hoboken, N.J.: Ktav, 1998.

Altshuler, Mor. "Prophecy and Maggidism in the Life and Writings of R. Joseph Karo," *Frankfurt Jewish Studies Bulletin* 33 (2006): 81–94.

———. "Revealing the Secret of his Wives: R. Joseph Karo's Concept of Reincarnation and Mystical Conception," *Frankfurt Jewish Studies Bulletin* 31 (2004): 91–104.

Angel, Marc D. *Foundations of Sephardic Spirituality*. Woodstock, Vt.: Jewish Lights, 2006.

Arzy, Shahar, Moshe Idel, Theodor Landis, and Olaf Blanke. "Speaking with One's Self: Autoscopic Phenomena in Writings from the Ecstatic Kabbalah," *Journal of Consciousness Studies* 12, no. 11 (2005): 4–30.

Ashkenazi, Tzvi Hirsch. *She'elot u-Teshuvot Chacham Tzvi*. Jerusalem: Makhon L'Hotzas Sefarim, 1995.

Ashlag, Yehudah L. *In the Shadow of the Ladder: Introductions to Kabbalah*. Translated from the Hebrew with additional explanatory chapters by M. Cohen and Y. Cohen. Safed, Isr.: Nehora, 2002.

Azoulay, Yehuda. *A Legacy of Leaders: Inspiring Stories and Biographies of Sephardi Hachamim*. Lakewood, N.J.: Israel Book Shop Publications, 2008.

Bachrach, Yair Chaim. *She'elot u-Teshuvot Ha'at Ya'ir*. Ramat Gan, Isr.: Makhon E'ed Sefarim, 1997.

Bahir. Translation, introduction, and commentary by Aryeh Kaplan. New York: Weiser, 1979.

Ben-Shlomo, Yosef. *Poetry of Being: Lectures on the Philosophy of Rabbi Kook*. Translated by Shmuel Himelstein. Tel Aviv: MOD Books, 1990.

Berlin, Naftali Tzvi Yehudah. *She'elot u-Teshuvot Meishiv Davar.* Vol. 3. Jerusalem: Hotza'as Yeshivas Volozhin B'Eretz Yisroel, 1993.

Bilu, Yoram. "Oneirobiography and Oneiorocommunity in Saint Worship in Israel: A Two-Tiered Model for Dream-Inspired Religious Revivals," *Dreaming* 10, no. 2 (2000): 85–101.

———. "Modernity and Charisma in Contemporary Israel: The Case of Baba Sali and Baba Baruch," *Israel Affairs* 1, no. 3 (1995): 224–236.

———. "Dybbuk and Maggid: Two Cultural Patterns of Altered Consciousness in Judaism," *AJS Review,* 1996, 341–366.

Bindman, Yirmeyahu. *Rabbi Moshe Chaim Luzzatto: His Life and Works.* Northvale, N.J.: Aronson, 1995.

Bleich, J. David, ed. *With Perfect Faith: The Foundations of Jewish Belief.* Hoboken, N.J.: Ktav, 1983.

Bokser, Ben-Zion. *The Maharal: The Mystical Philosophy of Rabbi Judah Loew of Prague.* Northvale, N.J.: Aronson, 1994.

Book of Creation. Translated by Irving Friedman. New York: Weiser, 1977.

Buber, Martin. *Tales of the Hasidim: Books One and Two.* Translated by Olga Marx. New York: Schocken, 1975.

Carlebach, Elisheva. "Redemption and Persecution in the Eyes of Moses Hayim Luzzatto and his Circle," *Proceedings of the American Academy for Jewish Research* 54 (1987): 1–29.

Chajes, J. H. *Between Worlds: Dybbuks, Exorcists, and Early Modern Judaism.* Philadelphia: University of Pennsylvania Press, 2003.

Cordovero, Moses. *The Palm Tree of Devorah.* Translated and annotated by Moshe Miller. Southfield, Mich.: Targum, 1993.

Dan, Joseph. *The Heart and the Fountain: An Anthology of Jewish Mystical Experiences.* New York: Oxford University Press, 2002.

———. *Jewish Mysticism and Jewish Ethics.* Northvale, N.J.: Aronson, 1995.

Duran, Shimon. *Magen Avot.* Jerusalem: Makhon L'Hotzas Sefarim, 2003.

Elior, Rachel. "Messianic Expectations and Spiritualization of Religious Life in the Sixteenth Century," *Revue des Etudes juives* 145, no. 1–2 (1986): 35–49.

Faierstein, Morris M. "Charisma and Anti-Charisma in Safed: Isaac Luria and Hayyim Vital," *The Journal for the Study of Sephardic & Mizrahi Jewry* 1, no. 2 (October/November 2007): 1–20.

———. *All in the Hands of Heaven: The Teachings of Rabbi Mordechai Joseph Leiner of Isbica.* Hoboken, N.J.: Ktav, 1989.

Fine, Lawrence. *Physician of the Soul, Healer of the Cosmos: Isaac Luria and His Fellowship.* Palo Alto, Calif.: Stanford University Press, 2003.

———, ed. *Judaism in Practice: From the Middle Ages through the Early Modern Period.* Princeton: Princeton University Press, 2001.

Finkel, Avraham Y., ed. *Kabbalah: Selections from Classic Kabbalistic Works from Raziel HaMalach to the Present.* Southfield, Mich.: Targum, 2002.

Gabbai, Meir ben Ezekiel ibn. *Sod ha-Shabbat.* Translated and with a critical commentary by Elliot Ginsburg. Albany: State University of New York Press, 1989.

Giller, Pinchas. *Shalom Shara'bi and the Kabbalists of Beit El.* Oxford: Oxford University Press, 2008.

———. "Leadership and Charisma among Modern Kabbalists in the Footsteps of Shar-abi-Contemporary Kabbalistic Prayer," *The Journal for the Study of Sephardic & Mizrahi Jewry* 1, no. 2 (October/November 2007): 21–41.

———. *Reading the Zohar: The Sacred Text of the Kabbalah.* New York: Oxford University Press, 2001.

Goldish, Matt, ed. *Spirit Possession in Judaism: Cases and Contexts from the Middle Ages through the Present.* Detroit: Wayne State University Press, 2003.

Gordon, Hirsch. *The Maggid of Caro: The Mystic Life of the Eminent Codifier Joseph Caro as Revealed in his Secret Diary.* New York: Pardes Publishing, 1949.

Green, Arthur. "Abraham Joshua Heschel: Recasting Hadisim for Moderns," *Modern Judaism* 29, no. 1: 62–79.

———. *Tormented Master: A Life of Rabbi Nahman of Bratslav.* New York: Schocken, 1981.

Hayyim ben Elijah al-Hakam, Joseph. *The Power of Torah: The Ben Ish Hai on the Eternal Truth of Torah and on the Relationship Between the Torah and the Jewish People.* English adaption by Daniel Levy. Jerusalem: Yeshivat Ahavat Shalom Publications, 2001.

Heschel, Abraham. *God in Search of Man.* New York: Farrar, Straus, and Giroux, 1976.

Hoffman, Edward. *The Wisdom of Maimonides.* Boston: Trumpeter, 2008.

———. *The Way of Splendor: Jewish Mysticism and Modern Psychology, Updated 25th Anniversary Edition.* Lanham, Md.: Rowman & Littlefield, 2007.

———, ed. *Opening the Inner Gates: New Paths in Kabbalah and Psychology.* Boston: Shambhala, 1995.

———. *Despite All Odds: The Story of Lubavitch.* New York: Simon & Schuster, 1991.

———. *The Heavenly Ladder: The Jewish Guide to Inner Growth.* San Francisco: Harper & Row, 1985.

Idel, Moshe. "Leadership and Charisma: Maimonides, Nahmanides and Abraham Abulafia," *The Journal for the Study of Sephardic & Mizrahi Jewry* 2, no. 1 (2008): 2–34.

———. "Abraham J. Heschel on Mysticism and Hasidism," *Modern Judaism* 29, no. 1, 80–105.

————. "Jewish Mysticism among the Jews of Arab/Moslem Lands," *Journal for the Study of Sephardic & Mizrahi Jewry* 1, no. 1 (2007): 14–39.

————. *Messianic Mystics.* New Haven: Yale University Press, 2000.

————. *Studies in Ecstatic Kabbalah.* Albany: State University of New York Press, 1988.

Jacobs, Louis. *Jewish Mystical Testimonies.* New York: Schocken, 1976.

————. *Theology in the Responsa.* Boston: Routledge & Kegan Paul, 1975.

Jacobson, Simon. *Toward a Meaningful Life: The Wisdom of the Rebbe Menachem Mendel Schneerson.* New York: HarperCollins, 1995.

Kadish, Seth (Avi). "The Book of Abraham: Rabbi Shimon ben Zeman Duran and the School of Rabbenu Nissim Gerondi." PhD diss., Faculty of Humanities, University of Haifi, 2006.

Kagen, Israel Meir. *Ahavath Chesed: The Love of Kindness as Required by God, by the Chafetz Chaim.* Translated by Leonard Oschry. 2nd ed. New York: Feldheim, 1976.

Kook, Abraham Isaac. *The Lights of Penitence, The Moral Principles, Lights of Holiness, Essays, Letters, and Poems.* Translation and introduction by Ben-Zion Bokser. New York: Paulist Press, 1978.

Kurzweil, Arthur. *On the Road with Rabbi Steinsaltz: Twenty-Five Years of Pre-Dawn Car Trips, Mind-Blowing Encounters, and Inspiring Conversations with a Man of Wisdom.* San Francisco: Jossey-Bass, 2006.

Lenowitz, Harris. *The Jewish Messiahs: From the Galilee to Crown Heights.* New York: Oxford University Press, 1998.

Luzzatto, Moses Chaim. *The Way of God.* Translated by Aryeh Kaplan. Jerusalem: Feldheim, 1978.

Maimonides, Moses. *The Guide for the Perplexed.* Translated and with an introduction by Shlomo Pines. Chicago: University of Chicago Press, 1963.

McGaha, Michael. "The Sefer Ha-Bahir and Andalusian Sufism," *Medieval Encounters* 3, no. 1 (1997): 20–57.

Meltzer, David, ed. *The Secret Garden: An Anthology in the Kabbalah.* New York: Continuum, 1976.

Mopsik, Charles, ed. *Les Grandes Textes de la Cabale.* Paris: Verdier, 1993.

Nachmanides. *Writings and Discourses.* Translated and annotated with index by Charles B. Chavel. New York: Shilo Publishing House, 1978.

Papo, Eliezer. *The Essential Pele Yoetz: An Encyclopedia of Ethical Jewish Living.* Condensed and translated by Marc D. Angel. New York: Sepher-Hermon Press, 1991.

Pinto, David. *La Genese: Bereshit I, II.* Paris: Bibliophane Daniel Radford, 2004.

Rabow, Jerry. *50 Jewish Messiahs.* Jerusalem: Gefen, 2002.

Raviv, Zohar. "Fathoming the Heights, Ascending the Depths—Decoding the Dogma within the Enigma: The Life, Works and Speculative Piety of Rabbi Moses Cordoeiro (Safed 1522–1570)." PhD diss., University of Michigan, 2007.

Rosenblatt, Yaakov. *Maharal: Emerging Patterns: Ten Representative Essays Culled from the Work of Rabbi Yehudah Loew of Prague.* Jerusalem: Feldheim, 2001.

Roth, Ahrele. *Reb Ahrele's Heart.* Translated and edited from the Hebrew sources by Hillel Goelman and Zalman M. Schachter-Shalomi. Philadelphia: ALEPH, Alliance for Jewish Renewal, 2006.

Sacks, Jonathan. *To Heal a Fractured World: The Ethics of Responsibility.* New York: Schocken, 2005.

———. *A Letter in the Scroll: Understanding our Jewish Identity and Exploring the Legacy of the World's Oldest Religion.* New York: Free Press, 2000.

Schachter, Zalman M., *Fragments of a Future Scroll: Hassidism for the Aquarian Age.* Edited by Philip Mandelkorn & Stephen Gerstman. Germantown, Pa.: Leaves of Grass Press, 1975.

——— *Wrapped in a Holy Flame: Teachings and Tales of the Hasidic Masters.* San Francisco: Jossey-Bass, 2003.

Schachter, Zalman M., and Edward Hoffman. *Sparks of Light: Counseling in the Hasidic Tradition.* Boulder: Shambhala, 1983.

Schapiro, Moshe. *The Book of Yonah: "Journey of the Soul," An Allegorical Commentary Adapted from the Vilna Gaon's Aderes Eliyahu.* Brooklyn: Mesorah, 1997.

Schneersohn, Yosef Y., and Schneerson, Menachem M. *Basi LeGani: Chassidic Discourses.* Based on a translation by S. Weinberg, edited by U. Kaploun. Brooklyn: Kehot, 1990.

Schneur Zalman of Liady. *Tanya.* Translated by N. Mindel. Brooklyn, N.Y.: Kehot Publication Society, 1973.

Scholem, Gershom. *Kabbalah.* New York: Meridian, 1978.

———. *Major Trends in Jewish Mysticism.* New York: Schocken, 1974.

———. *On the Kabbalah and Its Symbolism.* Translated by Ralph Manheim. New York: Schocken, 1965.

Schwartz, Howard. *Tree of Souls: The Mythology of Judaism.* New York: Oxford University Press, 2004.

Sefer Hayashar: The Book of the Righteous. Edited and translated by Seymour J. Cohen. New York: Ktav, 1973.

Sefer Yetzirah: The Book of Creation. Translated by Aryeh Kaplan. York Beach, Maine: Weiser, 1990.

Shapira, Kalonymus Kalman. *To Heal the Soul: The Spiritual Journal of a Chasidic Rebbe.* Translated and edited by Yehoshua Starrett. Northvale, N.J.: Aronson, 1995.

Silver, Abba Hillel. *A History of Messianic Speculation in Israel: From the First through the Seventeenth Centuries.* Gloucester, Mass.: Peter Smith, 1978.

Steinsaltz, Adin. *The Thirteen Petalled Rose.* Translated by Yehudah Hanegbi. New York: Basic Books, 2006.

———. *The Candle of God: Discourses on Chasidic Thought.* Edited and translated by Yehuda Hanegbi. Northvale, N.J.: Aronson, 1998.

———. *The Long Shorter Way: Discourses on Chasidic Thought.* Edited and translated by Yehudah Hanegbi. Northvale, N.J.: Aronson, 1993.

Tishby, Isaiah. *Messianic Mysticism: Moses Hayim Luzzatto and the Padua School.* Translated by Morris Hoffman. Portland, Ore.: Littman Library of Jewish Civilization, 2008.

Twersky, Isidore. *A Maimonides Reader.* New York: Behrman House, 1972.

Unterman, Alan, ed. *The Kabbalistic Tradition: An Anthology of Jewish Mysticism.* New York: Penguin, 2008.

Volozhiner, Chaim. *Ruach Chaim: Rav Chaim Volozhiner's Classic Commentary on Pirkei Avos.* Rendered into English by Chanoch Levi. Southfield, Mich.: Targum/Feldheim, 2002.

Wein, Berel. *Triumph of Survival: The Story of the Jews in the Modern Era 1650–1990.* Monsey, N.Y.: Shaar Press, 1990.

Werblowsky, R. J. Zvi. *Joseph Karo: Lawyer and Mystic.* Philadelphia: Jewish Publication Society of America, 1977.

Zohar. Vols. 1–5. Translated by Harry Sperling and Maurice Simon. London: Soncino Press, 1931–1934.

CREDITS